D0875554

Paris and the Arts, 1851–1896:
From the Goncourt Journal

M. Prudhomme, the bourgeois incarnate, by Henri Monnier (courtesy of the editors)

Paris and the Arts, 1851–1896: From the Goncourt Journal

Edited and translated by
George J. Becker *and* Edith Philips

With an Afterword on Japanese Art and Influence by Hedley H. Rhys

Cornell University Press / ITHACA AND LONDON

Also edited and translated
by George J. Becker

Paris under Siege, 1870–1871:
From the Goncourt Journal

First published 1971 by Cornell University Press.
Published in the United Kingdom by Cornell University Press Ltd.,
2-4 Brook Street, London W1Y 1AA.

International Standard Book Number 0-8014-0655-2
Library of Congress Catalog Card Number 72-161309

PRINTED IN THE UNITED STATES OF AMERICA
BY VAIL-BALLOU PRESS, INC.

Acknowledgments

The portions of the *Journal* here presented, which attempt to give a comprehensive view of the literary and artistic life in Paris during the last half of the nineteenth century, are drawn from the full range of the "integral" text published by Fasquelle-Flammarion from 1955 to 1959. These materials are translated with the permission of the publishers and of Oxford University Press, holder of the English translation rights.

An entry for a particular date normally covers a variety of topics. It has seemed best, therefore, to indicate only deletions in the topic presented or a hiatus between topics in the same entry. This has been done by the addition of three ellipsis dots to the normal punctuation of the passage. Such deletions when they occur are in the interest of readability.

Illustrations, with the exception of the frontispiece, were reproduced by the Photographic Service of the Bibliothèque Nationale in Paris and are used with its permission. They were selected from the compendious Vinck Collection by Jean-Jacques Tourteau and his daughter Elisabeth, to whom we owe a special debt of gratitude, as we do also to Professor Hedley H. Rhys of Swarthmore College for his "Afterword on Japanese Art and Influence."

Acknowledgments

Edith Philips has assumed primary responsibility for that portion of the *Journal* written by Jules de Goncourt, and George J. Becker for that written by Edmond. Each has reviewed the work of the other, and both wish to acknowledge the helpful advice of present and former colleagues in the French department of Swarthmore College, notably that of Professor Simone Smith.

George J. Becker
Edith Philips

Bellingham, Washington
Swarthmore, Pennsylvania
July 1971

Contents

Acknowledgments v
The Literary Scene, *by George J. Becker* 1

Goncourt *Journal*
1851–1869 15
1870–1896 115

Afterword on Japanese Art and Influence
by Hedley H. Rhys 327

Writings of the Goncourts 337
Biographical Notes 339
Index 365

Illustrations

frontispiece

M. Prudhomme, the bourgeois incarnate, by Henri Monnier

following page 118

1. Edgar Degas, apotheosis of the artist *en famille*
2. Victor Hugo, romantic exile on the island of Jersey
3. Jules de Goncourt, by Edmond de Goncourt
4. Alphonse Daudet, by Bacard *fils*
5. Edmond de Goncourt, based on a photograph by Nadar
6. Hippolyte Taine *en bourgeois*
7. In the studios, by Daumier
8. Edouard Drumont, anti-Semitic gladiator
9. Gustave Flaubert dissecting Madame Bovary, by Lemot
10. The sinister Catulle Mendès, by Cappiello
11. Charles Sainte-Beuve, voluptuary, by Gill
12. Emile Zola's taste for ordure, by Le Bourgeois

Paris and the Arts, 1851–1896:
From the Goncourt Journal

To give the feverish accent of nineteenth-century life—which I find set down nowhere—without the staleness and loss of warmth of things put down in writing, that is, basically, what we are trying to do.

(From the *Journal*, February 10, 1880)

The Literary Scene

by George J. Becker

When the curtain rose on the literary career of the Goncourt brothers, and fortuitously on the Second Empire, on December 2, 1851, it revealed an artistic milieu made banal by outworn convention and empty doctrine. Balzac had died in 1850 leaving an ambiguous heritage of massively documented social novels, which were to provide the model for a new literature but which were vitiated by the hectic and impossible plots and retrograde philosophy belonging to the old. Stendhal, another innovator, had died in 1842; at the moment his ghost was disturbing no one. The great figure of the day was Victor Hugo, the revolutionary dramatist of *Les Burgraves* and *Hernani*, plays now twenty years in the past. With Lamartine in eclipse after the failure of the Revolution of 1848, Hugo seemed to tower alone in the literary landscape. Within a few days he would go into exile for the duration of the Empire, thereby acquiring an authority and respect that were somewhat anachronistic. The field was left to such popular novelists of adventure as the elder Dumas and Eugène Sue and to sentimentalists like George Sand. The theatre was filled with trivia written to formula or with the rigidly respectable vehicles of the past. The best that could be said about the popular or accepted works of the day, in painting and in literature, was that they were destined for quick and merciful oblivion.

Nor was the new regime with its blatant opportunism and crassly material goals likely to revivify the arts. The Emperor's reading a book is unimaginable. The Empress did read with a passionate prejudice that boded ill for innovation. The taste of the Duc de Morny, the energetic impresario of the reign, rose no higher than the music hall. Unfortunately, France, which was growing more and more centralized, could expect no renovating spring to gush forth in the provinces. Yet, in spite of this unpromising prospect, the two decades of the Empire proved to be seminal. Romanticism, still officially regnant, died of a surfeit of its own excesses—mortally stricken by its own Toledo blades, to paraphrase a comment by Gavarni. The early fifties were the time of realist manifestos in painting and literature, manifestos that were less clear about what realism was than emphatic in their insistence that the arts must come back to earth, to the observed, to "modern and popular subjects," as Champfleury demanded. These were the years when new works appeared in repudiation of the romantic past: Courbet's sidewalk Salon des Refusés in opposition to the official painting of the annual Salons; novels like *Madame Bovary* and *La Vie de Bohème* in France and *A Sportsman's Sketches* and *Sevastopol* in Russia to form the vanguard of the new prose fiction. In painting, in literature, and in the broad area of scientific and philosophical speculation the roots of the modern are to be found in those decades, though paradoxically set in the most imitative and anodyne of social and political backgrounds.

This then is the great value of the Goncourt *Journal.* The Goncourt brothers were there. They witnessed, participated in, contributed to, and were buffeted by major currents of change. The *Journal* in its forty-five-year span gives a record of four literary generations: the romantics on their way out; the realists on their way in; the second realist generation of the naturalists, who carried their efforts to a calculated extreme; and the anti-realists of the end of the century, who were variously determined to desert the orthodoxy temporarily imposed by Zola in pursuit of other doctrines. Just as the social structure was often in upheaval, as evidenced by the coup d'état of 1851, the Commune of 1871, and the Dreyfus case of the last years of the century, so there was continual tumult over the arts, particularly literature, a tumult recorded in vituperation, feuds, cabals, and occasional duels. To be a man of letters was to engage in battle, to be shot at from every quarter, including one's own, to engage in skirmishes that took on the magnitude and strategy of war.

The *Journal*, in which are set down the particular experiences and observations of its authors, by its scope and variety becomes a general record of the times. When they began to write it, Edmond and Jules de Goncourt were twenty-nine and twenty-one respectively, young men with a rather diffuse enthusiasm for the arts, recently emancipated from the need to earn a living, determined to make a name for themselves in the world of letters without knowing exactly how to go about it. For a time they lived on the fringes of Bohemia, leading a mildly libertine existence, associating with a subsociety of artists, journalists, actors, and whores, writing for the "little papers" and pursuing a passion for the prettiness of the eighteenth century, an activity and a taste that at first seemed to stamp them as amateurs. They were rescued from an aimless life by their innate fastidiousness, by their bourgeois good sense, and by their enthusiasm for documents revealing the intimate social life of the eighteenth century. It was by way of this passion that they came to the writing of documentary novels of increasing seriousness and depth. Almost without being aware of it, they provided the necessary link between Flaubert and Zola—though retrospectively Edmond never tired of harping on that fact. Their critical pronouncements also marked them as belonging to the current of change. They repudiated the classics in art and literature as being sterile and imitative. They extolled Diderot and Balzac among their immediate predecessors in the novel (though ignoring Stendhal); they considered Victor Hugo rhetorical and false; and with frequent reservations they aligned themselves with Flaubert, Zola, and the young realist-naturalists in prose fiction and less consistently with Baudelaire in poetry. In painting too, though without any great depth or consistency, they were on the side of the modern, as is especially evident in Edmond's comments on Degas, Manet, Monet, and Rodin, and his depreciation of Delacroix, Ingres, and Puvis de Chavannes.

The most substantial of the diarists' entries have to do with their literary friendships or associations. Of the hundreds of figures mentioned, five or six receive detailed and continuing attention: Gavarni, Gautier, and the novelists Hugo, Flaubert, Zola, and Daudet. Gavarni was their great idol; the early years of the *Journal* with its collections of "Gavarniana" show them to be fascinated by him. It was he, they said, who opened their eyes to the possibility of an artistic notation of modern life. They were completing their book about him when Jules was stricken. Edmond published the book and continued his praise of Gavarni in the *Journal*; on July 2, 1889, he wrote to Gavarni's son offering to buy such works as remained in the latter's possession with the 12,000 francs received from the play *Germinie Lacerteux*. Although the

Goncourts recognized they must not imitate Gautier's style because it was too literary, they considered him one of the moderns and evidently prized his company. It is a matter of interest that his daughter Judith was elected to the Goncourt Academy in 1910.

Much as they disapproved of what Hugo wrote, they were impressed by his personality and by his sexual prowess. Flaubert and Zola were competitors as well as friends, and feelings of professional rivalry frequently evoked acerb comments that seemed to undermine, if not deny, friendship. Their association with Flaubert was very close during those years when he lived for long periods in Paris. In 1880 Edmond and others spent Easter weekend with him at Croisset only weeks before his unexpected death, which profoundly upset Edmond, who realized that he and Flaubert were the old masters of the new school and that he was now very much alone. The relationship with Zola was always uneasy. By the power of his personality and his skill at self-advertisement Zola became a household name and, in Edmond's opinion, dimmed the reputation of deserving writers like himself. There was a degree of truth in his recurring charge that Zola plagiarized from the Goncourt novels. The Manifesto of the Five in 1887 produced a great strain. Zola let it be known that he thought Edmond might have encouraged the manifesto. Goncourt snubbed Zola at a performance of *Soeur Philomène* six weeks later. Zola wrote a letter demanding clarification of their relationship. Then a little later, when he presented himself for election to the French Academy, Zola was removed from the list of members of the Goncourt Academy. A reconciliation took place in 1895, however, when Zola helped to initiate a grand testimonial dinner for Edmond.

The Daudet friendship, which came after Jules' death, was

the most stable and enduring of Edmond's relationships, giving a fixed point to his lonely later years. He spent part of every summer at Champrosay, the Daudet country estate, and it was fitting that his death should take place there. From the many entries relating to Daudet we get a full-length portrait of the volatile Southerner and his family—in particular his wife, an author in her own right, as prickly and excitable as her husband, and the appealing and talented elder son, Léon. Alphonse, however, holds the center of the stage with his sprees, his recollections of a debauched youth, his popular success as novelist and dramatist, his fierce suffering from syphilis in later life, his sense of honor which made him ready to fight a duel even though he could not lift a sword and was unsteady on his feet. Above all he was loyal and tender—words which he applied to Edmond, who regarded one of the later volumes of the *Journal* as essentially a monument to their friendship.

The Goncourts and their contemporaries were intent on making their mark in the theatre. The *Journal* is a record of failures or only qualified successes in this field. Flaubert had the good sense to resist putting *Madame Bovary* on the stage, but his comedy *Le Candidat* fell flat. Many of the novels from Zola's Rougon-Macquart series were transformed into plays but none was of more than passing interest. Of these major writers only Daudet achieved lasting fame with his *Sapho*, which remains part of the standard repertoire of the French theatre.

For the Goncourt brothers the theatre was both an obsession and a humiliation. They came to the premiere of *Henriette Maréchal* in December 1865 expecting a triumph. Instead the evening degenerated into a battle equal to that provoked by Hugo's *Hernani*. When the play was put on again twenty years later the old antagonisms were revived and the performance was almost as tumultuous as the first one. *Germinie Lacerteux* and *La Fille Elisa* were theatrical causes célèbres, targets of furious abuse from the press, of interpellations in the Chamber of Deputies, and of censorship, or, in the case of *La Fille Elisa,* outright prohibition. Yet Edmond never gave up hope. In 1896 a play drawn from *Manette Salomon* was produced; it closed after twenty-eight performances, but to his surprise he did earn 7,600 francs from it.

What Paris needed was an experimental theatre where the traditional plays of the Comédie Française and the banal well-made fare of the boulevard theatres might be challenged. Such a stage came into being in October 1887 with the establishment of the Théâtre Libre by André Antoine. This was the first of the "new" theatres in Europe and ranks in importance with the Freie Bühne in Berlin, the Moscow Art Theatre, and the Abbey Theatre in Dublin. Significantly, the first play performed at the Théâtre Libre was the Goncourts' *Soeur Philomène.* Later Antoine put on *La Fille Elisa,* but *Germinie Lacerteux,* the most successful of their plays, was presented at the Odéon by Porel with Réjane in the leading role.

If the theatre was a world of intense and partisan passion, the various informal literary groupings of the capital were not far behind. Above all, the press was noted for literary passion as well as political partisanship. Under the Empire the press was considered dangerous. It was not surprising that the Goncourts and the literary paper *Paris* were prosecuted in 1853 for offense against public morals, a charge that was ostensibly literary but covertly political. Under the Third Republic a freer press took sides in literary controversies. Generally hostile to Edmond de Goncourt, it was for a time subservient to the energetic Zola, and was usually adulatory of lesser figures. At the end of his life, however, Edmond was unexpectedly asked by *Le Figaro* to succeed Albert Wolff as its art editor. He refused, not without wistful thoughts of the power he would have been able to wield in that role.

Social groups flourished and influenced public response to plays and novels. There existed, for example, various dinner groups, some political in orientation, some literary. Among the latter were the Magny and Brébant dinners, named for the restaurants where they were held, which brought together major writers for uninhibited talk. The salons continued to be a factor in French literary life. The salon most in view in the *Journal* is that of Princess Mathilde Bonaparte, created as a counterinfluence to the notoriously unliterate and dull Imperial court at Compiègne and setting off a rivalry that the Goncourts claimed to be the source of the government's attack on *Henriette Maréchal.* For a time a group of young naturalists clustered around Zola at Médan, and in February 1885, no doubt in rivalry to the Médan group, Edmond inaugurated his *Grenier,* Sunday gatherings in the renovated attic of his Auteuil house that continued until a month before his death. A variety of men of letters and artists passed through his doors on these occasions—in addition to the body of the faithful, such interesting outsiders as the Spanish novelist Countess Emilia Pardo Bazán, the Danish critic Georg Brandes, Stéphane Mallarmé, Robert de Montesquiou-Fezensac, and the American painter John La Farge.

Such groups and personalities are abundantly chronicled by the *Journal* almost from its inception. During his lifetime the younger brother, drawing on their joint observations and sensibility, composed the diary entries. In 1870 Edmond thought of closing the record at the page where Jules had laid down his pen, but he was soon caught up by a desire to record his brother's last months, then by the catastrophic events of the Prussian siege and the Commune that followed, and increasingly by a kind of compulsion to record the life of his times. In 1887 he published the first volume of selected entries, following this with eight more, the last of which appeared on May 26, 1896, his seventy-fourth birthday. In his will he directed that the manuscript of the complete *Journal* be deposited at the Bibliothèque Nationale and that it be published in its entirety by the Académie Goncourt twenty years after his death. In fact, because of representations by people of importance, law suits, and the involvement of France in two major wars the first of the twenty-two volumes of the "integral" text did not appear until 1955.

Judging by the response to the early volumes, we must conclude that this delay was well advised. Nine days after the first volume appeared Taine demanded that in the future the author eliminate mention of living persons. Others felt that their privacy had been invaded and their characters impugned. As Edmond commented on May 12, 1890: "Basically everyone wants the truth about others but will not permit it to be said about himself," concluding that if he were to consult everyone mentioned, his *Journal* in twelve volumes would be reduced to twelve printed pages. Even the Daudets were uncomfortable about the candid accounts set down and asked that no mention be made of the *Evénement* article about Madame Daudet that nearly provoked a duel.

Stylistically the *Journal* has considerable importance. Edmond made a point of this in his 1887 preface: "And in this work which sought above all to give *life* from a memory that was still warm, in this work hastily set down and not always reread—without concern for faulty syntax or words without a passport—we have always preferred the phrase and the expression which least blunted or *academicized* the liveliness of our sensations and the vigor of our ideas." The authors also took evident delight in the vulgar, the scatological, the slangy word; they made a point of setting down the spoken language of the time with a freedom not possible in the novel and drama.

As to the accuracy and objectivity of the diarists, which have sometimes been called into question, such omissions as Edmond's failure to mention that his brother probably died of the effects of syphilis seem insufficient reason to question the veracity of the *Journal* at large. The brothers were not historians seeking to render a balanced and many-sided judgment for posterity. Rather they were impressionists, seeing through a temperament, to borrow Zola's phrase. They varied their shading in depicting those whom they saw from day to day. They had a quick eye for the truth of character underneath a façade; they took delight in pointing to incongruity, in puncturing pomposity. There is little evidence of spiteful or deliberate distortion, though certainly they may overemphasize a salient trait, such as Hugo's eroticism, Taine's pedantry, or Burty's self-seeking.

It must be admitted, however, that they reveal no great warmth of human sympathy, or genuine compassion for others. We find an egoistic frame of reference that is as unvarying as it is spontaneous. For example, when their servant Rose dies a horrible death, the brothers' reaction is primarily one of pique that she should die on the day they are first invited to Princess Mathilde's and, later on, of outrage over the way their servant had pulled the wool over their eyes. For the most part they are detached observers, making no effort to get inside the people whom they observe or to find out why they act the way they do. They are content to record *sur le vif*. In short, they have a discerning eye but little heart.

Only in the relationship of the two brothers (and to a certain extent in that between Edmond and Daudet) is this emotional deficiency corrected. We can discern a warm affection and a degree of idolatry in the way Jules wrote about Edmond. The latter identified painfully with Jules in his illness and never recovered from his brother's death. His grief in some ways resembles that of a lover rather than of a brother. Their "twinned nature," of which Edmond wrote so eloquently, was a collaboration in being, in observing, and ultimately in creating which was so complete, so satisfying that they felt no emotional needs outside it. And Edmond, widowed, left truly empty of love, never seriously considered attaching himself to or identifying with another human being. There might have been more gaiety in the *Journal* if Jules had lived, but I doubt that it would have been greatly different in other respects. The exclusivity of the Goncourt brothers would have continued reinforced, not diminished. From where the diarists stood it was always a matter of *them* —other people to be observed in their incongruous behavior —and *us*, a unique and satisfying unity of mind and soul that set them apart from the world and buttressed them against it.

Goncourt *Journal*

1851–1869

1851

December

On the great day of the Last Judgment, when all the souls are brought before the bar by huge angels who sleep during the trial like gendarmes, their chins resting on their two white gloves crossed over the pommels of their swords, when God the Father with his long white beard—as members of the Institute paint him in the domes of churches—when God the Father, after questioning me about what I have done, asks me about what I have seen, that is, about everything to which I have lent the complicity of my eyes, he will doubtless say to me: "Creature whom I made human and good, have you by any chance seen the bullfight at the Barrière du Combat, or five great starving bulldogs tearing some poor old, thin, defenseless donkey with their teeth?" "Alas, no, Lord," I will say; "I have seen worse. I have seen a coup d'état!"

"Well, the revolution has come!" It was the companion of our Villedeuil cousin, M. de Blamont—Cousin Blamont, a former royal guard, now an aging conservative, asthmatic and ill-tempered—who gave us this news as he came into our rooms. It was eight o'clock. With a gesture that was habitual with him, crossing the tails of his coat across his belly, in the way one binds a sash, he took his leave and went to carry the triumphant news into all the homes of his half-awake acquaintances from the Notre Dame de Lorette district to the Faubourg Saint Germain.

A leap! Quick out of bed; trousers, shoes, and the rest, and into the street! Posters at the street corner announcing the order of march and the route. In the middle of our Rue Saint Georges troops were filling the building of *Le National.*

To go to our uncle's we went along the quays of the Cour des Comptes and of the Légion d'Honneur. All along them a regiment was encamped in luxury. Guns stacked, jugs of wine and all kinds of sausages on the benches, the men were having a public and praetorian feast, looking tipsy from last night's and this morning's drinking, their hearts full of gaiety. A stack of guns, badly arranged by these well-lubricated warriors, collapsed as we passed. Fortunately the guns were not drunk; they weren't feeling festive and didn't go off. . . .

Our uncle's old concierge, on the Rue de Verneuil, had a well-preserved tear in her owllike eyes: "Sir, I told him not to go there! They arrested him at the municipal building of the Tenth Arrondissement. He was determined to go; I told him . . ." We went to the barracks on the Quai d'Orsay. It was rumored that all those from the municipal offices were there. The door was closed. Some police were hiding the sword of the sergeant on duty. They told us: "They aren't here any more!" "Where are they?" "We don't know." And the sergeant said: "Beat it!"

I am sure that coups d'état would be even better if there were seats, stalls, boxes, so that one might see well and not miss anything. But this coup d'état almost misfired. It dared to spoil one of Paris's favorite pastimes: the strollers were not pleased. It was played in a low key—no drums; it was played fast like a curtain-raiser. There was hardly time to sit down. The fact was that we, the curious spectators, counted for nothing. At the most interesting moments the supernumeraries even shot at the windows—I mean the audience—and the worst of it was that they had forgotten to forget to load their guns. I assure you, this almost spoiled everything. Even I, who thought it was a bad play and yet, like a well-trained critic, patiently watched the police kicking men in the chest and the terrible cuirassiers, pistols in hand, charging against every cry of "Vive la République!"—watching the poor little barricades made of small boards often set up on the boulevards single-handed, and Deputies beaten up as they were arrested—even I, I say, who watched it all, tense, with rage in my heart, choking down a little anger with a great deal of shame, but silent as a carp, I almost hissed when at the end of the Rue Notre Dame de Lorette a woman walking past me got a bullet in her dress as the huntsmen of Vincennes took pot shots from the Rue Laffitte at the passersby.

Among all the posters that covered the walls on this December 2 and the following days to announce the new company, its repertory, its rehearsals, the hiring agents, and the new address of the director, moved from the Elysée to the Tuileries, there was one notice that did not appear, and yet was supposed to appear—a fact, indeed, of which Paris had no suspicion. Nothing was disturbed by this lack of a notice, neither the order of the elements nor the order of things. And yet it was no ordinary notice, this one which was to present to the world and to France, by means of two letters and two figures, *En 18 . . ,* two more men of letters, Edmond and Jules de Goncourt.

But Republics which want to be Empires, or rather men with debts and a star, care little about such things!

But the Gerdès Press was surrounded by troops. Gerdès

was frightened. *En 18 . .*, that suggested the 18th *Brumaire.* So Gerdès, who happened to be at the same time the printer of *La Revue des Deux Mondes* and of *En 18 . .*, threw the pack of posters that had been printed into the fire. The result was that we appeared on December 5 without notices—but with cuts in a political chapter. According to our printer we had, six months before, made the most dangerous allusions to what had now taken place.

So *En 18 . .* appeared, our first child, so cherished, so beloved, worked over and reworked for a year, an unfinished work marred by certain imitations of Gautier, but for a first work original to the point of strangeness, a first-born for which there was no need to blush, for it contained in embryo all the aspects of our talent, and all the colors of our palette, a little extreme still and too sharp. The first word of our sceptical credo had been spoken, and, as befitted us, with a smile.

Poor *En 18 . .*, what bad timing! A symphony of ideas and words in the midst of that rush for spoils!

Sunday, December 21

Janin had told us: "If you want to succeed, you know, there is nothing like the theatre." As we left him the idea came to us of doing a review of the year for the Théâtre Français in the form of a conversation by the hearth between a society man and woman during the last hours of the old year.

When we have finished this trifle and christened it *La Nuit de la Saint Sylvestre*, Janin gives us a letter for Madame Allan.

We climb up to the sixth floor, Rue Mogador, to the apartment of the actress who brought Musset back from Russia. A Byzantine Virgin in her salon reminds us of that fact.

Madame Allan is dressing before a theatrical mirror with two wings, a triptych mirror in which one can see oneself almost completely, even from behind. She welcomes us, and we are quite astonished at her voice, her everyday voice, rough, husky, and common compared to her theatre voice, so delicate, musical, caressing, and full of wit. With actors the voice plays a role like everything else.

And here we are, keeping the appointment she has made for today to listen to the small part we bring her. She listens, and we are in a cold sweat; she applauds in the middle with those little murmurs for which one could kiss the slippers of an actress, and accepts the part!

It is one o'clock. At two o'clock we rush to Janin's. But we have forgotten his column. Not possible to get off a letter now. "I'll speak of you tomorrow to Houssaye."

At three o'clock we enter the office of Arsène Houssaye, who receives us standing in front of his desk, without asking us to be seated. After we state our business, a play called *La Nuit de la Saint Sylvestre* which Madame Allan has agreed to learn between now and the thirty-first of December and which would be performed on New Year's Eve, he looks at us as a minister would look at an impertinent schoolboy and crushes us: "We shall not put on any new plays this winter. It is impossible. I can do nothing about it." Finally, "Have Lirieux read it and make a report. I'll arrange a special reading for you if I can!" A director's unctuous promises which he tosses out to you, as icy and suffocating as water thrown in your face.

We dash to Lirieux's, on some sixth floor or other. A mistress of his opens the door. "But you know that M. Lirieux is not to be disturbed! He is writing his column."

"Come in, gentlemen," Lirieux calls out, and we go into a

sort of den of a bachelor and man of letters, smelling of man and ink and an unmade bed. Lirieux is very pleasant, promises to read our piece this evening and make a report tomorrow.

From there we rush to see Brindeau. Out! His mother says he will be back at five. At four-thirty we write to Lirieux. At five we ring again at Brindeau's. We find the whole family. He will be back for a cup of bouillon. We chat with the actor's family till a quarter to six. No Brindeau!

At half-past seven we track him down in his dressing room at the Comédie Française.

"Tell me about it," he says as he dresses, dashing about the room in a white robe. "Impossible—sorry—to hear the play read." He continues to run around looking for a comb or something. "This evening?" "Impossible. I am going to dine with friends when I leave here. Oh, wait a moment; during the play I have a quarter of an hour off stage. I'll read it then. Wait for me in the theatre."

They were playing a thing by Gozlan. Finally it ends. Brindeau accepts and says he will speak to Houssaye. At eight o'clock we leave the manuscript at Lirieux's with a letter. At nine we are at Madame Allan's. She is surrounded by her family and students, playing the bourgeoise. We tell her about our day. So went our first day of literary emotions.

Two days later, sitting on a bench on the stairway of the Théâtre Français, we are trembling and shaking. We hear the voice of Madame Allan coming out of Houssaye's office: "That is not very nice!"

"Sunk!" one of us says to the other, with that physical and moral collapse so well depicted by Gavarni in the young man fallen on a chair in a cell at Clichy.

It was all over. Our soap bubble had burst. And really our little trifle deserved nothing better. It is the story of first literary dreams. They are made only to be followed in the sky by the eyes of children who watch them shine and burst.

1852

End of January

L'Eclair, a weekly review of literature, the theatre, and the arts, makes its appearance on January 12, 1852.

And here we are playing at journalism. Our paper has a ground-floor office on the Rue d'Aumale, a street that has barely been finished. We have a manager, to whom we give five francs per signature; he is Pouthier, a Bohemian painter, a school friend of Edmond. The review has one line: romanticism pure, raw, crude, and undiluted. It gives free advertisements and even promises of bonuses. Villedeuil, in whose ideas of business there is some of the extravagance of his dress—a little of his velvet waistcoats and his watch chains that make him look like an Italian prince at the table d'hôte of a cheap restaurant—Villedeuil suggests giving a ball as a bonus to subscribers. In fact, it is a review which lacks nothing, nothing except subscribers.

We spend two or three hours a week at this office, waiting each time a footstep passes by in this new street where few people pass, waiting for subscribers, readers, or contributors. Nothing comes, not even a manuscript—which is inconceivable—and, even more miraculous, not even a poet!

We intrepidly continue our review in a vacuum, with the faith of apostles and the illusions of stockholders. Villedeuil is forced to sell a collection of the *Edicts of the Kings of France* in order to keep it going; then he discovers a moneylender and gets five or six thousand francs from him. No change. The world obstinately ignores us. Our painter manager is replaced by one named Cahu, as fantastic as his name, a bookseller near the Sorbonne and a member of the Academy of Avranches. He is followed by another manager who looks like a nutcracker, an ex-soldier who has a nervous tic which causes him to look constantly at the place where his epaulettes would be and to spit over his shoulder.

I put the idea of Gavarni into Villedeuil's head; he takes fire and now the paper comes out with lithographs by Gavarni. . . . [1]

One fine day there at last came a subscription from an actress, the only one to subscribe to *L'Eclair*. She was a singer at the Théâtre Lyrique. Her name was Rouvroy. Her six francs were well invested. Villedeuil was later to squander with her a good part of his two millions.

One of Villedeuil's mistresses, a redhead named Sabine, came into the office one day and asked: "And why is that gentlemen so sad?" We answered in chorus: "He is our accountant!"

[*undated*]

On the road to Versailles at the Point du Jour gate near a cabaret with a sign "A la Renaissance du Perroquet Savant" a wall juts out. Its gates are so rusty one would think they would never open. Above the wall one could see the roof of a house and the top branches of pollarded chestnut trees, in the midst of which is a little square building, an ice house, with a scaly plaster statue on top of it—Houdon's *La Frileuse*.

In this dingy wall is a door with a broken bell-pull. Its cracked tinkling stirs up the barking of some big mountain dogs. There is a long wait. Finally a servant appears and con-

[1] This advocacy of Gavarni was decidedly effective. He provided a daily drawing for Villedeuil's next venture *Paris* for an entire year.

ducts us to a little studio in the garden, lighted from above and very gay. That is where we pay our first visit to Gavarni.

We go over the house with him—endless corridors on the third floor where old carnival costumes, badly packed, are falling out of women's hat boxes.

A monastic interior, a narrow little iron bed, two bookcases, a knife in a book entitled *Le Cartésianisme.*

He has a theory about the theatre: admiration for *Le Bourgeois Gentilhomme* and *Les Précieuses Ridicules* as excellent conventionalized farces; only likes the conventionalized. "Good plays are the ones that don't let you forget for a moment that they are plays, that they are on the stage." The audience must see that they have only flats and painted backdrops. The moment there is moonlight, illusion, a diorama, down it all falls! He has a horror for local color—for *Toledo blades. . . .*[2]

One day we decide to go on an excursion to Fontainebleau, to Marlotte, to "Papa" Saccault's place, the favorite locale of modern landscapists and of Murger. Amélie puts on her most elegant dress and all her jewelry, and we arrive in that forest where every tree seems to be a model surrounded by a circle of paint boxes.

There we take long walks, following the painters and their mistresses, who are sniffing the country air like working girls; it is like a working man's Sunday. We live as one family. Sounds of lovemaking can be heard through the partitions. We borrow each other's soap. We have enormous appetites for meager stews, all seasoned with wit, which makes us forget the bad wine and which fills the whole forest with a spirit of comedy, even in this Bas Bréau region, where it seems we

[2] A cliché which had come to represent the romantics' love of local color.

might expect to see Druids passing by. Everybody pays his share goodnaturedly. The girls get their shoes wet without complaining. Amid all the greenery Murger is gay like someone recovering from too much absinthe. Sitting on the rocks, we tell jokes.

We try playing billiards at Saccault's on a miserable table with cracks in it which cause the balls to carom back. On special days Palizzi puts on a kitchen apron and makes a leg of lamb *à la Juive,* which we devour down to the bones.

At night we sleep like plowmen; the day's sketches are hung up to dry; and as they are making love, Murger's mistress asks him how much *La Revue des Deux Mondes* pays per page.

August

I find Janin happy and beaming in spite of gout in one foot. "When they came to take my grandfather to the guillotine, he had gout in both feet. Anyway I'm not complaining; they say it adds ten years to your life! I have never been ill, and as for what makes a man, I still have that," he adds smiling.

He shows us a letter from Victor Hugo, brought over by Mademoiselle Thuillier: "It is gloomy here, it is raining; it is as if tears were falling." He goes on to thank Janin for his article on the Hugo furniture, says that his book [*Napoléon le Petit*] will appear in a month, and that he will send it to him in a basket of fish or a box of type. "They say after that Bonaparte will put me out of the Academy. I leave my chair to you."

November

Paris made its first appearance on October 22, 1852. It is the first daily literary paper since the beginning of the world. We wrote the first article.

1853

January

The offices of *Paris* were first at Number 1 Rue Laffitte on the ground floor next to the Maison d'Or restaurant. From there after a few months *Paris* moved to the Rue Bergère over the offices of *L'Assemblée Nationale.*

The center of attention in these premises was Villedeuil's office, where he had the black upholstery and the curtains with silver fringe from his salon in the Rue de Tournon—a millionaire undertaker's dream, in the midst of which Villedeuil took pleasure in scaring himself to death by drinking punch with all the candles out. This mortuary chamber where one seemed to be waiting for the corpse was the holy of holies of the paper. Next to it was the cashier's office, where Lebarbier, grandson of the eighteenth-century vignettist, held forth behind a barred window. We had picked him up along with Pouthier in the depths of Bohemia, and he was already putting on airs though still wearing old shoes of ours.

A fugitive from *Le Corsaire* did the make-up of the paper in a small salon. He was a little man with yellow hair and a round eye like an evil eye—a dubious man of letters, a suspect journalist. Only he and Villemessant had escaped the net which had gathered in all the legitimist journalists after December 2; he was a man who always seemed to me the police spy on the paper. He was a family man and a pillar of the Church, preaching good morals, crossing himself like a man astray in a sacrilegious crowd, yet in spite of all that using dirtier language than any of us. He was, ironically, assigned to editing *Les Mémoires de Madame Saqui.*

To the table in the *grand salon* the regulars of the editorial staff came daily: Murger, with his weepy eye, his fine wit of a taproom Chamfort, his humble, ingratiating drunkard's manner. Scholl, with his eyeglass in his eye and his ambition to make, within a week, fifty thousand francs a year from novels in twenty-five volumes. Banville, with the pale face of a Pierrot, his birdlike falsetto voice, his subtle paradoxes, the pretty silhouettes he drew of people. Karr, his head shaved like a jailbird's, accompanied by his inseparable Gatayes, looking like a calf's head at a picnic. A thin dirty fellow with stringy hair and the look of an onanist who was called Eggis and who had it in for the Academy. The inevitable Delaage, ubiquity made flesh and banality turned into a handshake, pasty-faced, grimy, sticky, looking like a kindly white of egg. Forgues, a frozen Southerner, who resembled the meat jelly Chinese cooks make and who with the air of a diplomat brought in sharp little articles written with needles. Louis Enault, who, adorned with cuffs, had the obsequious manner, the sinuous ingratiating air of a singer of romances. . . .

Charles in the midst of all these people arranged things, hurried about, went this way, ran that way, wrapped up in self-importance, as fatuous as a child and as serious as a minister, as proud as if he were in the shoes of Girardin. Since the paper was not getting any subscriptions, he was constantly full of projects, of innovations; every day he thought up a new system of advertisements or bonuses, some scheme, some man or some name that would get him ten thousand subscribers in a week.

In spite of everything the paper had found its niche: if it didn't make money it did make quite a stir. It was young and free; it was alive with real literary convictions. It was imbued with the spirit of 1830; there were in its columns the ardor and accuracy of aim of a band of sharpshooters. No order, no discipline; on principle, scorn on the part of everyone for subscriptions and subscribers; brilliance, zeal, imprudence, daring, wit, devotion to a certain ideal, illusions, a little madness, a bit of the ridiculous—such was this paper which never concerned itself, and that was its uniqueness and its glory, with being a business enterprise.

Sunday, February 20

At the end of December, Villedeuil came back from the Ministry of Police and in a voice full of tragedy said:

"The paper is being prosecuted. Two articles are under attack. One is by Karr. The other is an article in which there is some verse. Who put verse in an article recently?"

"We did."

"So, it is you! That's just fine."

Here is the pretext for the prosecution, which would force us to appear in police court and would smear us with an accusation and doubtless a conviction for offense against public morals and morality in general, before a court from which there is no appeal and whose judgment alone would be published, mentioning the nature of our offense in such a way that we would scarcely be distinguished from homosexuals or Ignorantine friars who molest little boys.

On December 15 we had published an imaginative article made up of bits and pieces. The title of the article was "Journey from Number 43 Rue Saint Georges to Number 1 Rue Laffitte." A journey in the manner of Sterne from our street to the office of the paper, giving a series of fanciful descriptions of the businesses, the shops selling odd objects, the dealers, male and female, in paintings and bibelots that we passed on our way, and among others the shop of a woman once famous as a model in various studios. In this we had inserted without names the story of a nude by Diaz sent by Nathalie to Rachel, who sent it back. Nathalie then took revenge on Rachel's prudery in a letter. There were two letters in Janin's possession which he kept in the front of a copy of *Gabrielle*, and in referring to Diaz we had quoted these lines by Tahureau:

> Croisant ses beaux membres nus
> Sur Adonis, qu'elle baise,[3]
> Et lui pressant le doux flanc,
> Son cou douillettement blanc
> Mordille de trop grand aise.

It was for the quotation of these five lines that the courts of our country were holding us to account and for which they were going to punish us.

But behind this incredibly puerile pretext for the suit there was a reason. There were undercurrents to the affair, a secret order given by the powers-that-be to the judges, the fine hand of the Ministry of Police, the resentment of minor officials, the suspicions of the bureau head, the literary opinions of the Ministry, perhaps an actress's revenge. These are all the things that in a Late Empire can build up a storm over the head of an honest man.

We had sensed the coming of this blow for a long time. The paper was not in good odor. "They" didn't like the editor's title of count or his financial independence. *Paris* was considered to be the continuation of *Le Corsaire*. It seemed too that we personally were objects of displeasure. We were supposed to be ardent Orleanists, and in the Faubourg Saint Germain, to be people who had refused to sing

[3] At least some of the difficulty over this article must be imputed to the verb *baiser*, which in the sixteenth century meant *to kiss*, but by mid-nineteenth century had degenerated to *to copulate* in the vulgar.

the right tune. They even held against us our reply to the charge, a Roman reply. We were under suspicion also for vivacity of style and violent epithets.

In spite of everything disquieting rumors increased. Dumas, who was connected with the supervisor of the press at the Ministry of Police—a certain Latour-Dumoulin, a sort of Bohemian of industry, whom he had once taken to see Girardin to offer him a new type of button for his gaiters—Dumas *fils* kept us informed of all the wounded feelings and all the ill will that was piling up there. "M. de Villedeuil comes to the Ministry in his carriage. When he sends in his card and I tell him to wait, he leaves. The proof of the paper's hostility to the government is shown by this: everyone else humbles himself to get invitations to the Tuileries or to M. de Nieuwerkerke's; this paper has never made such a request!"

M. de Maupas told the Abbé de Susini, who was sent to him by Villedeuil: "M. de Villedeuil has gambled on a falling market. We don't want anything to do with his paper." And we must not forget that Rachel had been Prince Napoleon's mistress.

We waited, and we slept badly, as one sleeps while waiting for justice from a police court under an Empire. Nothing is less reassuring and more frightening in such a case than a good conscience. Not to feel guilty is to be sure to be condemned. The slow meshing of the gears of this heavy wheel made us hope at times that the thing would not go through to the end; and then one evening at home, while we were entertaining friends, in the midst of the tobacco smoke, there arrived two of the four summonses, the others were for Karr and for Lebarbier, the manager of the paper.

I sent my de Courmont uncle to see Latour-Dumoulin, who said: "Sir, I am glad to have the information you have given me about these two young men. I must admit that as the matter was first presented we believed that there was a question of blackmail. At any rate, now that I am better informed, I have sent my private secretary to M. de Royer to tone down the proceedings, and I authorize you to report to the young men the steps I have taken."

Making another approach, a councillor of state, M. Armand Lefebvre, also a member of my family, wrote to M. de Royer in our behalf. M. de Royer replied that we were not being proceeded against for the lines we had quoted but for quite another reason. I am holding in reserve the admission by the state prosecutor. And orally he told M. Lefebvre that we would be convicted, that we would get a prison sentence, but that we had only to make a plea to the Emperor for mercy, and that he would be the first to support it. This was straight to the point and the plan in the prosecutor's mind was all worked out: we would first be somewhat dishonored by the conviction and then completely so by the plea for mercy. The Empire, it appeared, had need of two more low acts; at least M. de Royer thought so. It was an illusion that he lost later, or so I like to think.

Upon being summoned, we appeared at the Palais de Justice before one of those men who have raised interrogation to the level of torture. Our examining magistrate was named Braux. He questioned us rather as if we had smothered our mother in flannel vests. Perhaps he was brutal in order not to appear embarrassed. When we pointed out to him that we had taken the lines of Tahureau from *L'Essai sur la Littérature du XVIe Siècle* by Sainte-Beuve, a book that was practically a classic and which had raised its author to the Academy, he took the blow head on and, not knowing what to reply, he forgot whatever manners he had, which weren't much to speak of! As we went out, we said to Karr: "We are being prosecuted for offense against bad manners!"

We had to have a lawyer. It would have been lacking in respect for our accusers not to have one. A connection of our family, a lawyer at the Cour de Cassation, M. Jules Delaborde, advised us not to employ a brilliant lawyer whose talent might wound and irritate the judges. We needed a lawyer who had, as they say, the ear of the court, one of those honest, stupid men whose nonentity draws a sort of pity to his client. . . . The man he suggested, who answered to all these conditions, was named Mahon. . . . When I explained our case to him, he was quite embarrassed. He did not know quite what to make of us. We were for him a sort of combination of men of the world and criminals. He would have entrusted his watch to us with one hand and taken it away with the other. . . .

We were summoned to appear in police court before the sixth chamber on February 2. That was the court specializing in this sort of case, a court in which "they" had confidence, one which had proved itself. Its complaisance had gained it the honor of specializing in cases against the press and in political cases. . . .

Just before our case they brought in a skinny little young man who, after December 2, had on his own authority condemned the Emperor to death, and had sent notice of his condemnation to all the embassies. They quickly sentenced him to three years in prison for having had more courage than the High Court. . . .

Finally we were called up. . . .

. . . Paillard de Villeneuve, Karr's lawyer, very cleverly

and with a certain degree of eloquence made holes in the oratory of the prosecution, showed it for what it was, and asked how they dared proceed against us for an article which was not incriminating and when the author in question was not present with us at the bar.

My lawyer was just what we expected. He described us as two nice young men and cited in our favor the fact that we had had the same old servant for twenty years, a patriarchal plea, all very paternal, which, however, for a moment, in view of the incredible accusation, rose to the occasion like a goose taking wing. We sensed that the spectators were won over; we felt the murmur that greets a successful plea in the courtroom, the unconscious sympathy in an audience which rises up and takes a stand against an accusation. A conviction was impossible in these circumstances. The court adjourned the case for a week. "That's it!" we said. "They think they can get away with a conviction at the beginning of a session. Today they didn't dare."

But the postponement was our salvation. During the week the prosecutor was changed. Rouland replaced Royer. Rouland still had Orleanist connections. He was a relative of Janin's wife, who had spoken to him about us. There were ties between him and the Passy family, who had also worked hard for us.

We came back at the end of a week. The handing down of the sentence was put off to the end of the session. We went to lunch with Karr, on the Place du Palais de Justice, feeling very resigned, hoping for nothing. We returned to the courtroom. We rose to hear the judgment and were greatly astonished to hear issuing from Legonidec's mouth an acquittal with censure!

July 27

I go to see Rouland to find out whether I can publish *La Lorette* without getting into trouble with the police again. And in the conversation with him about our prosecution he confirms one thing that had already been told me, that the Ministry of Police in addition to what it was prosecuting us for was really attacking certain literary ideas: "They did not want *any literature which is heady and excites others.* That was their idea, which it was not my place to comment on." Yes, there was the crime of romanticism in our affair, in this year of grace 1853! Had not Latour-Dumoulin said to our cousin on February 10: "I must say that I am very sorry about the prosecution of these gentlemen. You know how magistrates are . . . very fussy, those people. However, I think they are on the wrong literary track, and I think I am doing them a favor by this prosecution."

1854

End of February

All this winter working like mad at our *L'Histoire de la Société pendant la Révolution.* We carry away some four hundred pamphlets all at one time from M. Perrot, who lives on the Rue des Martyrs, a poor, very poor collector who has made a collection of very rare pamphlets, bought for two sous on the quays, sometimes pawning his watch, a silver watch. We excerpt from them all day. At night we write our book. We have given away our old evening clothes and haven't had any new ones made, so it is impossible for us to go anywhere. No women, no pleasures, no amusements; work, constant work, and mental strain. To get a little exercise in order to avoid falling ill, we allow ourselves a walk after dinner, a walk in the dark on the outer boulevards so as to avoid any distractions which would entice us away from our work and our complete mental immersion in our writing.

May 20

M. Hiltbrunner, the director of the Théâtre des Délassements, to the architect Chabouillet:

"Sir, my theatre is a brothel!"

"Oh, sir!"

"No, sir, my theatre is a brothel! It is quite simple. I only pay my actresses fifty or sixty francs a month. I have to pay 30,000 francs rent, so I can't pay them more than that. My actors get scarcely any more. They are all pimps or homosexuals. Often a woman comes to me and says the fifty francs is not enough, that she will be obliged to solicit, to pick men up in the audience at five sous. It is none of my business. I have to pay that 30,000 francs rent!"

1856

May 10

When Murger wrote *La Vie de Bohème* he had no idea that he was writing the history of something which would become a force in five or six years, and yet that is the case. The world where they scrounge for a five-franc piece, this free masonry of publicity, now rules and governs and ostracizes anyone who is well born. "He's an *amateur!*" and with that word they kill him. He might have back of him the learning of a Benedictine or the imagination of Heine, but he will be dubbed an amateur by one of Villemessant's *hirelings* who has neither verve nor talent. Without anyone's suspecting it, socialism is ruling literature and shooting red bullets at the literary capital. And yet the movement of 1830 was for the most part led by men who had independent means, Hugo, etc.

July 16

After reading Poe. Something that the critics have not seen, a new literary world, the portent of the literature of the twentieth century. The scientific miracle, a story on mathematical lines, a morbid and lucid literature. No more poetry! Imagination through analysis, Zadig an examining magistrate, Cyrano de Bergerac a pupil of Arago. Something of monomania. Things having more importance than men; love giving place to deduction and other sources of ideas, of phrasing, of narration, and of interest; the foundation of the novel displaced from the heart and removed to the head; from passion to ideas, from drama to solutions.

August 1

Met Banville on the boulevard, slovenly, long beard, just back from a museum trip from Paris to Bordeaux with Arsène Houssaye, paid for by the latter in return for Banville's taking notes for him. Took him to dinner at Maire's.

Banville, even before the wine, a delightful talker, full of the best irony, the most amusingly malicious remarks, overflowing with backstage gossip, reporting what one never reads, with insights and paradoxes that are new and charming, superb philosophy, thumbnail sketches, scenes like engravings, a *Comédie Humaine* which charms me, delights me, instructs me.

The truest, most intimate, most informal portrait of Houssaye, that blond director who hides and takes refuge behind his beard; the king of inertia, from whom one can get neither a look nor a word; the clever man with the vague expression, who avoids everything, agreement or answer, with a grunt; Houssaye of the great company of the absentminded, the preoccupied, the heads-in-air of our century, Beauvoir, Gaiffe, etc., the wisest and most sensible madmen imaginable, playing the ambiguous role of Julius Caesar; strong men, marvelous actors, stirring up tempests in dirty teapots, the equals of Talleyrand!

October 30

Realism is born and breaks out when the daguerreotype and photograph show how much art differs from reality.

December 25

Sold to Dentu the twenty *Portraits Intimes du XVIIIe Siècle* for 300 francs—that doesn't pay for the oil and wood we burned—two volumes for the making of which we bought two or three thousand francs' worth of autograph letters.

1857

January 20

As we were talking at the office of *L'Artiste* about Flaubert, who like us had been dragged before the police court, and as I was explaining that the higher-ups wanted the death of romanticism and that romanticism had become a crime against the State, Gautier went on to say: "Really, I blush for the profession I practice! For the very modest sums which I must earn because without them I would starve to death I say only the half or the quarter of what I think, and even then with each sentence I risk being dragged into court!"

March 16

Publication of the first volume of our *Portraits Intimes du XVIIIe Siècle.* Barrière of *Les Débats* reproaches us for wasting talent on trifling things. The public needs solid and compact bodies of work in which it meets people it has seen before, in which it hears things it knows already. Things that are too little known, virgin documents, frighten it. A history of the eighteenth century as I understand it, in a long series of autograph letters and unpublished documents providing a pretext for developing all aspects of the century, a history that is new, subtle, exquisite, differing in form from histories in general, will not bring in a quarter of what I would get from a solid history where my plan would be clearly stated in the title and where I would plod through whole pages of well-known facts. Barrière said that, and perhaps he was right. Now I have an idea for a book on Marie-Antoinette.

Met Rosa Bonheur at a dinner at the Passys'—she looks like a little humpbacked Polish Jew. She is accompanied by her ever-present friend, Nathalie, who looks like an exhausted Pierrot, an old Deburau, lacking only the black headband.

April 11

At five o'clock went to the office of *L'Artiste.* Gautier, Feydeau, Flaubert there. Feydeau always like a child whose first article has just been printed; an infatuation, an admiration for himself, so self-satisfied and so puffed up in such good faith and so naively insolent that you are disarmed. Asking Gautier apropos of the first of his *Saisons,* which will appear at each solstice: "Don't you think it is a pearl? I should like to dedicate a pearl to you!"

A great discussion about metaphors. "His opinions had no need to blush for his conduct," from Massillon, was acquitted by Flaubert and Gautier. "He rode horseback, that pedestal of princes," by Lamartine, was condemned without appeal.

After that a wild discussion of assonance. An assonance, according to Flaubert, should always be avoided even if it takes you a week to get around it. Then between Flaubert and Feydeau a thousand rules for style were tossed back and forth; little mechanical tricks emphatically and seriously explained, a discussion that was both puerile and serious, ridiculous and solemn, of ways to write and of rules for good prose. So much importance attached to the clothing of the idea, to its color and texture, that the idea was no longer anything but a rack on which to hang sound and light. It seemed to us that we had stumbled into a discussion by grammarians of the Late Empire.

May 4

Louis Passy came to see us this morning to tell us about Sainte-Beuve's long article on *Madame Bovary*, as eager as a friend who comes to tell you a bit of bad news. Went on at great length about the importance of such an article and, not having enough tact to grasp the fact that we had understood perfectly and that the shot had hit the mark, finally told us with a certain insistence: "It is an article such as I would have liked to see written about you."

May 12

Gautier—the stylist in the red waistcoat for the benefit of the bourgeois—the most astonishing common sense on literary matters, the sanest judgment, a terrific lucidity coming out in short, simple sentences, in a voice like a soft caress. This man who seems at first reserved and shut within himself certainly has great charm and is extremely congenial. He says that when he wanted to do something good he always started with verse because there is always uncertainty about form in prose, whereas verse, when it is good, is like a stamped medallion. But the exigencies of life have made him write many stories in prose which he began in verse.

Musset is dead, one of the least authentic originalities, a talent completely suffused with the originality of Shakespeare, of Byron, and even of Joachim du Bellay, from whom he did not disdain to plagiarize a whole passage.

Those who labor over form in this century are not lucky. Really, to observe the hostility of the public to carefully wrought style, the style of all works that have survived, one would think that the public had never read a classic, that it seriously believed that all works of imagination were written by M. Dumas and all history by M. Thiers. The public seems to want to read as it sleeps, without fatigue, without effort, and its hatred seems to turn into the fury of ignorance.

May 19

Baudelaire, coming down from a prostitute's room, meets Sainte-Beuve on the stairs. Baudelaire: "Oh, I know where you are going!" Sainte-Beuve: "And I, where you have been! But wait, I'd rather go somewhere and talk." They go to a café. Sainte-Beuve: "You know, what disgusts me about philosophers—Cousin and the rest—what makes them odious to me is that they do nothing but talk about the immortality of the soul and the good Lord. They know very well that there is no such thing as immortality of the soul or a good Lord. It is disgusting!" And thereupon a tirade on atheism which makes the most daring philosopher of the eighteenth century seem like Saint John—getting more animated and excited, attacking God so fiercely that all the domino games in the café come to a stop—this by that same Sainte-Beuve who made Cardinal de Bernis practically an early father of the Church!

June 4

At the Hôtel Drouot saw the first sale of photographs. Everything is becoming black in this century: photography is like the black clothing of things.

Château de Croissy,
September 3 to 21

Read Balzac's *Les Paysans.* No one has thought or spoken of Balzac as a statesman, and yet he is perhaps the greatest one of our times, a great socially minded statesman, the only one who has got to the bottom of our malaise, the only one who has seen in broad perspective the disturbed condition of France since 1789—the customs behind the laws, the deed behind the word, the anarchy of unbridled interests behind the apparent order in the competition of talents; abuses replaced by influence, privileges by other privileges, inequality before the law by inequality before the judge; the falsehood in the program of 1789, money instead of a name, bankers instead of nobles, and communism, the executioner of fortunes, at the end of it all. Strange that only a novelist should have seen this!

Read *La Mare au Diable* by George Sand, in which it is said that "purity of morals is a sacred tradition in certain rural areas remote from the corrupting influence of great cities." The eighteenth century—Boucher, the narcissistic painters and novelists—only put ribbons on the peasants;

Madame Sand gives them a soul—her soul. Fake genius and false spirit, which comes down from *Paul et Virginie* by way of *L'Astrée*. From Mademoiselle de Scudéry to Madame Sand, not omitting Madame de Staël, women have a genius for the false. . . .

Read Sainte-Beuve's *Causeries du Lundi*, that dictionary of conversation and biography. There is a phrase of Heinrich Heine about himself which characterizes this man perfectly: "unfrocked romantic." That is it, the man and the style completely unfrocked: part Saint-Simon for young ladies, part suggestiveness, part trickiness, part a quality of being ill at ease, part moral cowardice in an effort to curry favor, compromises of conscience and of propriety, the violence of a priest, the attitudes of an old man at once disavowed and denied. A sermonizing content, a sour smile, a prudish criticism, reciting the *mea culpa* of youth and of the romantic spirit mounted on the backs of the sturdy, bold, and frank geniuses of France. On the one hand, corrupted by his novel *Volupté* into making little inquiries into the petty and unwholesome side of human nature; but on the other, constantly exorcising the demon with high-sounding words, the sign of the cross, invoking God, society, the world, and human nature, and reciting the litany of the classic saints.

A small mind, after all, ambitious but low, a better judge of phrases than of books, an analyst of bits and parts, judging style by grammar, an enemy of wit out of envy, a lover of platitudes, running his little arms over the statues of great men and ending by clinging to their feet of clay.

Paris, October

The Café Riche seems at the moment to be trying to become the gathering place for men of letters who have gloves.

An odd thing how places create their clientele. Beneath that white and gold, onto that red plush, none of the vagabonds dares to venture. Murger, with whom we are dining, makes his profession of faith. He renounces Bohemia and is going over, bag and baggage, to the men of letters of good society. He is becoming the Mirabeau of the group. . . .

Baudelaire at supper nearby—no necktie, neck bare, head shaven as though ready for the guillotine. A single nicety; small hands carefully washed, nails trimmed and polished. Looking like a madman but having a voice as sharp as a steel blade. Pedantic style of speech, tries to be a Saint-Just and succeeds. Denies obstinately, and with a surly passion, that he ever was guilty of outrage to morality in his poetry.

1858

Tuesday, April 13

Reread *Le Neveu de Rameau.* What a man Diderot was, what a river, as Mercier said! What a book that is, genius probing into human consciousness! A terrible refutation of the justice of posterity: Diderot having a second-rate popularity, one that is almost suspect; Diderot, the Homer of modern thought, considered dull in comparison with the figure who dominated his time, interested everyone, invaded the future—that Voltaire with the mentality of the National Guard, no more! Take away from the latter his success, his tragedies, his books touching on everything, and what is left? *Candide,* his one glory, his only claim to fame.

April 23

At Gavarni's we meet Guys, the artist for the *Illustrated London News,* who, with high style and strong brush strokes, presents brothel scenes conveying the moral physiognomy of prostitution in this century.

He is a strange man who has experienced all the ups and downs of life, who has ranged widely through the world and its hazards, who has impaired his health in all sorts of climates and loves; a man who has known the furnished lodgings of London, fashionable great houses, German gambling dens, Greek massacres, Paris boarding houses, newspaper offices, the trenches at Sevastopol, mercury cures, the plague, Oriental dogs, duels, prostitutes, thieves, roués, usury, poverty, cut-throats, and the lower depths where all fallen creatures swarm as in the sea—all those nameless and shoeless men, all those submerged and terrible beings who never come up to the surface in novels.

A small man, he has survived all that with energy, a terrific energy concealed behind his grey moustaches; he is strange, chameleonlike, diverse, changing his voice and his appearance, seeming multiple and various, making you forget for a moment the grumbler you have next to you, and with his lively speech and mobile face continually changing his mask, becoming all the characters he depicts for you; limping along the road and bumping into you as he is blown along by the wind; with a quick and nervous gesture of the palm of his hand constantly pushing up his sleeves over his bony arms; diffuse, verbose, overflowing with parentheses, zigzagging from idea to idea, losing the thread, finding it again, never letting go your attention for a moment, holding you constantly under the spell of his brilliant, colorful speech, which is loud and almost visible to the eye, like a painting. An eloquence which is loquacious, felicitous, and very personal. And all of a sudden when your attention is about to wander, he catches it again with a vulgar image or a slangy metaphor, and out of the disorder and bedazzlement there suddenly issues a phrase worthy of one of the great German thinkers, or an object is defined by a word from the technical vocabulary of art with the sharpness of relief of the Elgin Marbles.

He evokes a thousand things in his promenade through memory, tossing out from time to time handfuls of irony, sketches, memories, landscapes, pictures, profiles, vignettes of streets, crossroads, or sidewalks where you hear the clattering of women's sandals; views of cities riddled with bullets, gutted and bleeding, hospitals teeming with rats. Then in contrast with all that—as in an album you find a thought by Balzac on the back of a drawing by Decamps—he comes out with social sketches, comments on the English species and the French species that are new and have not been moldering in books, a comparative philosophy of the national character of peoples, two-minute satires, pamphlets in one word.[4]

1859

February 17

I am in a room on the ground floor. Two windows without curtains letting in a white light and showing a small scrubby garden with spindly trees. In front of me a large wheel with little wheels geared to it. At the wheel a bare-armed man, his sleeves rolled up, a man in a grey smock who is wiping with gauze tampons a copper plate covered in black and is edging it with Spanish white. On the walls two drawings, caricatures, fastened up with pins, and a cuckoo clock which seems to breathe the time. At the rear a cast-iron stove, some

[4] Edmond de Goncourt in a late *Journal* entry on April 22, 1895, gave a radically unfavorable judgment of Guys, calling him a clumsy draftsman and dirty colorist.

large boxes standing upright and separated into two rows. At the foot of the stove a black dog, flat on his side, asleep and snoring, two feet stretched out.

The door continually opens, making the panes rattle, and three little children, their cheeks fat as buttocks, press their faces against the panes, come in, run around the press amid all the copper and acid under the tables and into the legs of the man who is wiping the plates.

And in my chair I sit waiting, like a general who has made a plan of campaign and is leaving the rest to Providence, or like a father who is waiting for a son, a daughter, or a monkey. A true emotion. I am having my first etching pulled at Delâtre's, the portrait of Augustin de Saint-Aubin. For days now we have been plunged in acid up to the neck and over the head! It is a strange thing: nothing in our life has taken hold of us like these things, first, drawing, now, etching. Never have things of the imagination gripped us with such power, making us forget absolutely not only time, but life, troubles, everyone and everything. For whole days one lives entirely immersed in it from morning till night; one seeks a shape as one never seeks an idea; one pursues a line and a dry point effect as one would not pursue the scenario for a book! That is the way it is with us. Never perhaps in any situation in our lives such great desire, such impatience, such longing for the next day—for the great test, the great culmination in the pulling of the print.

And watching the plate being washed, blackened, and cleaned, watching the wetting of the paper, the raising of the press, the placing of the covering, the two turns of the wheel—all that makes your heart beat and your hands tremble at the touch of the damp paper which bears the more or less viable line.

1860

Thursday, January 12

At our table are Flaubert, Saint-Victor, Scholl, Charles Edmond, and in the way of women Julie and Madame Doche, who has a red net over her hair, which has a touch of powder in it. We talk of the novel *Lui* by Madame Colet, where Flaubert appears under the name of Léonce, and from time to time Scholl, in order to call attention to himself, jokes about something or lambastes an absent friend. Finally he swears on his honor that he will give Lurine a beating.

At dessert Doche leaves for the dress rehearsal of *La Pénélope Normande,* which is to open tomorrow, and Saint-Victor, who has nothing for his column, leaves for the rehearsal too with Scholl.

And so the rest of us begin to talk theatre, and Flaubert takes the bit in his teeth and is off: "The theatre is not an art, it is a secret. I stole the secret from those who possess it. Here it is: First, you must drink several absinthes at the Café du Cirque, then say of any play: 'It isn't bad, but it needs cutting!' Repeat: 'Yes, but it isn't a play!' Above all always sketch out a play but never write one. When one has written a play, even when one has written an article in *Le Figaro,* one is done for! I have studied the secret in an idiot who possesses it, La Rounat. It was La Rounat who coined the sublime phrase, 'Beaumarchais is a prejudice!' Beaumarchais!" Flaubert exclaims, "filth and fire! Let him try to create even a character like Chérubin."

Has never wanted to let *Madame Bovary* be put on the stage, believing that an idea is right for one medium and that it can't be used for two purposes, also not wanting to put her in the hands of a Dennery. "Do you know what is necessary for success in the boulevard theatres? That the audience should be able to guess everything that is going to happen. I once found myself next to two women who from scene to scene told each other what would happen next. They made up the play as they went along!"

Then the conversation turns to various people of our acquaintance, the difficulty of finding people one could live with who are not corrupt, or unbearable, or bourgeois, or bad mannered. Charles Edmond promises to name ten but only comes up with three or four....

Then we give actresses a going over, discussing the oddities of those singular creatures. Flaubert gives his recipe for making them: one must be sentimental and take them seriously. Then the question is raised as to whether they sleep with men as much as the latter say they do, whether care of their health, the fatigue and demands of the theatre do not reduce their affairs to mere flirtations....

Then we are alone with him in the room filled with cigar smoke, he pacing the floor, bumping his head on the hanging lamp, overflowing, letting himself go as one does with kindred spirits.

He talks about his withdrawn, unsociable life—even in Paris—one that is shut in and closed off. Hating the theatre, having no diversion except for Madame Sabatier's Sunday dinner—the President, as they call her in Gautier's circle—hating the country. Working ten hours a day, but wasting a great deal of time, losing himself in books and always ready to play truant from his work. Not getting really warmed up till five in the afternoon, though he starts at noon; not being able to write on blank paper, needing to cover it with ideas as a painter places his first colors.

Then we talk of the few people who are interested in a thing *well done,* the rhythm of a phrase, a thing that is beautiful in itself:

"Can you understand the idiocy of trying to remove all assonances from a sentence, all repetitions from a page? For whom? And then too, even when the work succeeds, the success that comes is never the one wanted. It is the entertaining aspects of *Madame Bovary* which have made it a success. Success always comes for the wrong reasons. Yes, form—who in the public takes delight in or is satisfied with form? And notice that form is what makes you suspect to the law, in the courts which always have classical tastes. But no one has read the classics! Not eight men of letters have read Voltaire. I mean *read.* Not five who know the titles of Thomas Corneille's plays. Yet as for imagery, the classics are full of it. Tragedy is nothing but images. Pétrus Borel would never have risked this mad image:

> Brûlé de plus de feu que je n'en allumai . . .
>
> [in Racine's *Phédre*].

"Art for art's sake? It has never been honored as in the Academy speech of a classic—Buffon: 'The manner in which a truth is expressed is more useful to humanity than that truth itself.' I trust that is art for art's sake! And La Bruyère, who said: 'The art of writing is the art of defining and depicting.' "

Then he tells us his three breviaries of style: La Bruyère, a few pages of Montesquieu, a few chapters of Chateaubriand, and he is off, his eyes bulging from his head, his face flushed, his arms raised as in a theatrical embrace, with the exaltation of Antaeus, bringing forth from his chest and his throat fragments from Montesquieu's *Le Dialogue de Sylla et d'Eucrate*, to which he gives a brassy sound like the roar of a lion.

Flaubert quotes to us the sublime comment made by Limayrac on *Madame Bovary*, of which the last sentence is: "How could anyone indulge in such an ignoble style when there is on the throne the greatest writer of the French language—the Emperor?"

March 4

As we talk about *Madame Bovary* [Flaubert] tells us that there is a single character sketched from life, but very remotely—the elder Bovary, who is drawn after a certain Enault, a former paymaster in the Imperial armies, boastful, debauched, good for nothing, threatening his mother with a sword in order to get money, wearing a policeman's cap, leather trousers, and boots; a man who at Sotteville was the support of the Lalanne Circus, whose members used to come to drink hot wine with him which they made in basins on the stove, and whose girl riders used to give birth to their children at his place.

Thursday, May 17

Dinner with Gavarni. Concerning his portraits tells us that he wants to move somewhat in the direction of idealization, toward a generalized physiognomy. Photography only gives one aspect, and besides it is time for painting to show a little enthusiasm for the beauties that do not show up at all in the darkroom.

A Thursday at the end of May

On Gavarni's easel there is a sepia representing a grotto in the Pyrenees, dating from the time when he kept to a minimum of white spaces or margins. Beside the sepia, a very curious drawing representing Gavarni's room at Tarbes. The room, with the footboard of the bed, the painter's folding seat leaning against it, his dilapidated felt hat on the counterpane, his sandals under the bed, the wallpaper in a trellis pattern with a man's portrait hanging against it, the parquet floor with its inlay forming designs, a partly open door on which is hanging a hunter's game bag, and in the open hallway the reflection of the slats of the blinds forming a perspective which seems to rise before the eye. Perhaps the most curious and characteristic drawing, showing Gavarni's point of departure, a drawing made with a compass which seems to have some of the conscientiousness and patience of a Van Eyck. Never has an artist gone so far from one extreme to the other of art.

Feydeau is there. When it comes to literary vanity, his is one of the most monstrous I have ever seen. It goes from insolence to childishness with a naiveté and impulsiveness which really stun you. And I think, on my honor, that of all literary "egos" he is the one who least knows how to live. Whoever or whatever comes up, he always places that person or thing in relation to *Fanny*. Any man who dares touch *Fanny* is a monster, a homosexual—at the very least—a man without convictions, homeless, shoeless, sexless. It would be enough to make you give up literary animosities in disgust, if you had any.

July 12

I go to an important exposition of paintings and drawings of the eighteenth century, a showing of the art I love. I scarcely recognize the paintings I have already seen and which I used to be fond of. The masters who charmed me, I seek in vain their charm. Perhaps all of it, the charm of a work of art, is in ourselves and, so to speak, in the momentary mood of the eye. The words people say to me seem grey. I feel that I have seen brighter, gayer sunlight. I have happened on one of those days where you would like to be somewhere else, somewhere far off from where you are. If a whole populace were overcome by such prostration, by such an emptiness in the head, they would start a revolution that very evening for the interest of seeing what got broken or who got guillotined.

July 15

I heard recently how the government buys scholars. It does not take long. I had been told that in order to corrupt men it was necessary to feel one's way, to make careful approaches, to have a third party open the subject, in short, to spend a little time and exercise some delicacy.

The Emperor sends for Monsieur Renan, tells him that he has been following his work with interest, asks him if he would not like to see the peoples and the places of which he speaks in his books—Syria, Palestine. Renan replies that he would but does not have the money for such a journey. "How much do you want?" asks the Emperor. The other replies, just like ushers in the theatre:

"I don't know; whatever you wish."

"But I want you to be the one to fix the amount. You must know approximately."

"Well, it seems to me that 25,000 francs . . ."

There's one case!

August 17

Daumier, whom we see for the first time [at the offices of *Le Temps*], long white hair swept back behind his ears, a bit in the fashion of Béranger, a full face, rather pale, two very black small eyes, a little nose shaped like a potato, a large man with a sharp voice and with nothing kind or open in his physiognomy.

August 24

We were naive enough to enter our *Histoire de Marie-Antoinette* in the Academy competition. I admit frankly that it was not for honor, but for money. The Academy, which resembles certain institutions in the provinces where they give consolation prizes to pupils who don't get any others, has honored many books that the public has made the mistake of not reading, and also many people whose names I have been very glad to learn.

August 30

Flaubert, whom we had asked to put us in touch with some hospitals for our novel *Soeur Philomène*, takes us to see Doctor Follin, a great surgeon and one of his friends. A stout, well-fed man with intelligent eyes, who understands immediately what we want and that we need to enter *in medias res*, to observe the clinic and dine with the internes and the nurses.

We feel a sort of shudder at the world he is going to open up to us; we feel in it a sense of drama without words, which sends chills down the spine, and our book grows in our imaginations to the point that it frightens us.

October 11

Once more that criticism of Gavarni that he doesn't depict virtuous people, that he represents them with dark rings under their eyes, with faces that are tired and pale. Nonsense! Gavarni shows Parisians, people of the capital, exhausted people. In the nineteenth century he cannot paint the innocents and saints and the calm and stupid bourgeois louts of the German primitives. It is as if one asked one's wife to be the type of a Virgin by Schongauer.

November 1

A big dinner at Gavarni's. . . .

Monnier is still the unforgettable Prudhomme,[5] even improvising pantomimes, with infinite delicacy of detail, such as the egotist at table or the arguer at table or the country woman in the Salon of the Louvre, crossing herself in front of all the religious pictures. . . .

As we go along the road to the station, Monnier tells me that Flaubert is an epileptic. Is he? Isn't he? The fall he had last winter would seem to lend support to Monnier's statement. Perhaps this is also the explanation for his great disappointment in love: perhaps a woman left him or was unwilling to have him when she discovered this.

November 29

Flaubert drops in on us. He is here for his friend Bouilhet's play [*L'Oncle Million*] at the Odéon. Still in his Carthage novel, buried in it like a grub, working like an ox. Has gone nowhere except for two days at Etretat. In his novel he has now reached the copulation scene, a Carthaginian copulation, and he says: "I must set it up for my public. I must create the illusion of a man, who thinks he is penetrating the moon, coupling with a woman, who thinks she is receiving the sun." . . .

I know that with all allowance for differences there are

[5] Joseph Prudhomme, the creation of the caricaturist Henri Monnier, is the incarnation of bourgeois platitudes.

many points of resemblance between us and Chateaubriand. He was fundamentally a sceptic like us, yet a defender of religion. He was both a monarchist and a liberal. He was essentially an aristocrat. We have all those characteristics, with their apparent contradiction, but like him, without any doubt, in complete good faith. For a man is not all of one piece. He is made up of feelings and ideas which are often contradictory, but it is enough for him to hold them with conviction to be an honest man.

Perhaps the ability to observe, that great quality possessed by the modern writer, comes from the fact that the writer lives little and sees little. In this century he lives, as it were, out of the world, so that when he does enter it, when he sees a corner of it, that corner strikes him the way a foreign country strikes a traveler.

On the other hand, how few *well-observed* novels there were in the eighteenth century! Writers of that period participated in the life that surrounded them, naturally, as in an atmosphere. They lived without seeing in the midst of the dramas, the comedies, the novels of their society, which habit prevented them from noticing and about which they did not write.

December 10

Flaubert was telling us that while he was writing about the poisoning of Madame Bovary, he suffered as if he had a copper plate in his stomach, and this suffering made him vomit twice. Then citing as one of his most agreeable impressions the fact that while working on the end of his novel, he had been obliged to get up and go find a handkerchief, which he soaked with tears! And all that for the sake of entertaining the bourgeois! . . .

Fundamentally and in fact, *Madame Bovary*—a masterpiece in its genre, the last word of truth in the novel—represents a very material side of art and thought. The accessories in it live as vividly and almost on the same level as the people. The physical setting is in such high relief around the feelings and passions that it almost stifles them. It is a work which paints for the eyes much more than it speaks to the soul. The noblest and strongest part of the book is much closer to painting than to literature. It is the stereopticon pushed to its furthest illusion.

The true is the basis of all art; it is its foundation and its conscience. But why are the mind and the soul not completely satisfied with it? Shouldn't there be an alloy of the false in order for a work to be regarded as a masterpiece by posterity? How does it happen that *Paul et Virginie*—that romantic novel in which I do not feel the real, but always the imagined life of the characters, their dreamlike nature—will always be considered an immortal masterpiece, whereas *Madame Bovary*, a stronger book, having the force of maturity instead of youthfulness, of observation instead of imagination, of being composed from life instead of poetically imagined, will be looked on merely as a prodigious feat but never will achieve the standing of books like *Paul et Virginie*, a kind of Bible of the human imagination? Because it lacks that grain of falsehood which is, perhaps, the ideal of a work of art?

Tuesday, December 18

It is rather strange that it should be the three men of these times who are the purest professionals, the three pens most dedicated to art, who under this regime have been brought before the magistrate's court: Flaubert, Baudelaire, and ourselves.

1861

January 30

Gestures of sympathy have come from all sides to Murger's deathbed. Michel Lévy, his publisher, who made 25,000 francs from *La Vie de Bohème,* for which he paid 500 francs, generously sent 100 francs. M. Walewski, as soon as he heard the news, sent 500 francs with a very cordial letter which may even have been in his own hand, and the Minister will bear the cost of the funeral. Ministers are always very generous about burying men of letters. It is a pity that men of letters cannot draw on their funeral expenses before death.

January 31

We are in the courtyard of the Hospice Dubois, tramping in the mud, the air damp, icy, misty. The chapel is too small: there are more than fifteen hundred of us outside. All of literature and the schools, brought out by an appeal made every evening for the last three days in the cafés of the Latin Quarter; and there is also Dinochau the wine seller and Markowski the pimp.

Looking at this crowd, I reflect that the distributive justice of funerals is a strange thing; this justice on the part of contemporary posterity which follows the corpse of a reputation or a man of value while it is still warm. Behind the hearse of Heinrich Heine there were six people; behind Musset, forty. The coffin of a man of letters has its luck, like his books.

February 3

The columns, the articles, the funeral orations have been written. Pens have shed their tears. Sorrow has been sung in all keys. They have begun to create a legendary Murger, a sort of hero of poverty, an honor to the world of letters. They have poeticized him from all angles. . . . They have spoken not only of his talent but of his virtues, his qualities of heart, and his dog.

Come now! Enough of bunkum, sentimentality, and publicity! Murger, penniless, lived as best he could. He lived by borrowing from newspapers. He squeezed out advances here and there. The man had no more sensitivity than the writer. Amusing and droll, he let himself drift into parasitism—dinners, suppers, parties at brothels, glasses of wine for which he did not pay and could not reciprocate. As a comrade neither good nor bad. I always found him very indulgent, especially toward those who had no talent; he was more ready to speak of them than of any others. The perfection of egotism. There you have what Murger was. He may have brought honor to Bohemia; he honored nothing else.

Sunday, March 17

Flaubert says to us: "The story, the plot of a novel, that is nothing to me. I intend, when I write a novel, to create a color, a tone. For example, in my novel of Carthage I want to make something purple. Now the rest, the characters, the plot, all that is a mere detail. In *Madame Bovary* I had the idea of creating a grey tone, the color of moldy dampness where grubs live. The story to put in it meant so little to me that a few days before starting it, I conceived of *Madame Bovary* quite differently; using the same environment and seeking the same tonality, it was to be the story of a pious old maid with no sex life. Then I realized that this would be an impossible character!"

In his resounding voice, which has the hoarseness of a wild animal's, mixed with the dramatic cadences of an actor, he reads to us the first chapter of *Salammbô.* An astonishing translation by the imagination into a country of fantasy, a seemingly real invention whose local color is deduced from that of all the ancient and Oriental civilizations; very ingenious, and by its very profusion of tones and perfumes producing a kind of intoxication. But more emphasis on detail than on a harmonious ensemble, and two things lacking: the color of Martin's paintings and Hugo's ringing sentences.

Sunday, April 7

We go to spend Sunday afternoon with Flaubert. In his work room cheerfully lighted by the daylight from the Boulevard du Temple, there is a clock in the form of a gilded wood Brahma, a large round table with his manuscript on it next to the window, a large metal plaque with Persian arabesques, and over the leather couch at the end of the room a cast of the *Psyche* of Naples. . . .

When everyone has left, we stay on for a while to talk to Flaubert. He speaks of his mania for acting out and furiously declaiming the novel as he writes, shouting so much that he empties whole pitchers of water, intoxicating himself with his noise until he causes the metal plates, like the one here, to vibrate to such an extent that, one day at Croisset, he felt something hot rising from his stomach and was afraid that he was going to spit blood.

Tuesday, April 9

Visit by Flaubert. There is really in Flaubert an obsession with Sade. He wracks his brain to make sense out of that madman. He makes him the incarnation of *antiphysis* and goes so far as to say, in one of his finest paradoxes, that he is the last word in Catholicism, hatred of the body. Everybody has to have his crotchet. One should find out whether Sade is not, like Marat, a product of '93. Is it really true that his books were written before the blood of the Terror?

Sunday, April 28

At Flaubert's.

Before going to Lévy he offered *Madame Bovary* for publication to Jacottet, and at the Librairie Nouvelle Jacottet told him: "Your book is very good, *it is chiseled*. But you cannot aspire to the success of Amédée Achard. I cannot commit myself to bringing you out this year."

" 'It is chiseled!' " roars Flaubert. "I consider that insolence on the part of a publisher! A publisher may exploit you but he has no right to judge you. I have always been grateful to Lévy for never having said a word about my book."

July 29

An anxious return to Paris, to our life, to our book [*Soeur Philomène*], to news of success or failure. What a life is this life of letters! I curse it at times and hate it. What hours when emotions pile up on you! Those mountains of hope which rise up and then collapse in you, that constant succession of illusions and disillusions; those hours of dullness, when one waits without hope, those moments of anguish, like this evening, when with constricted throat and beating heart one questions the fortunes of one's book in front of the window displays, and something terrible and poignant seizes you in front of a bookshop where you do not see your book, your child, in the window. Then the wild dreams over which you have no control: that the book is not there because it is sold out! All the breathtaking activity of your mind, of your whole soul, torn between confidence and despair—all that beating on you, rolling you about, turning you over as waves do a shipwrecked man!

Sunday, October 6

Balzac is perhaps less a great physiological anatomist than a great painter of interiors. It seems to me sometimes that he has observed furniture much more than people.

October 10

Saint-Victor and the Charles Edmonds have dinner with us at home. We talk about this great little theatre, the Figaro of theatres, les Bouffes. About all the importance it has taken on, all the curiosity it arouses, all the groups it appeals to. . . . The whole gang is there, a little world that hangs together, running the gamut from Halévy to Crémieux, from Crémieux to Villemessant, from Villemessant to Offenbach, chevalier of the Legion of Honor: bargaining, selling a little of everything, selling even their wives by having them mingle with actors and actresses. They range from Commerson at the bottom to Morny, the Maecenas of Offenbach, the amateur musician, the typical man of the Empire, shopworn and soiled in all the corruption of Paris, representing its decadence without grandeur, a collector who traffics in paintings, a dilettante minister, one of the authors of December 2 as well as of *Monsieur Choufleury*, doing business as an auctioneer, producing music to play at la Farcy's, a high liver with no taste, a typical Parisian brain, so entranced by the wit of Crémieux that he takes him along to the country as his court fool.

Monday, October 28

Sainte-Beuve, who has written that he would like to call on us, comes at two o'clock. He is a small man, rather plump, a little heavy, almost rustic in manner, simple and countrified in dress, a little like Béranger without the decorations.

A high bare forehead, receding up to a bald white skull. Big eyes, a long, inquisitive, sensitive nose, a wide mouth of an ugly rudimentary shape, an expansive smile which shows white teeth, cheekbones projecting like wens, somewhat frog-like, all the lower part of his face pink and well nourished. The general appearance is that of an intelligent provincial coming out of a library, a bookish cloister, beneath which there might be a cellar generously stocked with burgundy, accounting for his jolly, fresh look, his sanguine cheeks beneath his white forehead.

He speaks in a gossipy manner, easily, with little touches like a woman painting pretty, well-designed pictures from a little palette. His speech reminds one of a sketch by Metzu which is tentative and not drawn together by any grand sweep of the brush. His wit is to be found in nuances, his color in finesse. . . .

He talks about *Soeur Philomène*: there is no value except in works that come from the real, from the study of nature. He has little taste for pure fantasy, takes little pleasure in the pretty stories of Hamilton; in fact, as to this ideal one hears so much about, he isn't sure that the ancient writers had it; their works were based on reality, only perhaps their authors worked from a reality that was finer than ours. . . .

Speaking of Flaubert: "One shouldn't be so slow; one gets there too late for one's own times. For works like Vergil that is understandable. And as for the book Flaubert is doing now, it will just be a repetition of *Les Martyrs* of Chateaubriand. After *Madame Bovary* he should have written more works about real life, and then his name would have stayed in the battle, the great battle of the novel, whereas I have been forced to carry on the fight on an inferior field, that of *Fanny*."

November 12

One reason for the weakness of the works of the eighteenth century is that their authors went out too much into society; they found their level there instead of in themselves—this is also the weakness of modern journalism. . . .

The future of modern art, will it not lie in a combination of Gavarni and Rembrandt, the reality of man and his costume transfigured by the magic of shadows and light, by the sun, a poetry of the colors which fall from the hand of the painter?

1862

January

Art is not one, or rather there is no single art. Japanese art is as great an art as Greek art. Greek art, frankly, what is it? The realism of the beautiful. No fantasy, no dream. The absolute of line. Not a grain of opium, so soft, so caressing to the soul, in representations of nature or of man.

February 19

Women have never done anything remarkable except by sleeping with many men, absorbing their moral fiber: Madame Sand, Madame de Staël. I believe that one would never find a virtuous woman who has two sous' worth of intelligence. A virgin has never produced anything.

Monday, March 3

It is snowing lightly. We take a cab and go to deliver our *L'Art Français* to Gautier, 32 Rue de Longchamp in Neuilly.

He lives in a street of poor, rustic-looking buildings—courtyards full of hens, fruit stores which have little brushes made of black chicken feathers hanging beside the doors; a street like those suburban streets that Hervier paints with his dirty brush.

We push open the door of a stucco house and are in the home of the Sultan of the Epithet. A salon with furniture upholstered in red damask, gilded woodwork, all in heavy Venetian style. Some old paintings of the school of Andrea del Sarto with fine yellow flesh tones. Over the mantelpiece a mirror with no backing, decorated with colored arabesques and Persian designs in the style of the Café Turc. A sumptuousness that is shabby and hit-or-miss, like the house of an old retired actress whose pictures came from a bankrupt Italian director or a Venetian patrician on his uppers.

We ask if we are disturbing him. "Not at all, I never work at home; I work only in the press room at *Le Moniteur*. They print me as I write. The odor of printer's ink, that is the only thing that keeps me going. Then too there is the force of urgency. It is fate; I must finish my copy. I can only work there. I could not now write a novel except in that way, printing it as I go along, ten lines at a time. On the proof sheet one judges oneself. What one has done becomes impersonal, while a manuscript is you, your handwriting; it holds you by many threads; it is not detached from you." . . .

He turns to a discussion of *La Reine de Saba* [an opera by Gounod]; we confess to him our utter deficiency, our musical deafness—liking and appreciating only military music. "Well, it pleases me to hear you say that! I am like you, I prefer silence to music. I have managed to learn to distinguish good music from bad, because I lived part of my life with a singer. But it is a matter of complete indifference to me.

"And the strange thing is that all the writers of these times are like that. Balzac hated it, Hugo can't stand it, even Lamartine, himself a piano for sale or for rent, has a horror of it. I don't know a single one! There are only a few painters who have a taste for it.

"Music has fallen into a stupefying Gluckism. Broad, slow things going back to the plainsong. This Gounod is a pure donkey! In the second act there are two choruses of Jewesses and Shebans who chatter beside a pool before washing their backsides. Well, this chorus is rather nice but nothing to rave about! However, the whole audience breathed a sigh of relief, the rest was so boring!"

The name of Verdi comes up and we naively ask Gautier what he is like. "Well, Verdi is a Dennery, a Guilbert de Pixérécourt, you know. He had the idea that when the words were sad, the music should go 'trou, trou, trou' instead of 'tra, tra, tra.' For a funeral, for example, he will not write an air for a flute. Rossini would not have hesitated: in *Semiramide* he has the shade of Ninus enter to a delightful waltz tune. Well, that is all Verdi's musical genius amounts to!" . . .

Then the talk turns to Flaubert, his strange way of working, his conscientiousness, his patience, his seven years of labor: "Imagine, the other day he said to me: 'It is finished; I have only about ten sentences to write, but I have the endings to all of them!' So he already has the rhythm for the ending of the sentences which he hasn't written—he has his 'diminuendos.' Funny, isn't it? As for me, I believe that a sentence must have visual rhythm. For example, a sentence which has a very long first part should not end up briefly and brusquely, except when you want a special effect. A book is not written to be read aloud. . . . And then in Flaubert the rhythm very often is only for himself; it escapes the reader. He roars it out to himself. You know, he has his 'roarings' which seem very harmonious to him, but you have to read as he does to get the effect. Well, we have our pages, all of us—you in your *Venise*—which are just as rhythmic as anything he has done, and without taking such great pains!

"He has one remorse which poisons his whole life and will follow him to the grave; it is for having put into *Madame Bovary* two genitives on top of each other, 'une couronne de fleurs d'oranger.' That grieves him, but try as he would, he could not get around it."

March 11

I have been to see the famous *La Source* by M. Ingres. It is a recreation of the body of a young girl of antiquity, a rendering that is worked over, polished, naively stupid. The female body is not immutable. It changes according to civilizations, periods, customs. The body of the time of Phidias is no longer that of our time. Other customs, another age, another line. The elongation, the free-flowing grace of Goujon or Parmigiano are only the woman of their time, caught in the elegance of the type. In the same way Boucher merely paints the frivolous woman of the eighteenth century, full of dimples. The painter who does not paint the woman of his time will not endure.

March 29

Flaubert is seated on his big divan, legs crossed in the Turkish fashion. He talks of his dreams, his plans for novels. He confides to us his great desire, one that he has not given up, to do a book on the modern Orient, the Orient in modern dress. He grows animated at the thought of all the antitheses that his talent would find in it: scenes taking place in Paris, scenes in Constantinople, on the Nile, scenes of European hypocrisy, savage scenes behind closed doors out there—like those boats which on the forward deck have a Turk dressed by Dusautoy, while in the stern, under the deck, there is the harem of this same Turk. He talks of heads cut off, for a suspicion, a caprice.

He brightens at the thought of depicting the European rabble, Jews, Muscovites, Greeks; he enlarges on the curious contradictions that will arise here and there as the Oriental becomes civilized, while the European returns to the savage state, like the French chemist who in the Libyan desert has kept none of the habits and customs of his country. . . .

In the evening after dinner we go to Gautier's in Neuilly, and find him still at the table at nine o'clock, entertaining Prince Radziwill, who is dining there, and having a simple Pouilly wine which he says is very pleasant. He is very gay, very childlike. It is one of the great qualities of intelligence.

We leave the table and go into the salon. They ask Flaubert to do "The Dance of the Drawing Room Idiot." He asks Gautier for his dress coat, pulls up his collar, does something to his hair, his face, his physiognomy, and all of a sudden he is transformed into a marvelous caricature of stupidity. Gautier, full of emulation, takes off his tail coat and, sweating and dripping, his big behind resting on his calves, dances for us "The Creditor's Dance," and the evening ends with gypsy songs, with terrible melodies of which Prince Radziwill renders wonderfully the strident and roaring notes.

April

Hugo's *Les Misérables* a great disappointment to us. I leave out of account the moral of the book—there is no morality in art—the novel's humanitarian point of view is nothing to me.

Besides, on thinking it over, I find it rather amusing to make two hundred thousand francs—which is the true figure of the sales—by pitying the miseries of the people!

Let us leave that and go on to the work itself. It makes Balzac greater, it makes Sue greater, it diminishes Hugo. Title not justified: no wretchedness, no hospital, prostitution barely touched on. Nothing living: the characters are of bronze, alabaster, everything except flesh and bones. Lack of observation obtrudes and irritates one throughout. Situations and characters: Hugo has constructed his whole book with the appearance of reality instead of the real, without that truth which completes all things and all men in a novel by providing the unexpected element. There lies the fault and the profound wretchedness of this work.

As for its style, it is inflated, strained, breathless, unsuitable to what he is saying. It is like Michelet on Sinai—no order, half of it irrelevant. Hugo is no novelist; he is always Hugo! Fanfare and no music. No subtlety. A predilection for the coarse and the too highly colored. Flattery and fawning on vulgar opinion: a saintly bishop, and a Bonapartist and republican Polyeucte; craven concern for success which goes so far as to deal gently with the honor of innkeepers.

That is the book from which, when we opened it, we expected revelation; when we closed it, we realized it was merely a commercial speculation. In a word, a novel for the lending library written by a man of genius.

May 20

One could make an encyclopedia of the stupidities and untruths spread abroad in print. Whatever may be written now, Greuze will always be thought a virtuous man and Watteau a libertine. Greuze? One has only to read his *Les Bordels de Thalie*. As for Watteau, there was much chastity in him, as well as the melancholy of Vergil. . . .

At Flaubert's this evening the end of the reading of *Salammbô*. In this work what dominates all criticism of detail is its materialization of the pathetic, its return to the past, a return to all that makes Homer inferior to works of our time. Physical suffering takes the place of moral suffering; it is a novel of the body and not a novel of the soul.

May 22

It is really extraordinary the idiocy Gavarni shows in the conduct of his life, his well being! Here he is, old, ailing, grown lazy, disgusted with drawing, able to summon up energy only for mathematics; in a word, ready to retire from that career in which he has fulfilled himself so magnificently, and, on top of that, without money. As luck would have it, his house was expropriated. He might have got 600,000 francs, paid what he owed, and with what remained provided for a comfortable old age given over to idleness and the pleasures of mathematics. Not at all! He is giving up only part of his property and with the money his creditors leave him he plans to build on the land that is left. He will continue to be penniless, paying a rent of 20,000 francs. Then what does he see but the possibility of a nursery at the foot of his garden in the meadow which goes down to the Seine: a huge nursery and a chance to make a fortune! But it is too much to expect middle-class rationality from a man of genius.

Gavarni has always retained his workingman's tastes; he has absolutely no need for the delicacies important to those of gentler birth. He likes forty-sou dinners; the adulterated wine from the wine merchant's is not distasteful. He is insensitive to all the subtleties which give quality to food, dress, or lodgings. He even has a certain tendency to economize without reaching the point of avarice; on the other hand, he is very charitable, very generous, very free-handed, always ready to lend or give money to all who ask, letting them extract from him twenty of the forty francs he has in the house.

August 16

This morning at ten o'clock the bell rings. I hear a conversation between the servant and the concierge. The door opens; the concierge enters with a letter. "Gentlemen, I bring you bad news." I take the letter, bearing the imprint of Lariboisière Hospital. Rose[6] died this morning at seven o'clock. . . .

Chance or the irony of existence! This evening, exactly twelve hours after the poor girl breathed her last, we must go to have dinner at Princess Mathilde's. For some reason, she was curious to see us and wanted to have us to dinner. . . .

On the train we meet Gavarni and Chennevières; at Enghien the Princess's little omnibus meets us and takes us to Saint Gratien. "Her Highness is not down yet," a servant tells us.

The house has nothing of a palace about it. The interior is not princely. Its luxury lies in its comfort. Large rooms, full of comfortable furniture all upholstered in a sort of antique Persian; flowers in little pots hanging on the walls; not a single objet d'art. The drawing room has a bay window of glass through which you get a view of a very fine lawn and a park which seems endless.

[6] Rose, their servant for many years, whose life of depravity was revealed after her death, provided the basis for the central character of *Germinie Lacerteux*.

The Princess comes down. We are introduced. She is a large woman, the remains of a beautiful woman: a rather mottled skin, a withdrawn face, rather small eyes whose expression one does not see very well, the manner of an aging courtesan, and a surface cordiality which does not entirely hide an underlying reserve. . . .

[After dinner] People arrive: Viollet-le-Duc, Admiral La Roncière-le-Noury, some Russians, some Cantacuzène princesses. The Princess takes her place in her second salon beside a basketful of little pug dogs which she adores and which follow her everywhere. She has two of these horrible dogs with protruding eyes in a basket in the salon; she never leaves them even when she is traveling, always holding them under her arms. "They look," says Nieuwerkerke, "like the two spigots on the tank of a soft drink vendor."

Giraud tells us how Musset went to dinner at the Princess's so drunk that he came in staggering and at the table sat down sideways in his chair. I recite with great success the fine philosophical song by Grassot on the National Guard:

> Vive à jamais la Garde nationale,
> Arc-en-ciel de nos libertés!
> Si elle ne fait pas de bien,
> Elle ne fait pas de mal:
> Voilà pourquoi qu'elle a mon amitié.

The Princess fulminates against that beast Haussmann, who has taken 1,200 meters of the park at her town house on the Rue de Courcelles for a boulevard. Then a deep bow and we take our leave of her Imperial Highness.

Bar sur Seine, September 4

It is prodigious the way Millet has caught the outline of the peasant woman, the woman of hard work and weariness, leaning over the ground and picking up clods of earth! He has made a rounded design, making the body into a bundle, with none of the provocative lines of the flesh of a woman; a body which poverty and toil have flattened out as if with a roller; a body which seems when it moves to be toil and weariness in motion; no hips, no breasts, a worker in a sheath, the color of which seems to come from the two elements in which she lives, brown of the earth, blue of the sky.

October 20

A shady side of Flaubert has come to light since he became Lévy's accomplice in saying that he had received 30,000 francs for *Salammbô.* The underside of his character, so frank in appearance, but which I sensed to be otherwise, has become clear to me, and I feel suspicious of this friend who used to say that the true man of letters should work all his life on books for which he should not even seek publicity, but whom I now see using such clever charlatanry in the sale of his.

Friday, November 21

Flaubert, whom I meet at Saint-Victor's, seems ill at ease with me. There is a coldness, I feel it, suddenly come between him and me, doubtless because of the article Sainte-Beuve spoke about Sunday, when he asked for proof sheets of *La Femme au XVIIIe Siècle.* There is, I am beginning to believe, a Norman quality, very sly but strongly developed, in this fellow who seems so open, so exuberant on the surface—such a hearty handshake, showing such open scorn for success, articles, publicity—but whom I see, after his pretended big contract with Lévy, underhandedly making use of rumors, contacts, working at his success like no one else and heading, with his modest manner, for out-and-out rivalry with Hugo.

December 1

We go to thank Sainte-Beuve for the article he did this morning in *Le Constitutionnel* on our *La Femme au XVIIIe Siècle*. He lives on Rue Montparnasse. . . .

We go up to his room, which is directly over the salon, by way of a series of small corridors. On entering one sees a bed with no curtains and an eiderdown quilt; opposite, two windows without curtains; on the left, two mahogany bookcases full of books in Restoration bindings with iron bands on the backs in the Gothic style of Clothilde de Surville. A table piled with books in the middle of the room; and in the corners next to the bookcases all sorts of piles of books and pamphlets —a heaping up, a disorder, a confusion such as you might find when someone is about to move, the appearance of the furnished room of a workman.

He is exasperated with *Salammbô*, in revolt, foaming at the mouth in short phrases:

"In the first place, it is unreadable, and then it is tragedy. It is classic to the last degree. The battle, the plague, the famine, they are set pieces for a literature course . . . like something from Marmontel or Florian! I prefer Numa Pompilius." For nearly an hour whatever we say in favor of the book—you have to defend your comrades against the critics—he gets more excited, he spews out the result of his reading.

December 6

Flaubert came to see me yesterday. I told him more or less what Sainte-Beuve had said to me. He couldn't contain himself. He exploded in a rage of humiliation. The word "tragedy" and the epithet "classic" wounded him deeply; and, opening up completely under this blow, he shortly said: "He is a cad, our friend Sainte-Beuve! He is a bootlicker of Prince Napoleon. What's more he is a low fellow, he is a dirty pig!"

Then his pride came to the surface. He was swimming in vanity. It was a matter of *Salammbô* and nothing else. Everything else had disappeared. At times the Norman burst out. He talked of sending process-servers to a paper which had shortened a quotation from him. And he talked openly and freely of Hugo as a competitor, to whom he no longer had to show consideration. He shook off all politeness toward that outmoded god, who is finished, out, dead as far as he is concerned.

December 28

There are two men in Gavarni. One curious about all important questions, for whom, as for Goethe, the Revolution of 1830 was a small event in comparison with an opinion of Cuvier at the Academy; highly intelligent, admirable at defining and explaining the boldest systems of science and philosophy concerning man, woman, character; having the most profound insights, sharp, concrete, compelling. That one is the man of solitude and intimacy, the man who most often veils and hides himself. Then there is another Gavarni, rather narrow-minded, full of the petty tastes of the Restoration, loving fables, songs, enjoying articles in minor reviews, recalling Désaugier's parodies of the opera—a man, in fact, who is to the other what his first drawings are to the *Vireloque* sketches.

1863

January 3

At Magny's. Our books, our way of working, have made a great impression on Sainte-Beuve, I know. The preoccupation with art in the midst of which we live disturbs him, worries him, tempts him. Being intelligent enough to understand all that this new element, unknown heretofore in history, has brought in the way of color and richness to the novelist and the historian, he wants to be up-to-date. He puts out feelers, he questions, he tries to get us to talk; he asks our indulgence for his article on the Le Nain brothers in his Monday column. He does not know, and he would like to know.

February 28

Our Magny dinner. Charles Edmond brings us Turgenev, the Russian with such a subtle talent, the author of *A Sportsman's Sketches*, *Antéor*, and *A Russian Hamlet.*

He is a charming colossus of a man, a gentle giant, with white hair; he looks like a mild old genie of forest or mountain; he is like a Druid or the good old monk in *Romeo and Juliet.* He is handsome, but with a kind of venerable good looks, handsome on a large scale like Nieuwerkerke. But Nieuwerkerke's eyes are blue as velvet; Turgenev's are like the sky. His benevolent look is accompanied by the softness of the slight sing-song of his Russian accent, melodious like that of a child or a Negro.

Very modest, and touched by the ovation he receives, he talks about Russian literature, now completely launched on the road of realism from the theatre to the novel. The Russian public are great readers of reviews. Turgenev and ten others like him, whom we do not know, are paid, he blushes to tell us, six hundred francs a sheet. But books pay little, scarcely 4,000 francs.

The name of Heinrich Heine is mentioned; we pick it up and affirm our enthusiasm for him. Sainte-Beuve, who knew him very well, says that the man was a wretch, a rascal, but then, in face of the general enthusiasm, he becomes silent, beats a retreat, taking refuge behind his hands, covering his eyes and hiding his face all the time we are praising Heine.

March 1

It is Flaubert's last Sunday. He is going off again to bury himself in work at Croisset.

A gentleman arrives, slender, a little stiff, slight, with a small beard; neither short nor tall, authoritarian in manner, bluish eyes behind glasses; a very thin face, somewhat featureless, which becomes animated when he talks; a gracious way of looking at you as he listens; gentle speech, flowing, almost falling from his mouth as he shows his teeth. It is Taine.

In his talk he is a sort of nice little incarnation of modern criticism, very learned, pleasant, and somewhat pedantic. A residue of the professor—one can't be defrocked from that profession—but saved by a great simplicity, worldly manners, polite attentiveness, and a willingness to give himself to others. . . .

As we were talking about what Turgenev had told us the night before, that there was only one popular writer in Russia, Dickens, and that since 1830 our literature had had little influence there, that English and American novels were carrying everything before them, Taine said that as far as he could see, this trend would be even stronger in the future, that the literary and scientific influence of France would continue to diminish, as it had been diminishing since the eighteenth century; that in all the sciences, for example, there are only ten remarkable men in France, a fine front line but with nothing back of it, no troops; that it is always the old story of Paris and the provinces. "Hachette refused to bear the expense of a translation of Mommsen's *History of Rome*, and he was right. In Germany at the present moment they are publishing a marvelous edition of the works of Sebastian Bach; out of fifteen hundred subscriptions, only ten in France."

March 28

Dinner at Magny's.

The newcomer whom we receive this time is Renan. Renan, a calf's head with red blotches and calluses like the backside of a monkey. He is a stocky man, short, not well built, his head down between his shoulders, making him look somewhat hunchbacked; an animallike head something between that of a pig and an elephant; small eyes, an enormous pendant nose, a mottled face, striped and spotted with red. From this unhealthy man, ill-shaped, ugly to look at, and morally ugly as well, there comes a little tinkling falsetto voice.

We talk religion: Sainte-Beuve says that paganism was at first a beautiful thing, then became rotten, a pox. Christianity was the mercury to cure that pox; but now we have too much of it and we must be cured of the medicine.

We hold a private conversation in which he tells me of the ambitions of his childhood, of how at Boulogne under the Empire the presence of soldiers stirred up in him a desire to be a soldier. He still feels a deep regret at not having followed that career: "There's nothing like military glory, nothing like it. Great generals and great geometers, those are the only people I admire." He says nothing about the uniform, but I think that was his dream, to be a colonel in the Hussars—because of women! Basically his real ambition was to be a pretty fellow; I have rarely seen anyone who missed the boat more completely!

A terrific discussion gets going on Voltaire. We two stand alone in our separation of the writer from the polemicist, from his actions and his social and political influence. We challenge his literary value and dare to defend Trublet's opinion: "He is the perfection of mediocrity." And we define him in these terms: "A journalist, nothing more!" His histories? The conventional lies of the old history, which have been destroyed by the science and the consciousness of the nineteenth century. Thiers descends from him and patterns himself after him. His science, his hypotheses? Objects of ridicule for contemporary scientists. What about the rest? His plays? *Candide?* He is a prose La Fontaine and an emasculated Rabelais. Yet right alongside him was the narrative of the future, *Le Neveu de Rameau.*

Everyone jumps on us, and Sainte-Beuve, in order to put an end to it, shouts: "France will not be free until Voltaire has a statue in the Place de la Concorde!"

We turn to Rousseau, whom Sainte-Beuve finds sympathetic, a man with the same kind of mind, a man of his own sort. Taine, rising to the heights of the discussion and tossing his academic robes to the wind, exclaims: "Rousseau! A masturbating lackey!"

In the midst of this violence of ideas and words Renan remains a little horrified, distressed, practically mute; curious nevertheless, interested, attentive, drinking in the cynicism of the words like a respectable woman at a supper of prostitutes. Then at dessert come the big questions.

"It is astonishing," says someone, "how at dessert we always talk about the immortality of the soul and God."

"Yes," says Sainte-Beuve, "when we no longer know what we are saying!"

April 9

There are certain flexible personalities which appear different according to the places where you meet them. The other day I was observing Taine at Princess Mathilde's. In his narrow coat, his elbows close to his sides, his head lowered, holding his hat in his hands to keep himself in countenance, his whole person flat, he seemed to me to be the amiable pedant out in society. Now I can hardly look at him without thinking of the silhouette of the son of Diafoirus [in Molière's *Le Malade Imaginaire*].

May 18

Our friend Flaubert is the greatest theoretician about books that ever was. In a book he is thinking about he wants to put all of *Tom Jones* and *Candide*. He continues to affect the greatest scorn and disgust for reality. Everything in him starts with a system, never from inspiration. I fear that masterpieces cannot come from so much premeditation.

June 22

At Magny's.

Gautier: "The bourgeois? Tremendous things happen among them. I have been in some households which were enough to make you hide your face. Lesbianism a normal thing, incest on a permanent basis, and bestiality . . ."

Taine: "I know some bourgeois; I am from a bourgeois family. First of all, what do you mean by bourgeois?"

Gautier: "People who have from fifteen to twenty thousand francs of income and don't work."

Taine: "Well, I will name for you fifteen bourgeois women whom I know who are chaste!"

Edmond: "How do you know? God Himself can't be sure!"

Taine: "Look, the women of Angers are so watched over that there is only one who gets herself talked about."

Saint-Victor: "Angers? Why, it's full of homosexuals! The recent trials . . ."

Jules: "They caused the bridge to collapse!"

Sainte-Beuve: "Madame Sand is going to do something on one of Rousseau's sons during the Revolution. It will show the most generous side of the Revolution. She is full of her subject. She has written me three letters in these last few days. She has the thing admirably worked out."

Soulié: "There is a vaudeville skit by Théaulon about Rousseau's children."

Renan: "Madame Sand, the greatest artist of our times, and the truest!"

The Table: "Oh, oh, hey!"

Saint-Victor: "It's a funny thing; she writes on letter paper!"

Edmond: "She will endure, like Madame Cottin!"

Renan: "By true, I don't mean realism!"

Sainte-Beuve: "Drink up . . . I'm drinking! Come on, Scherer."

Taine: "Hugo? Hugo is not sincere."

Saint-Victor: "Hugo!"

Sainte-Beuve: "How can you, Taine, put Musset above Hugo! Why, Hugo writes books! He has got away with the greatest success of our times right under the nose of this government, and yet this government is very powerful. He has penetrated everywhere. Women, the common people, everybody has read him. He goes out of print between eight o'clock and noon. After I read his *Odes et Ballades*, I took all my poetry to show it to him. The people at *Le Globe* called him a barbarian. Well, all that I have done it was he who inspired me to do it. In ten years those people at *Le Globe* had taught me nothing."

Saint-Victor: "We are all his descendants."

Taine: "Excuse me! Hugo is an immense event in these times, but . . ."

Sainte-Beuve: "Taine, don't talk about Hugo! Don't talk about Madame Hugo! You don't know her . . . only two of us here do, Gautier and I, but it's magnificent [*Victor Hugo Raconté par un Témoin de sa Vie*, by Madame Hugo]!"

Taine: "Well, I believe that nowadays you call it poetry to describe a church tower, a sky, to show things. That's not poetry, that's painting."

Saint-Victor: "I know her! I know Madame Hugo."

Gautier: "Taine, you seem to share the stupid bourgeois notion about poetry, to want it to be sentimental! Poetry isn't that. It is a core of light in a diamond, luminous words, the rhythm and music of words. A burst of light doesn't prove anything, doesn't tell anything! That's the way it is at the beginning of *Ratbert*; there is no poetry in the world like that, so lofty! It is a plateau in the high Himalayas. All Italy is emblasoned there! And it is nothing but names!" . . .

Scherer: . . . "Taste is nothing, there is only judgment. You must have judgment."

Jules: "On the contrary, taste and not judgment! Taste is temperament."

Saint-Victor, timidly: "I must admit I have a weakness for Racine."

Edmond: "Well, now, that is what has always surprised me, that one can at the same time like salad with a lot of vinegar and salad with a lot of oil—Racine and Hugo."

A final brouhaha.

A voice: "We don't understand each other!"

Gavarni: "We understand each other too well!"

Exeunt.

Journal, 1863

Monday, July 6

Sainte-Beuve has resigned as a member of the Academy commission on the Dictionary, that is to say, giving up 1,200 francs a year in order to write this morning's article on Littré. He puts passion into his hates!

This evening he demands forcefully that there be fewer police in the streets to control morals and becomes excessively heated as if arguing *pro domo sua* against the arbitrary regulation of prostitutes. He demands that an honest man rise at a meeting of the Corps Législatif to defend and protect them; then M. Thiers and all the others would have nothing to say.

Monday, July 20

At Magny's.

Apropos of Madame Hugo's book and the premiere of *Hernani*, Gautier says that he was not wearing a red waistcoat but a pink doublet. Laughter. "But it is very important! A red waistcoat would have indicated a political shading, republican. There was nothing of that. We were simply being *medieval*. And all of us, Hugo as well as the rest of us . . . a republican, we didn't know what that was . . . Pétrus Borel was the only republican. We were all against the bourgeoisie and for Marchangy. We were the 'crenelated wall' party, that is all. There was a schism when I celebrated antiquity in the preface to *Mademoiselle Maupin*. Crenelated walls, nothing but crenelated walls. Uncle Beuve, I realize, has always been a liberal, but Hugo, in those days he was for Louis XVII, I assure you!"

Monday, August 17

At Magny's. . . .

We talk first about the funeral from which we have just

come, that of Eugène Delacroix, of his death—obscure, hidden, veiled, secretive, like the death of a dog in his hole, without any of his friends having known anything or seen him for six months. We talk of this sequestration which was forced on him by an old servant, a sort of Madame Evrard, in order to be sure of the absurd legacy from the dying man. And already mystery and controversy are raging around the hardly cold corpse. Some say he died like a child; others, that he died in a state of excitement, his mind full of new methods and new techniques by which to realize his genius, feeling robbed of everything that he had promised himself to do and everything he felt at the tip of his fingers as he died.

Saint-Victor gives us a capsule sketch of that man so ravaged and bitter, whom I saw one day in the street with a package under his arm: "He looked like an apothecary of Tippoo-Saeb." Then we evaluate him and say: "He was in the line of Rubens. Yes, but by way of a wine merchant!"

September 14

At Magny's. . . .

"Oh, by the way, Gautier, you have just come back from Nohant, from Madame Sand's! Was it amusing?"

"Like a convent of Moravian Brothers! I arrived in the evening. It is quite far from the station. They put my trunk in some bushes. I went in by way of the farm, where the dogs frightened me. They gave me dinner. The food is good but there is too much game and chicken—that doesn't agree with me. Marchal the painter was there, and Alexandre Dumas *fils* and Madame Calamatta."

"Is Dumas *fils* still ill?"

"Do you know how he spends his time now? He is very unhappy. He sits in front of a blank sheet of paper and stays there four hours on end. He writes three lines. He goes and takes a cold bath or does gymnastics, because he is full of ideas about hygiene. He comes back, finds his three lines as stupid as anything."

"Well, that is lucidity at least," says someone.

"And he only leaves three words. From time to time his father comes up from Naples and says to him: 'Send for a chop for me. I am going to finish your play for you.' He writes a scenario, sends for a prostitute, takes some money from his son, and leaves. Dumas *fils* takes the scenario, reads it, thinks it is very good, goes to take a bath, rereads the scenario, finds it stupid, spends a year revising it. And when his father comes back, he finds the same three words that were left from the three lines of the year before!"

September 28

We come back [from Croissy] for the Magny dinner. The talk is of Vigny, who died today, and Sainte-Beuve is tossing anecdotes into his grave. When I hear Sainte-Beuve with his little phrases talk about the dead, I seem to see ants on a corpse. He disposes of a reputation, and what is left is a little skeleton of the individual, all tidy and neatly laid out.

October

The other day I bought some albums of Japanese obscenities. They delight me, amuse me, and charm my eyes. I look on them as being beyond obscenity, which is there, yet seems not to be there, and which I do not see, so completely does it disappear into fantasy. The violence of the lines, the unexpected in the conjunctions, the arrangement of the accessories, the caprice in the poses and the objects, the picturesqueness, and, so to speak, the landscape of the genital parts. Looking at them, I think of Greek art, boredom in perfection, an art that will never free itself from the crime of being *academic!*

October 8

It is astonishing how our way will be made from above and not at all from below! Recently Michelet, in the preface to *La Régence*, called us eminent writers! Hugo, Busquet tells me, is full of friendly curiosity concerning us. It is the upper levels of criticism which have discussed us, judged us, evaluated us. The comrades of our own generation, except for Saint-Victor, have accorded us only silence and insults.

Thursday, October 29
At Croisset near Rouen

On the station platform we find Flaubert with his brother, head surgeon at the Rouen hospital, a very tall, Mephistophelian-looking fellow with a great black beard, thin, a sharp profile like the shadow of a face, a well-balanced body as supple as a vine. We go by cab to Croisset, a fine house with a Louis XVI façade situated at the foot of a hill along the Seine, which at this point looks like the end of a lake but which occasionally has waves like the sea.

And here we are in the study, scene of the dogged and unceasing work and the tremendous labors from which *Madame Bovary* and *Salammbô* have come forth.

Two windows face the Seine and show the water and the ships which pass; three windows open on the garden, where superb shrubbery seems to support the hillside which rises behind the house. Bookcases of oak, with twisted columns, placed between these windows tie in with other bookcases which fill the whole end of the room. Opposite the view of the garden, above white woodwork, a mantelpiece bearing an ancestral clock in yellow marble and a bronze bust of Hippocrates. At one side a bad watercolor, the portrait of a little English girl, languorous and sickly, whom Flaubert knew in Paris. Then box tops with Indian designs, framed like watercolors, and an etching by Callot, a *Temptation of Saint Anthony*, are there like images of the master's talent.

Between the two windows facing the Seine, on a square pedestal painted bronze, the white marble bust of his dead sister by Pradier, with two curls and a pure, strong face which is like a Greek face found in a keepsake. To one side, a divan bed made of a mattress covered with Turkish material and piled high with cushions. In the middle of the room, near a table holding an Indian box with colored designs and bearing a gilded idol, is the work table, a large round table with a green cover, where the writer dips his ink from an inkwell in the form of a toad.

Gay draperies, antique and somewhat Oriental in style, with large red flowers, hang at the doors and windows. And here and there, on the mantelpiece, on the tables, on the tops of the bookcases, hanging from brackets on the wall, all sorts of Oriental bric-a-brac: amulets with a green patina from Egypt, arrows, weapons, musical instruments, a wooden bench such as African people use for sleeping, eating, and sitting; copper trays, necklaces of glass beads, and two mummy feet which he snatched from the grottoes of Samoûn and which stand out among the pamphlets, showing their Florentine bronze color and the congealed life of their muscles.

This interior is the man, his tastes, and his talent; his real passion is for the vulgar Orient; there is a barbarian base to this artistic nature.

November 1

We stay in all day. This pleases Flaubert, who seems to have a horror of exercise, and whom his mother has to nag even to get him to set foot in the garden. . . .

All day, without resting, in a thunderous voice with bursts of sound like an actor in a boulevard theatre, he reads to us his first novel, written while still in school, which has no title on the cover other than *Fragments in an Unformed Style*. The subject is a young man's loss of his virginity with the *ideal whore*. There is much of Flaubert in the young man, his hopes, aspirations, melancholy, misanthropy, hatred of the masses. All of it, except the dialogue, which is nonexistent, is astonishingly powerful for his age. There is already in it, in the small details of the landscape, the delicate and charming gift of observation we find in *Madame Bovary*. The beginning of this novel, the sadness of autumn, is something which he could sign even now. In a word, in spite of its imperfections, it is very strong.

For relaxation before dinner he went rummaging through his cast-off clothing, costumes, and travel souvenirs. With great enjoyment he went through all his Oriental masquerade; and then he dressed us up, and dressed himself up, looking superb in his tarboosh—a magnificent Turk's head with his handsome heavy features, his sanguine complexion, and his drooping moustaches. Finally he pulled out the old leather breeches he wore on his long trips, contemplating them with the emotion of a snake looking at its old skin.

November 23

We go to thank Michelet, whom we have never seen, for the very flattering words he wrote about us in his *La Régence*. . . .

He speaks with "admiration" of our study of Watteau, of that very interesting history which is still lacking, the history of French furniture. And he sketches for us, with the vivid words of a poet, the house of the sixteenth century, Italian in style, with great staircases in the middle of the palace; then the entensive spaces freed by the disappearance of the stairway, first occurring at the Hôtel de Rambouillet; then the Louis XIV style, inconvenient and barbaric; then the marvelous apartments of the Fermiers Généraux, apropos of which he wonders whether it was their money or the taste of the times or the taste of the workmen which produced them; then our modern apartments, even the richest of which are heavy, bare, bleak.

Then: "You, gentlemen, who are observers, you will write this history, the history of ladies' maids. I am not talking about Madame de Maintenon, but there is Mademoiselle de Launai . . . there is the Julie of Madame de Gramont, who had such influence on her, especially in the Corsican affair. . . . Madame du Deffand said somewhere that she had only two persons who were attached to her, d'Alembert and her maid. Oh, it is very interesting and important, the role of domestics in history. Male servants had less influence." . . .

. . . Gautier, although quite pleased and as flattered as a beginner by the articles which Sainte-Beuve has devoted to him, complains that in discussing his poetry the critic did not mention the poems into which he has put the most of himself, *Emaux et Camées*. . . .

"The two real strings to my work, the two really dominant notes, are buffoonery and black melancholy—a disgust for my times from which I have sought a sort of escape."

"Yes," we say, "you are nostalgic for the obelisk!"

"That's it! And that is what Sainte-Beuve does not understand. He does not understand that all four of us here are sick people: what distinguishes us is our sense of the exotic. There are two feelings for the exotic. The first is for the exotic in space, the taste for America, India, yellow women, green ones, etc. The second, which is more refined, a more lofty corruption, is the taste for the exotic in time. For example, take Flaubert, he would like to screw in Carthage; you would like to have la Parabère [an eighteenth-century courtesan], and as for me, nothing would excite me like a mummy."

"But how can you expect," we said to him, "that Papa Sainte-Beuve, in spite of his rage to understand everything, should completely understand a talent like yours? To begin with, they are very nice, his articles; they are very ingenious and make pleasant reading, but that is all there is to them! Never with his light touch and his little written talks has he characterized a man or given the formula for a talent. None of his judgments has struck off a bronze medal to a literary glory. And as for you, with all his desire to be agreeable to you, how could he get into your skin? All your plastic quality escapes him. When you describe the nude it is a kind of onanism of line. You just told us that you do not seek to put any sensuality into it. Well, for him, the nude, the description of a breast, of a woman's body, all that is inseparable from dirty thoughts and excitation. He sees Devéria in the Venus de Milo."

1864

January 24

I observe at the Princess's the curious way Flaubert works to attract the attention of the mistress of the house, to get himself noticed, to be asked to talk—all this by a variety of looks, attitudes, poses. I feel in everything about this man a need, which reaches the point of actual suffering, to attract and appropriate attention and hold it for himself alone; and I laugh to myself to see this great mocker of human glories so fiercely hungry for little bourgeois favors.

March 4

Do you know what makes Delacroix famous? He introduced into painting the movements of mechanical toys, a blacksmith shoeing horses, a dentist operating—pictures that move.

Saturday, March 12

We take our volume to Madame Sand. In the shadows where she obstinately stays we see in her a sort of mulatto type. She is more animated, more talkative, more lively than the first time, but just as much of a nonentity. It seems that the success of *Le Marquis de Villemer* has made her blood circulate a little more actively. . . .

Her chatter is pure nothingness, without either grace or wit, even in the compliments she pays you.

Monday, April 11

Hugo nowadays is Saint John on the island of Pathos.

Thursday, April 28

Literature can and must go down to the people, to the ugly, even the horrible.[7] On the other hand, painting must tend

[7] This idea was developed with almost sentimental emphasis in the famous preface to *Germinie Lacerteux*, 1865 (see George J. Becker, *Documents of Modern Literary Realism* [Princeton University Press, 1963], pp. 118–119).

toward the beautiful, the elegant, the pretty. The one is addressed to eyes that are shocked; the other to the heart which is moved.

May 5

Voltaire is the man of letters of the past, of old forms—tragedy, epic poetry, etc. From him are descended such Gallic spirits as Thiers, Béranger, etc. Diderot is the writer of the future. From him come the novel and written painting, Balzac and Gautier.

May 30

It is very strange that we should be the ones, surrounded and suffocated by all the prettiness of the eighteenth century as we are, who devote ourselves to the most severe and almost the most repellent studies of the common people; that we, in whose lives women have so small a part, should be the ones who make the most serious, the most profound, the most intimate study of women.

Paris, June 20

Renan is very excited, very talkative, very violent, this evening. He rants against the poetry of words, poetry which has no useful purpose, which has no content, the poetry of the Chinese, the Orientals, etc., which Gautier is introducing again.

Sainte-Beuve takes up the defense of useless poetry, saying that Boileau, who had a small mind, is a great poet, a hundred times greater than Racine. "Boileau!" says Renan. "What do you expect of a man who rose out of the palace dust." Thereupon a great commotion. Sainte-Beuve, Gautier, and Saint-Victor grow animated and excited and praise the genius of Boileau.

Victor Hugo's name comes up. Renan speaks bitterly of him as a sort of clown or juggler, putting him much lower than Madame Sand, "the only writer who will still be read in fifty years." "Yes, like Madame Cottin!" I emit that outburst along with the protestations of the rest of the table.

"Hugo is full of barbarisms," exclaims a newcomer, who has the manner and behavior of an intelligent workingman mixed with those of a ham actor. He is M. Berthelot, an important chemist, a man with down-to-earth divine powers, according to what I hear, who takes simple substances apart and puts them back together again. Then he proclaims *Notre-Dame de Paris* stupid.

July 19

This evening the sun looks like a wafer of cherry-colored sealing wax, glued onto the sky over a pearl-colored sea. Only the Japanese have dared, in their color albums, to give these strange effects of nature.

September 30

Chinese art, and particularly Japanese art, those arts which appear so incredibly fantastic to bourgeois eyes, are drawn direct from nature. Everything that they do is taken from observation. They represent what they see: the incredible effects of the sky, the stripes on a mushroom, the transparency of the jellyfish. Their art copies nature as does Gothic art.

Basically there is no paradox in saying that a Japanese album and a painting by Watteau are drawn from an intimate study of nature. Nothing like this in the Greeks: their art, except for sculpture, is false and invented. Their last word is the arabesque, a contorted monstrosity and an elegant geometry.

October 10

At Magny's. . . .

Renan tells us good-bye. He is going to the Orient to make what he calls his "Saint Paul cruise." We remark that as a result of the doctrine of the Immaculate Conception and the sanctification of Saint Margaret Mary Alacoque and others the Catholic religion has reached a feminine paganism.

Finally the intense bitterness of non-Senator Sainte-Beuve bursts out. He speaks of his fourteen years of service without a word of thanks from the powers-that-be, and he gives the Emperor just three weeks to call him to the Senate. If he does not, Sainte-Beuve will publish a letter renouncing his candidacy for the Senate, which he will address to a friend and send to *L'Indépendance Belge.* And bluntly, with brutal frankness, he tells us what the Senate means to him—30,000 francs, in other words, to be able to support a mistress decently, double the wages of his secretary, and pay the five-thousand-franc debt of his housekeeper. "For God's sake, favors ought to be given graciously!" Then he talks about the terrible obligations which counterbalance this favor, such as being forced to take sides if there is a regency, to put his name to a petition in which they say things that he does not believe.

October 12

Today we read some chapters of *Germinie Lacerteux* [to Charpentier].

At the place where she says that when she arrived in Paris she was covered with lice, Charpentier tells us we must put "with vermin" for the sake of the public. But who is this king the public, from whom one must hide the true and raw facts? Who is this little woman, from whom one must hide the existence of lice on the bodies of the poor? By what right should the novel lie to the public and conceal from it all the ugly side of life?

October 24

Dramatic movement, gesture, and life did not begin in the novel until Diderot. Up to then there were dialogues but no novels.

The novel, since Balzac, no longer has anything in common with what our ancestors understood by a novel. The novel of today is made from *documents*, recounted or copied from nature, as history is made from written documents.

Historians are the storytellers of the past, novelists the storytellers of the present.

November 12

We are anxious to finish the proofs of *Germinie Lacerteux*. Reliving this novel takes too much out of us, puts us in a state of nerves and sadness. It is as if we were *reburying* the dead woman. Oh, it is indeed a book which has come from our deepest viscera; it moves us too physically. We can no longer correct it, we no longer see what we have written: the horror of these things hides from us the commas and the typographical errors.

1865

January 12

I think the best literary education for a writer would be, after leaving school, and until he is twenty-five or thirty, to write down, without any action, what he sees and everything he feels, forgetting as far as possible what he has read.

January 17

Our *Germinie Lacerteux* came out yesterday. We are ashamed of our state of nervous tension. To feel conscious as we do of so much moral courage, and then to be betrayed by our nerves, by an unhealthy weakness, a cowardice in the pit of the stomach, a softening of the body. Ah, it is very unfortunate not to have physical strength equal to one's moral strength!

January 26

The best commentary on the genius of Michelet would be this: he is a historian with opera glasses; big events he looks at through the small end, little ones through the large end.

March 15

The other day, going down the Rue Taitbout, I saw some terrible watercolors by Daumier.

They represent judicial convocations, meetings of lawyers, processions of judges against dark backgrounds, grey places, illuminated only by the light from the chamber of an examining magistrate and the dim light of the corridors of the building.

They are washed in a sinister inky water and funereal blacks. The heads are horrible, with grimaces, laughs that frighten you. These men in black have something of the ugliness of horrible antique masks in a judiciary storeroom. The smiling lawyers take on the air of Corybants. There is something of the satyr in these macabre lawyers.

May 4

It is an odd group at table where we are seated at Gautier's. It is like a table d'hôte in a tower of Babel, the last caravansary of romanticism, a mixture of people of all nations which it is the custom and the pride of Gautier to assemble.

The other day at this table there were twenty individuals speaking forty different languages, with whom one could tour the world without needing an interpreter.

This evening, besides Flaubert, Bouilhet, and us, a real Chinese, with his slanting eyes and his coat of currant-red velvet, the Chinese teacher of Gautier's daughters. There is an exotic painter with seven-league boots up to his knees and the hooded eyes of a jaguar. There is the Hungarian violinist Reminy, with the bald head of a priest or a devil; there is his accompanist, an equivocal fat little man, youthful and effeminate, looking like an Alsatian, fair hair falling in strings from a part in the middle of his head, a frock coat like that of a German seminarist, with a spray of white lilac crushed in its opening—a strange and disturbing homosexual.

June 6

We are feeling scorn and disgust for the people at the Magny dinners. To think that this is a gathering of the freest spirits in France! Certainly for the most part, from Gautier to Sainte-Beuve, they are men of talent. But what poverty of ideas of their own, of opinions formed with their nerves and personal feelings! What absence of personality, of temperament! In all of them what a bourgeois fear of anything extreme, of any new ideas!

June 7

Read a trifling article by Taine written under a pseudonym.

There is something of the schoolboy in all these Normaliens.[8] They do not know men, women, or life; and, bear-

[8] Students at the Ecole Normale Supérieure are an elite group who attain the highest positions in education, government, and the arts. The intensity and narrowness of their intellectual formation is a frequent Goncourt target.

ing the stamp of what they have just read and what they have picked up here and there as they poke around, they take their revenge, they escape from the seriousness of their lives as professors in all sorts of small pieces of writing in which they play the frivolous, the knowing, the impertinent, the lighthearted, the followers of fashion, and the analysts of the hearts of women—rather like schoolboys at supper after their first evening at a dance hall.

Barbizon, June 16

A young American at our hotel, who has come here to paint and who talks very little. . . .

A nice young fellow, this American, a timid manner, a square head in which one senses prodigious nervous strength, the hardy, healthy, triumphant race to which he belongs. And apropos of this we say to ourselves: "The world has been and is now governed by physical force; the nations which have exhausted their health are passing away. The future belongs to Russia and America, virgin forces."

November 20

At Magny's this evening Taine was telling us about his life after his initial success. Although he passed first at the Ecole Normale, he was sent to a municipal college in a small provincial city, at 1,200 francs a year. Dismissed for refusing to write some Latin verses or a dithyramb in French verse to the Bishop; recalled to Paris and appointed substitute in the sixth form. In Paris in spite of all his degrees able only to find a tutoring job at five francs a month. That taught him, he said, to consider life a forest where one must look out for himself, a battle against others, in which in the Middle Ages it was necessary to go armed and in which, in the nineteenth century, one must have another kind of armor—capital. And since that time he has managed to acquire an income of 8,000 francs.

November 24

In reading Hugo I observe a separation, an abyss between the artist and the public of today. In other centuries a man like Molière merely represented the thought of his time. He was, so to speak, on a level with it. Today the great men are higher and the public is lower.

December 5

We arrive at the theatre.[9] It seems very lively with much movement all around the building. Feeling like victors, we go up the staircase which we have mounted so often, with such varied worries. We had been saying to each other all day that if, toward the end of the play, we saw that the enthusiasm was going too far, we would slip out quickly in order not to be dragged onto the stage in triumph. . . .

We go to the peephole in the curtain and try to see into the theatre, but all we can see is a sort of brilliant blur of faces. Then all of a sudden we hear the play going on. The raising of the curtain, the three knocks, all the ceremonial things that we were waiting for had completely escaped us.

Then in complete astonishment we hear a boo, two boos, three boos, a storm of catcalls, to which there is a hurricane of bravos in reply. . . .

The curtain falls; we go out without overcoats. We are very warm. The second act begins; the hissing resumes furiously, accompanied by animal noises and imitations of the actors' intonations. They hiss everything, even a period of

[9] This was the premiere of their ill-fated play *Henriette Maréchal.*

silence when Madame Plessy is alone on stage. And the battle goes on like that between the actors and a large part of the audience in the orchestra and boxes, who applaud, and the whole of the gallery, who wish to bring down the curtain by their shouts, their interruptions, their bursts of anger, their cheap music-hall jokes.

"Things are getting a little rough!" Got says to us from time to time. We remain leaning against a flat during the whole thing, taking it straight on, pale, nervous, but upright and unflinching, forcing the actors by our angry presence to carry on to the end.

December 6

The head of the claque tells me this morning that there has never been such a tumult in the theatre since the time of *Hernani* and *Les Burgraves*.

Dinner with the Princess, who returned home last night with burning hands after applauding so much; she is exasperated against the hissers, whose hissing, she feels, was directed more at her than at the play.

This evening my mistress tells me that after having been at the performance last night, she did not dare go out this morning; it seemed to her that the experience was written on her face.

December 11

Our first act is played absolutely like a pantomime. They don't let a word be heard.

In the midst of the hostile noise in the theatre Bressant is admirable for his courage in the role of "Gentleman in evening clothes," which is the best performance of the play.

This morning a notice is being circulated in the Latin Quarter urging that the curtain be forced to come down on the first act. Furthermore, the cabal's plan is now clear: it is to drown out all the effective scenes and especially the effective lines. The best parts of the play are hissed the most; the most dramatic parts are the most laughed at.

One thing which gives the measure of this cabal. As a curtain raiser to our play they put on *Les Précieuses Ridicules.* It was hissed. They hissed Molière's play, thinking it was ours.

December 15

Eugène Giraud tells us this evening in the wings that the Princess has received frightful anonymous letters apropos of our play, promising her that the first torch will be used on her town house and that they will hang "all her lovers!" All her lovers? We have been going to her house for three years now; we know it very well, and the devil take us if we have seen a single person called upon to put horns on Nieuwerkerke! Oh, the calumniating legends of political factions about the lovelife of princesses and queens!

December 23

At last we have a pretty good idea as to who finished off our play: it is the Empress. It is a matter of jealousy on the part of the mistress of the salon at the Tuileries toward the mistress of the salon on the Rue de Courcelles, toward the cousin who has established a court for arts and letters. An article signed Polin in La Guéronnière's "Premier Paris" column—yes, a "Premier Paris" article directed against a play!—and indications coming from various quarters make sufficiently clear the jealousy and bad will toward a play which has come from the Princess's salon.

1866

January 15

Taine maintains that all men of talent are products of their environment.[10] Gautier and we maintain the contrary, that they are the exceptions. "Where do you find the roots of the exotic in Chateaubriand? His exoticism is a pineapple grown in a barracks!" For Gautier the brain of the artist today is the same as it was in the time of the Pharaohs. As for the bourgeois, whom he calls "fluid nonentities," it is possible that there has been a modification.

February 12

Madame Sand comes to dine at Magny's today. She is there beside me with her fine and charming face on which with age the mulatto type shows up a little more from day to day. She looks at the group as if intimidated, whispering in Flaubert's ear: "You are the only one here who doesn't make me feel ill at ease."

She listens, says nothing, and sheds a tear over a bit of Hugo's verse at the point where sentimentality falsifies the poem.

She has small hands of marvelous delicacy, which she almost conceals in her lace ruffles.

February 25

How many intellectuals, passionately and excitingly devoted to things of the mind, live scarcely at all! I see Taine, going to bed at nine, getting up at seven, working till noon, dining at country hours; he makes his calls, visits the libraries,

[10] This passage recalls Taine's doctrine of the determinist influence of *race*, *milieu*, and *moment* expressed in the introduction to his *Histoire de la Littérature Anglaise*, 1864.

and spends the evening after supper with his mother and his piano. I see Flaubert, as if chained to a galley or in a dungeon by his work. I see ourselves immersed in our projects without any distractions or interruptions from family or social life, except for a dinner every two weeks with the Princess and a few crazy trips to look for curios on the quays, the maniacal recreation of bibliography and iconography.

March 28

At the Princess's the conversation at dessert is always a conversation about love. Gautier, who is in fine fettle, by a description of the nipples of a young girl which are hydrangea-colored gets Sainte-Beuve to admit that he has never gone at it a second time when making love. And the whole room bursts out laughing!

The character of men of letters today follows a natural course. Members of Sainte-Beuve's generation were under the tyrannical influence of romanticism, which, so to speak, regimented them in a certain hygiene, in theories, in poses, in ways of living, eating, and making love that were uniform and denied them any independence.

May 6

Flaubert said to me yesterday: "There are two men in me. One, you see, narrow-chested, leaden-assed, made to bend over a table; the other, lighthearted as a traveling salesman on a trip, with a taste for violent exertion!"

June 3

A new symptom of the envy, the hatred, stirred up by the good fortune of our name, of our books: there is now open anger not only against our style and our ideas but also against our dual being, our unique fraternal relationship. In the twelve pages of diatribe in *La Revue des Deux Mondes*, in the extreme ranting of *Le Figaro*, the bitterness is flagrant and unrestrained against our collaboration, the twinship of our thoughts and works. They resent the two brothers; it is the marriage, the domesticity, of our fraternity that they attack. They hate us because we love each other!

September 9

It is a curious thing that the three great French painters of the eighteenth century, Watteau, Chardin, La Tour, should be, so to speak, the only ones of their time who never were in Italy.

1867

February 15

The nineteenth century has operated on humanity for cataracts. A striking example: Rousseau, the great describer, went to Venice without being any more touched by the enchantment of the setting and the poetry of the place than if he had been embassy secretary at Pontoise.

February 22

Romanticism was not born in France. It was destined to come to us, like a tropical plant, from the New World. Bernardin de Saint-Pierre brought it from Mauritius, and Chateaubriand from America.

February 25

Why does a Japanese doorway charm me and amuse my eye, while all the Greek architectural lines bore me? As for people who claim to appreciate both, my conviction is that they feel nothing.

June 27

Apropos of *Hernani* [a successful revival].

It is sad to think that an author must live forty years, almost a half century, to be applauded as much as he has been hissed.

July 12

I find that around us, from day to day and everywhere in our world, all respect for posterity diminishes. Literature for the men of letters whom I meet seems no longer to be anything but a way of getting oneself on the "free list" for many things in life. It is the right to practice a certain parasitism without losing consideration. And more and more rarely does one find an artist, a man who lives only for his art. I know of only three: Flaubert and us.

August 4

Soulié was telling us that there are two Sainte-Beuves: the Sainte-Beuve of his upstairs room, his work room, the man of study, thought, and wit; and a quite different Sainte-Beuve, the downstairs one, in the dining room with his intimates, his secretary Troubat, the woman who corrects his proofs, his mistress *La Manchotte*, Marie the cook, and the two maids. In these humble surroundings he becomes the petit bourgeois, closed off on all sides from intelligence and his other life, a sort of vulgar small shopkeeper, flattened out, shut in, unrecognizable, made stupid by women's chatter, and soothed by the dullness and the idiotic repetitious talk of the Southerner, Troubat.

September 18

Nothing, nothing, absolutely nothing in this exhibition of Courbet. At most two seascapes. Aside from them, oddly enough in this master of realism, no studies of nature. The body of his *Woman with a Parrot* is, in its way, as far from the truth of the nude as in a painting by almost any academician of the eighteenth century.

Ugliness, always ugliness! And the ugly without that which gives it character, the ugly without the beauty of ugliness!

1868

February 5

Distance, excellent for the fame and reputation of living men. Voltaire at Ferney, Hugo on Jersey, two solitudes which rhyme and seem to echo each other. For a man of genius or talent to show himself is to diminish himself.

February 8

Buried all this week in our life of Gavarni.

What a woman chaser! What a seeker after the "feminine unknown!" What a pursuer of all the women he saw! And what assignations! And beneath all that, the new and painful things that we learn about him, that there was something dark and Machiavellian about him—the evil of *Les Liaisons Dangereuses*, an interest in cruel experiments, a bitter playing on the weaknesses of women.

And this man who talks of truth, even to himself, shows many sides without spontaneity, clarity, or frankness. The subterfuges of his thought and his expression are from his soul, his inner consciousness, a hair-splitting philosophy which is never the first impulse of a response straight from the heart. . . .

After all, there were many men in this man, and all of them very different from the man we knew!

Journal, 1868

February 24

How ridiculous the importance always given to the student, in everything touching on art, letters, the theatre, liberty! After all, what is a student? A future lawyer, a future notary —the embryo of the French Prudhomme.

March 23

If one only knew what makes Sainte-Beuve write a book! We find him now all excited over a project for a publication on Madame de Staël and her group, a sequel to his famous *Chateaubriand*, with nests of vipers in the form of footnotes—all this not because of any interest in or curiosity concerning the memory of Madame de Staël, not because of the attraction of unpublished documents, but in order to be disagreeable to the de Broglies. Down inside Sainte-Beuve there is a Chinese bourgeois.

May 6

Since on this occasion there were two poets presenting themselves to the Academy at the same time, one named Autran, the other Théophile Gautier, and the Academy has chosen Autran, it is my absolute, irrevocable opinion that the Academy is composed in the main of idiots or genuinely dishonest men. I leave the choice to it.

May 20

This evening at the Princess's we heard the wit of Dumas *fils* for the first time. A rather coarse animation but continuous; reparties that are cutting without regard for politeness; self-assurance which is close to insolence, and which permits him to say anything that occurs to him; and furthermore a cruel bitterness. But incontestably a very personal wit that is biting, cutting, incisive, which I find superior to the wit which as a dramatist he puts in his plays, because of the conciseness, the sharp edges which it has when it is really spontaneous!

July 22

Yesterday morning I read some chapters of *Madame Gervaisais* to Gautier. The latter, whose frank friendship makes him wish to increase our reputation, praised it to the Princess. So now she is full of curiosity, wishing to hear this reading, almost jealous not to have already heard it. We see that it is impossible to avoid satisfying this wish, though from experience we guess in advance how unpleasant it will be. Any reading, even of a masterpiece, arouses in her a boredom such as I have seen only in her, and for which she seems to blame the reader.

Finally in her pretty boudoir, next to her bedroom, I read seven or eight chapters. She listens in consternation, with the hostile expression of a person who is hurt in some way by our writing. But, my God, why do princes want to concern themselves with what does not interest them?

October 29

The taste for things Chinese and Japanese! We were among the first to have this taste. It is now spreading to everything and everyone, even to idiots and middle-class women. Who has cultivated it, felt it, preached it, and converted others to it more than we; who was excited by the first albums and had the courage to buy them?

In the first of our books, *En 18 . . ,* a description of a mantelpiece with Japanese ornaments brought us the honor of being called baroque fools, people without taste, and caused Edmond Texier to demand that we be committed to Charenton.

But let us go further back and revive some old memories. The elder of us was at that time a youngster of about fourteen and we had a fat old aunt in the country who had such small bones that although she was enormous, she weighed nothing. She adored us. And do you know the only quarrel we ever had with her? For her the Chinese were only people on screens. Never having seen them except on wall paper, she thought they were a sort of comic invention. From our schoolboy knowledge, we cited in their favor the compass, gunpowder, printing; she persisted in heaping scorn upon them: "So, your Chinese, that for them!" she said, with an old-fashioned belch. My aunt belonged to the good old days.

November 2

Ingres in his manifesto said that it took a week to learn to paint. Yes, like him . . . and even that we think is rather long!

December 1

We were, one of us especially, rather unjust toward the talent of Madame Sand. We have read the twenty volumes of *L'Histoire de ma Vie*, and in the midst of the disorganized stuff of a publication for profit there are admirable descriptions, priceless bits of information about the forming of a writer's imagination, impressive character sketches, scenes told with great simplicity—such as her grandmother's eighteenth-century death and her gentle heroism, her mother's Parisian death—which bring tears of admiration to the eye!

It is a great document—unfortunately diffuse—of psychology and analysis, in which Madame Sand's talent for truth, for observation of others and herself, and her vivid memory astonish and surprise one.

December 14

At lunch we met our admirer and disciple, Zola.

It was the first time we had met him. Our first impression was of the wreck of a Normalian, thick-set and sickly-looking at the same time, a posture like Sarcey's and a pale and waxy complexion; a vigorous-looking young man but with the delicate quality of a fine piece of porcelain in his features, the outline of his eyelids, the strong planes of his nose, and his hands. The whole person of the same cut as his characters, which he creates with two contrasting natures, in whom he mingles the male and the female; and in his moral nature as well he betrays a resemblance to his creations and the ambiguous contrasts in their character.

The dominant side, the ultranervous sickly side, gives you at times a vivid impression of a frail victim of heart disease. All in all, a being difficult to grasp, profound, confused, suffering, full of anxiety, disturbed, ambiguous.

He tells us about his hardships, about the desire and the need he has to find a publisher to support him for six years at a cost of 30,000 francs, assuring him 6,000 a year for food for him and his mother and freedom to write his *History of a Family*, a novel in ten volumes.

For he wants to do something big, no more of "those mean and wretched articles," he says in a tone of anger at himself, "which at present I am forced to write for *La Tribune*, associating with people whose idiotic opinions I am forced to adopt. For it must be said that this government with its indifference, its inability to recognize talent or anything that is productive, forces us wretches to go over to the papers of the opposition, the only ones who give us enough to eat! It is true, that is all that is left! And I have so many enemies! It is so hard to make oneself known!"

And from time to time with bitter recrimination he repeats to us and to himself that he is only twenty-eight, a vibrant note of harsh will and angry energy bursting out:

"And I have so much to learn. Yes, you are right, my novel [*Madeleine Férat*] goes off the track. I should have had only three characters. But I will follow your advice: I will redo the play your way. We are the new generation; we know that you are our mentors, Flaubert and you. You! even your enemies recognize that you have invented your art. They think it is nothing; it is everything!"

December 24

We are glad to see Flaubert again; and in our trio of bears and antisocial hermits we soothe our scorn, our indignation against all the vileness of today, the nasty side of people, the decline of letters, and the bourgeois domesticity with which one of our masters and a friend whom we love compromises his dignity and that of each of us as well.

1869

Wednesday, January 6

I tell the Princess that I have seen Sainte-Beuve, that I found him tired, preoccupied, sad. She does not answer, passes ahead of me into the front salon, the room devoted to her intimate chats and confidences.

And there she explodes: "Sainte-Beuve! I will never see him again! Never! The way he has behaved toward me . . . he of all people! It is on account of him that I quarreled with the Empress . . . and after all I have done for him! The last time I stayed at Compiègne, he asked three things of me: I got two of them from the Emperor . . . and what did I ask of him? I did not ask him to give up a conviction, I only asked him not to commit himself by a contract with *Le Temps;* and I offered to get him anything he wanted from Rouher. He could have been on *La Liberté* with Girardin, that would have still been acceptable, they were his kind of people, but *Le Temps!* our personal enemies! where every day they insult us!"

February 19

We go to see Sainte-Beuve and find him sad about his condition, sad about politics, sad about the state of literature. He tells us about the shameful behavior of the Academy, the bargaining for votes among the coteries, and the manipulations of Guizot. He tells us about this dialogue between Madame de Galliera and Lebrun, which Lebrun reported to him with the indignation and bitterness of an aging man of letters. As he went into her salon, she said to him:

"Well, M. Lebrun, the first chair is assigned . . . yes, to M. d'Haussonville . . . that is settled."

"I did not know about it," said the Academician, bowing.

"As for the second, it will doubtless go to M. de Champagny."

"Ah!"

"And as for the third, probably M. Barbier."

And on top of that the melancholy of five o'clock, of the end of a day, and the threat of solitude for the evening brought him back to talking in subdued thought and voice of all the privations he was suffering, the impossibility of going out to seek his own kind of society, an impossibility which makes one lose interest in the actions of others and of society.

Then, as if stirring a dying fire, he recapitulated for us his days following one on the other, still sometimes waking in the morning with a little illusion and brightness; then in the middle of the day feeling a slight interest in his work, in a few remaining faithful friends, and nothing more; and then the sad prospect of the evening. "Ah, my existence, you see, no! Such an existence! Life for me is no longer more than a bare wall; it needs hangings, ornaments." And with a little gesture in the air he indicated his regret for past things.

Night was softly falling and the words of the old man became more and more words of chiaroscuro, words approaching the great silence.

February 22

Since our book [*Madame Gervaisais*] appeared, painful days. Not a letter, not a word, no response by anyone except for a warm handshake from Flaubert. A profound sadness because of this, this conspiracy of silence that we feel, hostile and envious all around us, and the chill which is cast over all who come near us because the loftiness of the book diminishes them!

April 7

At Magny's.

They were saying that Berthelot had predicted that in a hundred years of science man would know the secret of the atom and would be able at will to extinguish or relight the sun; that Claude Bernard for his part was asserting that after a hundred years of physiological science it would be possible to know the laws of organic life, of human creation.

We raised no objections, but we firmly believe that at that point in the history of the world the good Lord with his white beard will arrive on earth with his bundle of keys and will say to human kind, as they say at the Exhibition of Painting at the Salon: "Gentlemen, it's closing time!"

April 16

We recently had an experience with Sainte-Beuve that was bizarre from beginning to end.

After his bitter and hateful outpourings against our novel and his almost personal hostility toward its heroine, he proposed to us, using Charles Edmond as intermediary, to write two articles about us in *Le Temps.* He warned us that he would expect us to accept the agreeable and the disagreeable, that furthermore he expected us to reply to his strictures in the same paper. . . .

After this was agreed upon during a visit, we met someone who informed us that Sainte-Beuve was not going to write the articles and that he said it was our fault. We wrote to him. He answered in a letter in which "Gentlemen" replaced "Dear Friends" as salutation, a letter full of embarrassment and evasiveness, in which he seemed to be saying in vague terms that his present situation with the Princess would prevent him from writing the articles he planned to write for us. At the first word of this letter I suspected the activity of hostile gossip, some spy at the Wednesday dinners—who knows, perhaps Taine.

So right up to the end, even to the edge of the tomb, Sainte-Beuve will be the Sainte-Beuve he has been all his life, a man always influenced in his criticism by the smallest, least important considerations—personal questions, the influence of domestic opinions around him! A critic who never judged a book freely and by his own standards!

And back of it all is the fact that he wants to break with all the friends of the Princess, while letting it be thought that the quarrel comes from them.

Wednesday, April 28

At the Princess's. As a touching surprise for the Emperor, who is coming tomorrow, she has ordered the court improviser, Théophile Gautier, to put into verse a piece of prose written by the prisoner of Ham on the return of his uncle's ashes—a rather substantial piece of prose. In the course of the day Gautier hastily wrested ninety lines from his muse. *O platitudo!*

April 29

We arrive at eleven-thirty. The Imperial ceremony is over. As we sadly shake hands with Gautier, who missed out in the Academy election today, he says: "Oh, I am quite consoled. My thing went over very well. We saw the Emperor weep!"

Poor naive fellow, who was led to compromise himself publicly by such obvious flattery, and whom the august mouths scarcely thanked, the Emperor having spent the rest of the evening talking with Ricord about the cultivation of pineapples, and the Empress talking for a whole hour with Dumas *fils* about his repentant prostitutes.

May 22

At Michelet's.

In spite of his years, his long labors, the hairy old man is still young and lively in spirit, still colorful, eloquent, and paradoxical.

We speak of Hugo's book. He says a novel is the creating of a miracle with great effort, the absolute opposite of historical science, "the great undoer of miracles." . . .

He pictures Hugo not as a Titan, but as Vulcan, a gnome, who beats out iron on great forges in the bowels of the earth. Above all a creator and lover of monsters: Quasimodo, *L'Homme Qui Rit,* his success always due to monsters; even in *Les Travailleurs de la Mer* the center of interest is the octopus. Hugo has strength, great strength, whipped up and overwrought, the strength of a man constantly walking in the wind and taking two sea baths a day.

May 23

Flaubert's book, his Parisian novel, is finished. We see the manuscript on his green baize table, in a box made especially for it and bearing the title to which he stubbornly clings: *L'Education Sentimentale,* with the subtitle *L'Histoire d'un Jeune Homme.*

He is about to send it to the copyist, for ever since he began to write he has kept for himself as a sort of religion the immortal monument of his manuscript. This fellow makes a somewhat ridiculous ceremony of even the slightest things connected with his painful creation. Decidedly, in our friend we do not know which is more gross, his vanity or his pride!

July 17

Flaubert comes to see us this evening, flourishing in strength and health, more exuberant than ever. He talks about the mortal illness of Bouilhet with plethoric unconcern, wounding us by the light and detached way in which he consoles us and comforts us. And as he leaves, the big fellow exclaims: "It is amusing how just now I seem to inherit the "vigousse" of all my sick friends!"

1870–1896

1870

His mortal illness caused Jules de Goncourt to lay down the pen in January of this year. After an interval his brother Edmond resumed the Journal, *continuing it for the rest of his life.*

Saturday, August 27

Zola comes to have lunch at my house. He tells me about a series of novels he wants to write, an epic in ten volumes, *The Natural and Social History of a Family*, which he is ambitious to try and in which he will show temperaments, characteristics, vices, virtues as they are developed by environment, and are as sharply differentiated as the sunny and shady parts of a garden.

He says to me: "After the analysis of the infinitesimally small expressions of feeling carried out by Flaubert in *Madame Bovary*, after the analysis of artistic, plastic, nervous things such as you have done, after these *jewel-works*, these finely chiseled volumes, there is no room left for the young, nothing for them to do, nothing in the way of creating characters. It is only by the number of volumes, the power of their creation, that they can impress the public."

Monday, November 7

I go to call on Hugo and thank the illustrious master for the sympathetic letter he so kindly wrote at the time of my brother's death.

He lives on the Avenue Frochot—at Meurice's, I think. I have to wait in the dining room among the remains of lunch and a mess of glass and porcelain bric-a-brac. Then I am ushered into a little drawing room, the walls and ceiling of which are covered with old brocade.

In the chimney corner are two black-clad women, whose features are vaguely visible against the light. Half-reclining on a divan around the poet is a group of friends, among whom I recognize Vacquerie. In a corner Hugo's fat son in National Guard uniform is playing checkers on a low table with a little blond-haired child in a cherry-red sash.

After shaking hands Hugo goes back to stand in front of the fireplace. In the penumbra of the antique furnishings, in the autumn light which is somewhat darkened by the faded colors of the walls and made blue by cigar smoke, against this background of another age where everything is a bit vague and uncertain, things as well as faces, Hugo's head in full light is properly framed and looks striking. He has some fine white disordered locks of hair like those of Michelangelo's prophets; on his face is a strange, almost ecstatic placidity. Yes, ecstasy, but now and then the dark eyes become lively again, it seems to me, and are infused with a sort of mean slyness.

1871

Thursday, May 4

At Burty's this evening Verlaine confesses something unbelievable. He declares that he has had to fight against a proposal that has been put forward to destroy Notre Dame.

Journal, 1871

Saturday, June 10

Dinner this evening with Flaubert, whom I had not seen since my brother's death. He has come to Paris to get some information for his *Temptation of Saint Anthony*. He is unchanged, a man of letters before everything else. The cataclysm seems to have passed over him without in any way detaching him from his impassive writing of his book.

October 18

I drop in on Flaubert just as he is leaving for Rouen. Under his arm is a ministerial portfolio with triple locks which contains his *Temptation*. In the cab he talks to me about his book, about all the trials to which he subjects his Theban hermit, trials from which he emerges victorious. Then, on the Rue d'Amsterdam, he confides to me that the ultimate defeat of the saint is due to the basic form of life, to the scientific *cell*. Oddly enough, he seems to be astonished at my astonishment.

Sunday, November 9

At Flaubert's I find Ramelli, to whom he wants the Odéon to give a part in Bouilhet's play. She is complaining about the theatre, which has adopted the custom of paying only the leading actors, giving Berton 300 francs a night for his role in *Le Marquis de Villemer* [by George Sand]. I have never seen any group of people who go more avidly after money than actors and actresses. Ramelli's lamentations resemble the angry outcries of a fishwife. She gets so red in the face that she has to stay in a room where there is no fire, and through the door we hear her furious complaints....

I stay for dinner, and afterwards Flaubert reads to me from *The Temptation of Saint Anthony*. My first impression: the Bible, the Christian past modernized in the fashion of Horace

Vernet, with Bedouin and Turkish color added. My second impression: an immense notebook on antiquity forced through the planing mill of the imagination by the stupid trickeries of the fairy tale, with a good many elements of the compilation stubbornly refusing to go through.

What is more serious is that I find no originality in this work, which some people are going to consider very original. In his sly way for some years past Flaubert has chosen the most colorful, the most eccentric, the most Carthaginian settings, the ones most likely to dazzle the bourgeois. But underneath the decor and the costumes his human beings are deucedly banal. He possesses none of the brilliant imagination of the poet under the influence of hashish, none of the psychological insight by which a *seer* could bring a dead humanity to life. In short, there is no personal invention, just intelligent, calculated appropriation. Of originality, nothing, absolutely nothing! Originality does not consist in turning the original into the commonplace, but in making something original out of the commonplace. Originality in Flaubert's Orientalism—again I say no! At most a laborious and assiduous exercise of ingenuity.

December 3

The composition, the narration, the writing of a novel—nothing to it! What is hard, painful, is the necessity of becoming a detective, a police spy, in order to search out the true reality, of which a contemporary story is made up—and most of the time to have to seek it out in repulsive locales.

But why, people will say, choose such locales? Because in the midst of the obliteration of a civilization it is at the bottom that the character of things, people, language, everything is

1. Edgar Degas, apotheosis of the artist *en famille*

2. Victor Hugo, romantic exile on the island of Jersey

3. Jules de Goncourt, by Edmond de Goncourt

4. Alphonse Daudet, by Bacard *fils*

5. Edmond de Goncourt, caricature based on a photograph by Nadar

6. Hippolyte Taine *en bourgeois*

7. In the studios, by Daumier

8. Edouard Drumont, anti-Semitic gladiator

9. Gustave Flaubert dissecting Madame Bovary, by Lemot

10. The sinister Catulle Mendès, by Cappiello

11. Charles Sainte-Beuve, voluptuary, by Gill

12. Emile Zola's taste for ordure, by Le Bourgeois

conserved, so that a painter has a thousand times more chance of making a work that has *style* out of a dirty streetwalker on the Rue Saint Honoré than out of a fancy piece from the Rue Bréda.

Again I ask why. Perhaps because I am a wellborn writer, and the people, the scum, if you wish, have for me the attraction of unknown and undiscovered peoples, possess a certain *exotic quality*—which travelers undergo a thousand discomforts to seek out in distant lands.

1872

Saturday, March 2

Théo, Turgenev, and I had dinner at Flaubert's today.

Turgenev, the gentle giant, the friendly barbarian, with his white hair falling into his eyes, with the deep furrow which cuts across his forehead from one temple to the other like the furrow left by a plow, with his childish speech, charms us from the start, "engarlands" us with pleasure—to use the Russian expression—by that mixture of naiveté and subtlety which constitutes the seductiveness of the Slavic race, enhanced in his case by the originality of a superior mind, by broad and cosmopolitan knowledge.

He tells us of the month he spent in prison after the publication of *A Sportsman's Sketches*, of the month when he had for a cell the police archives of the district, where he burrowed into the secret dossiers. With the strokes of painter and novelist he depicts the chief of police, whom he one day made drunk with champagne and who, giving Turgenev a nudge and raising his glass in the air, proposed a toast "To Robespierre!"

Then Turgenev pauses and says: "If I took pride in such

things, I would ask only that they inscribe on my tombstone what my book did for the emancipation of the serfs. Yes, that is all I would ask. Emperor Alexander had it conveyed to me that the reading of my book was one of the principal factors in his decision."

Théo, who climbed the stairs with one hand over his painful heart, has the vague eyes, the masklike white face of a Pierrot. Drawn into himself, mute, deaf, he eats and drinks mechanically in the way you would imagine a pale somnambulist dining in the light of the moon. In him you see already the dying man, who wakes up a bit and escapes from his sad concentration on himself only when he hears talk about poetry.

From a discussion of Molière's verse the conversation turns to Aristophanes; and Turgenev, giving vent to the tremendous enthusiasm he feels for the comic writer, the father of laughter, for that ability to which he accords so high a place and which he finds in only two or three men in the whole history of humanity, bursts out, his lips wet with desire: "Just think, if we were to recover Cratinus' lost play, the one that was considered superior to the plays of Aristophanes, the one the Greeks thought of as the masterpiece of comedy, the one called *The Bottle*, written by that old Athenian drunkard . . . I don't know what I wouldn't give for it . . . I just don't know . . . I think I would give everything for it!"

When we leave the table Gautier sinks down on a sofa and says:

"Basically nothing interests me any more; I feel as though I were no longer a contemporary. I am disposed to speak of myself in the third person and in the historical past tense. I have the feeling I am already dead!"

"For my part," Turgenev rejoins, "I have a different feeling. You know how sometimes in a room there is an indefinable odor of musk which you can't get rid of, which won't go away. Well, around me there seems always to be an odor of death, of nothingness, of dissolution."

After a silence he continues: "The explanation for that is to be found, I think, in one fact, in impotence—for a host of reasons, my white hair, etc.—in my absolute inability nowadays to love. I am no longer capable of it. And, you understand, that is death!"

As Flaubert and I question how important love is for the man of letters, the Russian novelist, letting his arms fall toward the ground, exclaims:

"As far as I am concerned, my life is saturated with things feminine. No book or anything else has ever been able to take the place of a woman for me. How can I express it? I find that love alone produces a kind of flowering of my being which nothing else brings about. Do you see?"

And as his memory searches into the past, his face lights up with happiness:

"Listen, when I was a very young man I had a mistress, a miller's wife in the outskirts of Saint Petersburg, whom I used to see when I was out hunting. She was charming, very white, with a cast in her eye—something fairly common among us. She would never accept anything from me, but one day she said:

'You must make me a gift!'

'What would you like?'

'Bring me some soap.'

I brought her the soap. She took it, disappeared, returned blushing, and said to me as she held out her perfumed hands:

'Now kiss my hands as you do those of Saint Petersburg ladies in their drawing rooms!' I dropped to my knees. Well, there has never been a moment in my life equal to that one!"

Monday, March 18

Today at the Regnault exhibition in the midst of everybody's enthusiastic admiration for the painter my own admiration, which preceded that of others, goes down a notch. To me he is definitely a decorator rather than a painter.

From there I am taken to the studio of Fantin, the immortalizer of beerhall geniuses. At the back of the room there is an immense canvas representing a realist apotheosis of Baudelaire and Champfleury. And on an easel there is an immense canvas representing a Parnassian apotheosis of Verlaine, d'Hervilly, etc., an apotheosis which has a big empty space in it, because, the painter tells us naively, so and so have not wanted to be depicted alongside colleagues whom they call pimps and robbers.

Certainly his painting has some good qualities, but it lacks firmness; it is painting which seems to be veiled by the vaporous ideas which haunt the flaming red head of the painter.

Friday, March 22

Turgenev, along with Flaubert, has dinner at my house.

Turgenev gives us a bizarre sketch of his Moscow publisher, a small-scale purveyor of literature who scarcely knows how to read and who, as far as writing goes, can barely sign his name. He describes this man surrounded by a dozen fantastic little old men, his readers and advisors at 700 kopecks a year. . . .

He soon turns to self-analysis. He tells us that when he is

sad and out of sorts, twenty lines of Pushkin will bring him out of it, pick him up, exalt him. Such reading gives him a feeling of tender admiration which no great and generous actions are capable of evoking. Only literature is able to give him this restoration of serenity, which he recognizes at once by a physical manifestation, by a pleasant sensation in his cheeks! He adds that when he is angry, he feels as though he had a great hole in his chest, in his stomach.

In the midst of the avid attention which he senses in us he becomes continually more expansive and reaches the point of telling us of the moment in his life which was most filled with sensations.

In his youth he courted a young girl but she married someone else. After a stay of eight years in Germany he returned to Russia. It was in July. He stayed at the home of the girl's mother during the three-day festivities that the mother provided for the birthday of her daughter, who was there alone, having left her ailing, hypochondriac husband at home. The mother was crazy for pleasure and the house was full of gaiety and dancing.

One evening he asked the young woman to dance a mazurka. As he led her to the floor he said: "Do you really want to dance or would you rather talk?" "As you prefer." They left the ballroom. Near it was a series of rooms where people were playing whist. Further on were other rooms, lighted only by the moon, into which dancers glided from time to time. They sat down in one of these rooms on a divan called a "paté" facing a big open window. They chatted, the woman's face being somewhat averted from his as she looked at the garden. Now and then a group of mazurka dancers would enter the room, wheel about in it, and disappear.

Suddenly the woman turned her big eyes toward him—

immense, slanting Chinese eyes. Then, he does not know how, he was unbuttoned and the woman's skirts were pulled up. In an instant the woman was on him and at him. He has kept the memory of the shock of teeth upon teeth, of contact with lips cold as ice, and of the furnace heat of all the lower part of her body. When the woman had left the room, he rushed out into the courtyard to get some air and let the cool breath of the wind soothe his face.

Next day he was told that the woman had left. Years later he saw her again, several times, but never dared allude to that evening. Sometimes he wonders if it really happened.

Sunday, March 24

Hugo has remained a man of letters above all else. In the sorry crowd of people with whom he lives, among the imbecile and fanatic contacts to which he is subjected, in the idiotic meanness of thought and speech which surrounds him, this famous man enamored of the great and the beautiful rages within himself. His rage, his scorn, his disdain, his high contempt show themselves by the way in which he is in opposition to his coreligionists over everything.

Yesterday at dinner he defended the former prefect, Janvier. The other day, apropos of a discussion about Thiers, he replied to Meurice, that doctrinaire Communard for whom he has a secret antipathy: "Scribe is just as guilty!" And when Meurice foolishly rejoined: "But Thiers suppressed *Le Rappel*," Hugo, in his indignation at seeing shoptalk intrude on the higher life, shouted at Meurice: "But what do I care about your *Le Rappel*?"

Sometimes in the face of the invasion of his drawing room by "men in soft hats" he lets himself sink back on his sofa with an air of indefinable weariness, muttering into a friendly ear: "Oh, those politicians!" Poor, unhappy great man who, under the threat of a visit by Schoelcher, said sadly to his intimates: "If Schoelcher comes, we won't get to read any poetry!"—something which, a few minutes before, he had been looking forward to as a special treat.

Recently on one of his visits to escape from his own house he said to Judith [Gautier]: "What if we were to do a little conspiring to get the Napoleons back? Then we could go back there, go to Jersey, and work together."

The Mendès couple are certainly a strange pair: the husband, that blond Portuguese Jew, that former ragged denizen of Bohemia, has assumed a correct demeanor, the face of a business man, the sharp look of an impresario who is exploiting a prima donna and living off her.

Tuesday, March 26

Hugo recently said to Burty: "It is a great effort for me to make a speech. A speech tires me as much as coming three times!" Upon reflection he added: "Perhaps even four times!"

Sunday, May 26

Today I am a half century old. That is a lot.

The manifesto of the realist school—no one would think of looking for it where it is. It is in *Werther*, when Goethe says through the mouth of his hero: "This confirmed me in my resolution of adhering in the future entirely to Nature." Adding, "Say what you will of rules, they destroy the genuine feeling of Nature and its true expression."

October 25

For the funeral of the father [Théophile Gautier] I am at the church in Neuilly where only a few months ago I attended the wedding of the daughter.

The funeral is full of pomp. The bugles of the Army pay

homage to the officer of the Legion of Honor. The most moving voices from the Opéra sing the requiem of the author of *Gisèle.*

We follow the hearse on foot all the way to Montmartre Cemetery. In a brougham I see Dumas reading the funeral eulogy by which we are menaced to big Marchal, who sits facing his illustrious friend on a little jump seat, which threatens to collapse under him. The cemetery is full of lower-class admirers, anonymous colleagues, scribblers for the little papers, who are accompanying the body of the journalist, not the poet, not the author of *Mademoiselle de Maupin.* For my part, it seems to me my corpse would feel revulsion at having behind it such a swarm of scribblers, and I ask only, when my time comes, for men of talent and the six devoted shoemakers who were at Heinrich Heine's burial.

Thursday, October 31

The bell rings. It is Feydeau. What brings him here?

I am at once struck by his ill-natured expression, the harshness of his voice, the way illness has given him a despotically imperious manner. The egoism of his personality, which used to be merely stupid, has become so aggressive that you would like to kick him out, if you did not feel sorry for the sick man. Everybody is rotten—publishers, relatives, friends. Everybody is ungrateful; during the whole visit he complains about and bursts out angrily at the lack of heart of the whole universe.

Famine has descended on his house. He is forced to sell the two portraits of his mother done by Gavarni; he wants 500 francs for them. I must find the money for him at once. Then he wants me to intercede with *Le Bien Public* for the placing of an article on Gautier which he alone is capable of writing. Then he has to take a piss, and I hold the pot, but he says it is my fault that he has trouble pissing. He goes beyond the impossible in his insupportability. I think that no attack of paralysis in the history of the world has ever made a man so disagreeable, so detestable, so morally repugnant as he!

As he is leaving he says: "There were only five francs in the house: I spent them to buy mourning for Gautier. My wife scolded me; she said that in my situation you don't buy mourning for friends."

And therewith the paralytic scrounger gets into an excellent middle-class brougham and goes off to join his wife, dressed in velvet and lace, in their pretty, flowery apartment on the Rue de Copenhague.

1873

February 26

Flaubert said rather picturesquely today: "No, it is indignation alone that keeps me going! Indignation for me is like the bar in a doll's back which keeps it upright. When I am no longer indignant, I shall fall flat on my face!" And he sketches the outline of a Polichinelle fallen on the floor.

Everywhere you go just now you run into a sort of stupid cult for the person of Littré. That superior Bescherelle is on the way to becoming a kind of deity as the result of the worshipful adulation of free-thinking folk.

March 5

I have dinner with Sardou at the Princess's tonight. I had glimpsed him two or three times in the drawing room but had not previously talked to him.

In Sardou there is nothing of the god that Dumas affects, nothing of the latter's overweening self-importance. Sardou is a good prince. He accepts everybody on a footing of equality.

He is talkative by nature, with the talkativeness of a man of business. He speaks only of figures, of box-office receipts. Nothing about him indicates the writer. If he tries to be merry, to be witty, it is the wit of the third-rate actor that appears on his thin lips, his hairless face.

A little overgenerous in his use of I, he tells us at length about the banning of his American play [*L'Oncle Sam*]. In this connection a pretty detail about Thiers. When the management of the Vaudeville begged Thiers for permission to put on the play, he let it be known that this was impossible: at the moment the Americans were the only people out of whom Paris was making any money and their feelings must not be hurt. Thiers really does have reason to boast of being a petit bourgeois.

Sunday, March 16

Alphonse Daudet, whom I had merely caught sight of at the performance of *Henriette Maréchal* but whom I now meet at Flaubert's, is talking about Morny, whose secretary he once was in a way.

Speaking of him with a certain reserve, his words of gratitude veiling the nullity of the man, Daudet grants him one quality—a certain understanding of people, an ability at first sight to distinguish an inept person from an intelligent one.

Daudet is very funny and reaches the highest flights of comedy when he depicts Morny the littérateur, the fabricator of operettas. He tells us about a morning when Morny ordered him to produce a song, a Madagascan triviality in the manner of "Good Negress love good Negro, good Negress love good leg of lamb." When this was concocted and delivered by Daudet, Morny, in the enthusiasm of the first audition, forgot that Persigny and Boitelle were in the anteroom. And there they were, Daudet, Lépine the musician, and Morny himself in the skull cap and big dressing gown in which he liked to play the Cardinal-Minister, jumping on footstools and beating out loud sounds of "zim boom, zim badaboom" while the Ministers of the Interior and of the Police chewed their nails!

March 18

All the lack of virility in Sainte-Beuve, all the feminine quality of his talent, all the shady, underhanded, miserable side of his character can be explained in one word. He was . . . no, he was not impotent, as Philips told the Princess, but with him the gymnastics of love-making were carried out with such difficulty, such embarrassment, such shame, that he might as well have been. Sainte-Beuve is one of the most interesting examples of the incomplete moral nature produced in a man by the defectiveness of his genitals.

Saturday, May 3

At Véfour's in the Renaissance Room, where I once brought Sainte-Beuve and Lagier together, I dine this evening with Turgenev, Flaubert, and Madame Sand.

Madame Sand has become more and more mummified but is full of the good nature and gaiety of an old woman of the last century. Turgenev talks, and we willingly let the soft-voiced giant hold the floor as he tells us tender little anecdotes with moving and delicate little touches.

Flaubert tells us about a play on Louis XI which he says he wrote in school, a play in which he evoked the misery of the common people in these words: "My lord, we are forced to season our vegetables with the salt of our tears."

This play takes Turgenev back to memories of his childhood—the harsh education under which he developed, the revolts against injustice which were generated in his young soul. He recalls, as the result of some misdeed or other, being sermonized by his tutor, then whipped, then deprived of dinner; he recalls walking in the garden and with a kind of bitter pleasure drinking the salt water which ran from his eyes down his cheeks and fell into the corners of his mouth.

Then he speaks of the "savorful" hours of his youth, the hours when, lying on the grass, he listened to the sounds of earth, the hours passed on watch in a dreamy observation of nature which is indescribable.

He tells us of a beloved dog which seemed to share his state of feeling, which would surprise him with a deep sigh in his moments of melancholy, a dog which one evening on the edge of a pond where Turgenev was suddenly caught up in a mysterious feeling of terror threw himself against his master's legs as if he shared his fright. . . .

Recently, in connection with Bouilhet's play, which he is working over, Flaubert said to me: "It will take only a month; it's a matter of writing it as simply as possible; and, moreover, I hate fine writing!"

His scorn for those qualities which he does not possess is amusing. No thank you! That's his response to wit and the gift of writing the language as it is spoken—language that does not seem to be written, the rarest thing there is in the theatre!

The older Flaubert gets, the more provincial he becomes. Truly when you take away the ox, the workhorse, the maker of books at one word per hour, you have left a being very *ordinarily* endowed, very little endowed with originality! And I am not speaking here only of originality of ideas and concepts; I am talking about originality of actions and tastes;

I am talking of a personal originality, which is always the mark of a superior man. By heaven, the bourgeois resemblance of his brain to everybody else's brain—which infuriates him deep down, I am sure—that resemblance he conceals by truculent paradoxes, antipopular axioms, revolutionary bellowings in brutal, and indeed ill-mannered, contradiction of all received and accepted ideas. He even gets away with it sometimes. But with whom? To perceptive observers the violence and exaggeration quickly reveal the lack of seriousness in what he says.

In short, Flaubert proclaims himself to be the most passionate man in the world. But over the years his friends have known and know that women play only a rather secondary role in his life. Flaubert proclaims himself to be most imprudent in the handling of money; in fact, he has no passions to indulge, doesn't buy anything—no compulsive fantasy has ever made a hole in his purse. Flaubert proclaims himself a man of extraordinary imagination when it comes to the comfort and elegance of a dwelling; up to now all he has come up with is the idea of making vases out of ginger jars, a creation about which, indeed, he shows himself rather proud. So it goes. The author of *Madame Bovary* has only the ideas, the tastes, the habits, the prejudices, the qualities, the vices of the common herd.

Now, is he an absolute liar when his words so completely contradict his inner being? No, and the phenomenon which takes place within him is rather complex. First of all, when you say he is a Norman, you say he is somewhat Gascon. Moreover, our Norman is very much given to violent language by nature. And lastly, the poor fellow undergoes a violent rush of blood to the head when he speaks. The result is, I think, that with one third gasconade, one third vituperation, and one third congestion my friend Flaubert manages to intoxicate himself almost sincerely with the counterverities which he purveys.

Saturday, June 14

Today to get some information about Watteau's *L'Enseigne* I went to the home of the Comte de Béhague. In millionaire collectors, pride of possession combined with nonappreciation of what they possess produces a strangely comic effect. If you saw very much of them, they would quickly succeed in making you detest what you have taught them to like.

Tonight Zola's *Thérèse Raquin* forces me once more to mingle with that firstnight audience which I hold in abomination—journalists as fat as old bawds, a whole feckless crowd whose job it is to make a lot of noise about stupid things.

July 26

When I get home this evening I find a letter which bears the imprint of the Ministry of Public Instruction and Religion. I am surprised, for I have nothing to do with ministries. I open the letter and read that, upon the suggestion of my dear colleague Charles Blanc, the Minister of Public Instruction has just bought, for the account of the Director of Fine Arts, 125 copies of *Gavarni, L'Homme et l'Oeuvre* at eight francs a copy.

First I smile at the irony of having such a psychologically loving study go into governmental libraries, at the irony that this book which contains such a fine profession of atheism should be encouraged by the Minister of Religion.

But then I become furious at the thought that this purchase, which people will think was solicited, will compromise our two names. What a family those Blancs are! attempting secretly to disarm hatred and to muzzle antipathy by means of a little money taken from the State.

But what can I do? As a well-bred man I can only express my thanks. What a misfortune not to have been born a mountebank! If tomorrow in a newspaper I refused in resounding fashion, I would get the reputation of being a man of inviolable honesty and would sell out my edition!

Thursday, November 20

Today I was in Manet's studio looking at his picture *Le Bal de l'Opéra*, which is, you might say, the setting for the first act of *Henriette Maréchal*.

1874

Sunday, February 8

This evening while we were having dinner at Flaubert's Alphonse Daudet told us about his childhood, a childhood that was precocious and disturbed. It was spent in a household without a sou where the father changed his trade or business every day, in the eternal fog of Lyon, already held in abomination by his young nature which was in love with the sun. At that time tremendous reading—he was only twelve—reading of poets, of imaginative works which overstimulated his brain; reading spurred on by drunkenness from stolen liquor; reading while riding whole days at a time in boats that he untied from the quay. And in the burning glare of the two rivers, drunk from reading and from alcohol, and shortsighted as he was, the youngster managed to live in a dream or in an hallucination in which, one might say, nothing of the reality of things ever came through to him.

Friday, February 13

Yesterday I spent the day in the studio of a bizarre painter by the name of Degas. After many trials, many experiments, much reaching out in all directions, he has become enamored of the modern; and in the modern he has fixed his choice on laundresses and dancers. Basically this is not a bad choice. He paints in white and pink, women's flesh in batiste and gauze, the most charming excuse for soft blond tints.

He places before our eyes laundresses, laundresses, laundresses, in their graceful poses and foreshortened attitudes, speaking as they would speak and explaining technically the difference between ironing and pressing.

Then dancers parade before us. There is their practice room: against the light from a window the fantastic silhouette of the legs of female dancers coming down a little staircase, with the stunning red spot of a tartan in the midst of all those white ballooning clouds, and with a ridiculous ballet master as a vulgar foil. There before us, caught as from life, are the graceful twisting movements and gestures of these little girl-monkeys.

The painter shows his pictures, supplementing his commentary from time to time by the mimicking of a choreographic movement, by the imitation of what the dancers call one of their "arabesques." It is really very amusing to see him on the tip of his toes, his arms held out, mingling the aesthetic terms of the painter with those of the ballet master, speaking of Velásquez' "soft muddiness" and the "silhouetting" of Mantegna.

An original fellow this Degas, sickly, neurotic, ophthalmic to such an extent that he is afraid he will lose his sight, but on that very account an exceptionally sensitive being who feels the subtle character of things. Of all the painters I have seen up to now he is the one who best catches the spirit of modern life in his depiction of that life.

Will he ever do anything finished? I have my doubts. He is too troubled a spirit. Moreover, can you imagine that instead of giving these delicately felt reproductions of beings and natures the rigorous setting of the ballet dancers' practice room at the Opéra, he has had a draftsman fill in a Panini-like architectural background?

From his studio I went on at nightfall to the studio of Galland, the decorator-painter, a studio which, with its cathedrallike grandeur, its little mockups of mythological beings, its lively wash drawings, seemed to present the crepuscular awakening of a Lilliputian Olympus as it came to life at night.

Thursday, March 12

Yesterday the atmosphere was funereal, a sort of glacial chill falling gradually on the performance of *Le Candidat*, on that audience warm with sympathy who in good faith expected sublime tirades, superhuman exhibitions of wit, language that would provoke battles, but instead found themselves confronted with nothing, nothing, nothing! At first on all faces there was sad pity; then, long held in out of respect for the person and the talent of Flaubert, the disappointment of the audience took its revenge in a sort of bantering whisper, a smiling mockery of the whole sorry business.

No, people who, unlike me, are not intimate with this man of genius could not believe their ears, had no idea that the comic discharges of his precise mind would be of such enormous caliber. Yes, there is nothing delicate about him, the good fellow!

And this badly restrained astonishment increased every moment in face of the play's lack of taste, lack of tact, and deficiencies of invention. For it is merely a pale imitation of Prudhomme; and the political satire it contains is nothing but a compilation of the stupidities put in print by all parties. The audience was always hoping for something of Flaubert, and there was nothing at all of Flaubert, absolutely nothing of an Aristophanes from Rouen come down to earth in Paris.

After the performance I went to shake Flaubert's hand backstage. I found him on the already empty stage among two or three Normans who had the thunderstruck air of Hippolyte's guards [in *Phèdre*]. Not one actor, not one actress left on the stage. It was a desertion, a flight from the author. You could see the stage hands, who had not finished their work, make haste with frantic movements, their eyes fixed on the exit door. In the stairways the extras rushed down silently. It was at once sad and a little fantastic, like a rout, a defeat shown on a diorama at dusk.

When he saw me, Flaubert gave a start as though he were waking up, as if he were trying to put on again his official mask of strong man. "Well, that's it!" he said with broad, angry movements of his arms and a scornful laugh which unsuccessfully simulated an "I don't give a damn!" attitude. And when I told him that his play would pick up at the second performance, he let himself go against the audience, against the cynical firstnight audience.

In the press this morning there is an effort to soften the impact of Flaubert's fall. I reflected that if I had written the play, if I had had an evening like last night, what a stomping on, what a flow of abuse, what a jawing I would have received from the press. And why? Mine is the same life of effort, of hard work, of devotion to art.

Sunday, March 15

I find Flaubert fairly philosophical on the surface, but the corners of his mouth turn down and his thundering voice is low at times, like a voice speaking in a sick room.

After Zola leaves, he lets himself go in concentrated bitterness: "My dear Edmond, there's no doubt about it; it's the most absolute flop . . ." And after a long silence he ends his sentence with: "Utter collapse of one's hopes does happen sometimes!"

When you come down to it, this fiasco is deplorable for every writer of books; not one of us will be performed ten years from now.

Friday, October 30

This morning I stopped by for Burty and we then went to *inspect* the arrival of two shipments from Japan.

We spent hours in the midst of those forms, those colors, those objects in bronze, porcelain, pottery, jade, ivory, wood, and paper—all that intoxicating and haunting assemblage of art. We were there for hours, so many hours that it was four o'clock when I had lunch. After these debauches of art—the one this morning cost me more than 500 francs—I am left worn out and shaken as after a night of gambling. I came away with a dryness in the mouth which only the sea water from a dozen oysters could refresh.

I bought some ancient albums, a bronze so greasy that it seems to be the wax mold of that bronze; I bought the gown of a Japanese tragedian on whose black velvet there are gold dragons with enamel eyes clawing at each other in a field of pink peonies.

Wednesday, December 2

"Blood? You can't get any"—it is Claude Bernard speaking—"they don't bleed people any more. In my day there was blood by the bucketful in the hospitals. I needed some recently for my course, and I couldn't get hold of any. And without the help of that old doctor—you know, Pasteur? the one who is taking my course—I wouldn't have got any! He bled himself . . . he is a former pupil of Broussais; he carries on the tradition; he bleeds himself whenever he is at the end of his tether. Didn't he say: 'I bleed myself every day and water my flowers with it!' "

That Claude Bernard is interesting to listen to and pleasant to look at! He has such a fine head of a good man, of an apostle of science! And too, when he talks of his own discoveries, he has such a distinguished way of saying "One has found that . . ."

Wednesday, December 16

This is Flaubert, pure Flaubert. We were talking in the Princess's smoking room about books which carnally excite the young, and some one mentioned *Faublas* among others. Thereupon Flaubert declared that he had never been able to finish it and that only one book had ever caused him to have an erection, the *Aloysia* of Meursius.[11] That man has such a superior nature, is of such a special cast, you must understand, that there is only one book, and that in Latin, capable of giving him a hard-on!

1875

Friday, January 22

It is paradoxical, really, the way prices go! Before me I have a Japanese bronze, a duck, which is remarkably similar to the antique animals in the Vatican Museum. If one like it turned up in the excavations in Italy you would probably pay

[11] Full titles of these works are: *Les Amours du Chevalier de Faublas* (1787–1790) by Louvet de Couvray, and *Aloisiae Sigaeae Toletanae Satyra Sotadica de Arcanis Amoris et Veneris* (1678) by Nicholas Chorier.

10,000 francs for it. Mine cost me 120 francs. Next to this bronze my eyes light on a Japanese ivory, a monkey in the armor of a Taikun warrior. The sculpture of the armor is a marvel of finish and perfection: it is like a jewel by Cellini. Imagine what this piece of ivory would be worth if the Italian artist had signed it with his point! It may well be signed with a name that is equally famous in Japan, but that signature is worth no more than twenty francs in France.

I do not regret having introduced a little, indeed a lot, of Japaneserie into my book on the eighteenth century. Basically eighteenth-century art is in some degree the *classicism of the pretty;* what it lacks is unexpectedness and grandeur. It could in the long run lead to a dead end. These albums, these bronzes, and these ivories have this in their favor: they bring your taste and intelligence back into the current of creations that have strength and imagination.

Sunday, February 7

Popelin told Flaubert recently that when the break between the Princess and Nieuwerkerke was official, she received a letter from Dumas, a very well-phrased letter, moreover. The author of *La Dame aux Camélias* proposed himself as Nieuwerkerke's successor, telling Her Highness that a woman like her, in company with a man like him, could conquer the world.

As a matter of fact, this amorous letter writer merely wanted to conquer a seat in the Senate.

Thursday, February 18

I have never been present at a session of the Academy, so I am curious to see with my own eyes, to hear with my own ears what that mandarin performance is like. The Princess is good enough to get me a ticket, and this morning after breakfast we set off, the Princess, Madame de Galbois, Benedetti, General Chauchard, and I, for the Institute.

These feasts of the intellect are not very well organized. We stand in line in the severe cold for a long time between surly policemen and foot soldiers, astonished at the jostling by fine ladies in carriages and gentlemen wearing the rosette of officer of the Legion of Honor.

At last we reach the door. A majordomo appears . . . no, it's the famous Pingard—a Parisian celebrity who owes his notoriety to his lack of politeness, a gelatinous man all in black, his teeth drawn back as though for defense, growling like an aroused bulldog. He ushers us into a vestibule which is decorated with statues of great men, who look very bored in their marble immortality. He disappears for a moment and on his return harshly rebukes the Princess—whom he pretends not to recognize—for having gone beyond a certain line on the tiled floor.

Finally we climb up a little winding stairway like the one in the Vendôme Column, and Madame Galbois begins to feel ill. Then we are in a little recess in the form of a theatre box, the plaster walls of which make us white like millers. From there, as through a window, our glance plunges down to the hall, making us a little dizzy.

The decoration of the dome—grey like the literature which is fostered beneath it—is enough to make you weep. Against a greenish-grey background, painted in the grey of half-mourning, are muses, eagles, wreaths of laurel, to which the painter has given about as much of a sense of illusion as a plank cut in two. The sculpture of the dome consists of a few plaster heads of Roman empresses, Messalina and her like, placed on pedestals, on one of which is inscribed, for no apparent reason, "To Virtue." The light of the dreary day, reflected by all that dreary painting, falls dull and icy on the skulls below us.

The hall is very small and Parisian society is so avid for this spectacle that you can't see an inch of the worn upholstery on the seats down below or of the wood on the amphitheatrelike benches of the large tribunes on the first floor, so pressed together and heaped on those seats are the behinds of nobles, men of ideas, millionaires, and heroes. Through a crack in the door of our box I see a very elegant woman in the corridor, seated on the top step of the stairway, planning to listen to the two speeches from there.

As we came in, we passed Marshal Canrobert; the first person whom we make out in the hall below us is Madame de La Valette, and everywhere there are men and women from the very highest society. However, among the women present at this solemnity there reigns a certain gravity of costume, the dark colors of the bluestockings in their dresses, set against which there is the striking contrast of the violet velvet cloak trimmed with furs worn by that superb Madame d'Haussonville, or of the extravagant hat worn by some actress.

The intimates of the establishment—several men and the wives of the Academicians—are gathered in a sort of circus enclosure protected by a balustrade. To right and left on two big tribunes against the walls the members of the other Academies rise up in rows of black broadcloth.

The sun, which has decided that it too will shine for Dumas, lights up faces on which all the lines turn upward, in those curves by which beatitude is represented on expressive faces. In all the men you feel an anticipatory admiration, impatient to overflow, and the women are somewhat moist eyed as they smile.

The voice of Alexandre Dumas makes itself heard. At once there is a sort of religious silence; then, soon, little benevolent laughs, caressing bursts of applause, ecstatic exhalations of "Ah!" The words which Alexandre is delivering he presents with the familiar off-handedness of a Lambert-Thiboust discussing a program with the actors of the Théâtre des Variétés.

The opening of the speech is full of playfulness and joking, thrusts of boulevard wit, gross lapses of taste. And the very flower of Parisian intelligence accepts this prose and this wit as though they were the very finest prose and the most subtle wit. Then, after a while, having made a show of himself in vulgar language, Dumas reaches a passage in which he seeks to reveal himself as a historian in the manner of Michelet. He declares solemnly that, thanks to his ability to read between the lines, he has discovered that Richelieu was never jealous of Corneille's poetry, that he was only briefly annoyed with him because his creation of *Le Cid* had delayed the establishment of the unities in French drama. But the Cardinal called the poet before him and said: "Take a seat, Corneille." There follows a monologue by the Cardinal, invented by Dumas, which is enough to make you laugh! No one, not even Houssaye, has ever put into the mouth of a historical figure anything of this ilk.

The audience was delirious: there was applause, the stamping of feet! In the midst of the enthusiasm provoked by Dumas' rehabilitation of Richelieu I was somewhat surprised by Benedetti's frenzy of admiration. I finally caught on: of everything flattering that Dumas addressed to the great French Minister in his quality of diplomat, Benedetti applied a large part to himself!

After that there was the address to the ladies, during which for a moment I thought they were going to throw their bouquets at the orator. Then a peroration in which Alexandre Dumas took up the pose of the literary Saint Vincent de Paul of prostitution, the tender redeemer of those who sell their love.

When the speech was over, everybody's face was drawn down in the falling lines of a horseshoe and profound sadness weighed on every forehead.

At this point an entr'acte, during which I looked at the auditorium and picked out the terrible Madame Dumas. I saw little Jeannine, not very responsive to her father's eloquence, busily taking her mother's lorgnette to pieces. I saw Lescure, right next to the balustrade which separated the elect and ready to slip under it, taking notes with the humble air of a servant. I saw the printer Claye, with the expression of a man who has been pleasantly brought to a sexual climax by Alexandre's eloquence. I saw a young gentleman pretentiously enfolded in a silver-embroidered coat, a cross on his breast and a part in the middle of his hair which was glued to his temples, whose head was bent over one hand in a yellow glove. I was told that he was the poet Déroulède. I saw the idiotic laugh of the Academician Sacy. I saw an Academician, whom no one could identify, with corkscrews of hair in his ears and the blue skin of a monkey on his cheeks. I saw another Academician in a black-velvet skullcap, swallowed up in a coachman's scarf and wearing woolen mittens—no one could name him either. I saw . . .

At that moment the vinegary voice of old Haussonville reached us, a voice that sounded like that of old Samson in the role of the Marquis in *Le Fils de Giboyer* [by Augier]. Then began the mandarin rite, that is, the execution of the newly received member, carried out with all the salutations, salaams, and ironic grimaces of Academic politeness. He conveyed to

Dumas that the latter was worth nothing at all, that he had always lived off prostitutes, that he had no right to talk about Corneille: an execution in which were mingled scorn for his writing and the disdain of a great lord for a man from Bohemia.

And after the mortal insult contained in the beginning of each sentence, uttered with his head raised toward the dome, the cruel orator let his voice drop down into his chest for the banal compliment at the end of the sentence, so that no one could hear it. Yes, it seemed to me that I was witnessing a Punch and Judy show with its ironically reverential bow after the victim's head had been beaten with a stick.

At last, *la commedia è finita.* Everybody leaves, and in the crowd I see Lavoix, Dumas' most assiduous *ass-licker,* pass by in company with Croizette, Lavoix as proud as a school boy at the way his lord and master has performed his stellar role.

Wednesday, February 17

This evening Dumas dined at the Princess's. The new Academician attempted to show himself to be a simple mortal, to let his success weigh as lightly as possible upon his fellow-writers.

After dinner he began to talk in a very interesting way about how to promote success, and at one moment, turning toward Flaubert and me, in a tone in which profound disdain was mingled with something resembling pity, he said: "You two have no idea, if you want to ensure the success of a dramatic work, of the importance of working up the first night, you have no idea how to go about it. Look, it's like this, if you don't surround yourself with well-wishers, with sympathetic people, the four or five members which each club sends to occasions like these . . . for that's an audience little given to enthusiasm! And if you don't pay attention to that, and to that . . ." And he informs us of a whole host of things of which we were completely ignorant and which, now that we know about them, we could never put into effect.

Sunday, February 28

At Flaubert's we are expressing our admiration for the poetry of the Englishman Swinburne when Daudet bursts out:

"By the way, they say he is a homosexual! There are some extraordinary stories of his stay at Etretat last year."

"It was longer ago than that; it was several years ago," young Maupassant breaks in. "I knew him a little at that time."

"In fact," Flaubert exclaims, "didn't you save his life?"

"Not exactly," Maupassant replies. "I was walking along the beach when I heard the shouts of a man who seemed to be drowning and I rushed into the water. But a fishing boat was ahead of me and had already pulled him out. He had gone in bathing completely drunk. Well, anyway, as I came out of the water, wet to the waist, another Englishman, who lived in the area and was Swinburne's friend, came up to thank me very warmly.

"The next day I was invited to lunch. A bizarre dwelling, a sort of cottage which contained some very fine paintings and which had an inscription over the door which I did not read at the time. And there was a big monkey frisking about inside. What a luncheon! I don't know what I had to eat—all I recall is that when I asked the name of the fish, my host replied with a strange smile that it was meat. I couldn't get any more out of him! There was no wine; we drank only hard liquor.

"According to what people said in Etretat the householder,

a man named Powel, was the son of an English lord living incognito under his mother's maiden name. As for Swinburne, imagine a little man with a cloven chin, the forehead of a hydrocephalic, an undeveloped chest, who trembled to such a degree that he caused his glass to do a Saint Vitus dance and who spoke always like a madman.

"One thing annoyed me immediately at the first luncheon: it was that from time to time Powel would play with the genitals of the monkey, whereupon the beast would escape from his fingers and come over and give me little taps on the neck when I bent over to drink.

"After lunch the two friends took out of gigantic portfolios some obscene photographs, life size, made in Germany—and there was nothing but pictures of men. Among others I recall one of an English soldier masturbating against a windowpane. Powel showed me these things in a state of complete drunkenness, and from time to time he sucked the ends of the fingers of a mummified hand, which was used, I think, as a paperweight. As he was showing me the photographs I mentioned, a young servant boy came in; at once Powel quickly closed the portfolio.

"Swinburne speaks French very well. He has immense erudition. He seems to know everything. On that day he told us a lot of curious things about snakes, saying that he often remained two or three hours observing them. Then he translated some of his poems for us, giving them an extraordinary charm. It was very fine.

"Powel too is out of the ordinary. He has brought a really extraordinary collection of ancient music back from Iceland.

"This household really intrigued me. I accepted a second invitation to lunch. This time the monkey left me alone: he had been hanged a few days earlier by the little manservant, and Powel had sought out an enormous block of granite to place on his grave and had made a big hollow in it where birds could find rainwater during periods of drought. At the end of the meal he served me a liqueur which laid me out flat. Immediately, in an access of fright, I escaped to my hotel, where I slept the sleep of the dead for the rest of the day.

"Finally I went back one last time in order to make up my mind whether I had to do with eccentrics or homosexuals. I pointed to the inscription over the door which read: 'Chaumière de Dolmancé,' and asked them if they knew that Dolmancé was the name of the hero of Sade's *La Philosophie du Boudoir*. They answered that they did. 'Well, then, it is the motto of the house?' I asked them. 'If you want it to be,' they answered with frightful faces. My mind was made up; I did not see them again.

"Yes, the two of them were living together and satisfying themselves with monkeys or young servant boys of fourteen or fifteen, who were sent over to Powel from England every three months or so, young servants of extraordinary cleanness and freshness. The monkey mentioned before, which slept in Powel's bed and beshat the sheets every night, had been hanged by the young servant boy, either out of jealousy or out of irritation at having to change the sheets all the time.

"The house was full of strange sounds, of sadistic shadows. One night Powel was seen and heard pursuing a Negro in the garden and shooting a revolver. They were true heroes of the 'Old Man' [Sade], who would not have hesitated to commit a crime. Then all at once this house with its mysterious life became silent, became suddenly empty. Powel was gone for months, and no one knew how he had gotten away. No one had seen him take a carriage and no one had met him on the road."

Sunday, March 7

When he came into Flaubert's, Zola fell into an armchair and murmured in a voice of desperation: "Oh, what trouble, what trouble Compiègne is giving me!"

Then he asked Flaubert how many chandeliers there were lighting the dining room table, whether the conversation was very loud, what people talked about, and what the Emperor said. Yes, there he was, trying to get from a third person, in a desultory conversation, the *physical features of a milieu*, which only eyes that have seen them can describe. And this novelist, who has the pretension of writing history in his novels, is going to base his portrayal of an important historical figure on what he is told in ten minutes by a colleague, who will keep the best of what he knows to himself in order to use it sometime in a novel of his own.

However, half out of pity for his ignorance, half out of satisfaction at the chance to inform the two or three visitors who are there that he has passed a fortnight at Compiègne, Flaubert in his dressing gown plays for Zola a classic Emperor, with dragging foot, one arm folded behind his back, twirling his moustaches, uttering characteristic idiotic phrases.

"Yes," he says, when he is sure Zola has got his sketch in mind, "that man was stupid, he was stupidity incarnate!"

"Certainly, I am of your opinion," I say to him; "but stupidity is usually loquacious and his was silent. That was his strength: it allowed people to suppose anything."

Then Flaubert recounts a curious episode in the amours of the Emperor with Bellanger at Montretout: the Emperor, a paper hat on his head, with his own Imperial hand pasted on the wallpaper of a small salon and the water closet of his mistress. "And I know well," Flaubert adds, "that it was a blue paper with little white crosses."

Saturday, March 13

I am taken to Stevens'. A Negro opens the door; beyond him there is an expanse of garden which I did not suspect existed on the Rue des Martyrs.

This very talented painter, this colorist of modern interiors, has nothing of the physique or the physiognomy of the artist. He looks somewhat like Villemessant, with short hair and a vulgar moustache; his age, rather well concealed by the uprightness of his torso, is given away by the weathering of his face which, you might say, is rhinocerized. In his black wool jersey, his stovepipe hat, which he does not remove at home, his stiff detachable collar, with his hands thrust in his pants pockets, he looks to me like a vulgar rake, a gentleman of uncertain antecedents, a shady racetrack tout.

He is in process of putting a little eighteenth-century lady into a landscape of one of his garden paths. His model is a tall, ugly, and sickly-looking girl who, in her faded cheap finery and an old blue-silk hat, seems to be a shadowy imitation of those slender elegant prostitutes shown in eighteenth-century aquatints of English Vauxhall Gardens.

Instead of his paintings, which have been sent away, he shows us an admirable sketch he has done of his wife lying down with her child—a sketch in a creamy tone resembling a painting done with the liquid interior of a Brie cheese spread on with a palette knife.

Knowing that I am an amateur of things Japanese, he opens up his Japanese room. It is decorated with two rolls of paper having a gold background on which are two carts, each carrying a gigantic bouquet of flowers—the gift of a young man to his fiancée. Japanese art is certainly full of charming inventions! In order to conceal the geometrical regularity of the wheels the artist has broken up his design by means of a cloud of dust, a cloud of golden dust.

Sunday, March 21

Alphonse Daudet lives in the Hôtel Lamoignon in the Marais district. This town house is like a part of the Louvre; the little dwellings that have been made out of the immense old apartments are inhabited by miserable little industries, whose names you see on all the doors opening onto the stone landings of the stairways. This is the kind of place one would have had to live in in order to write *Froment et Risler*. From the author's study you look out onto big, melancholy glassed-in workshops, little gardens with greenish stones, dark trees whose roots grow into the gas mains, and an enclosure made of packing boxes.

Daudet, who has been living there for seven years, tells me that this building has been good for him, that it has calmed him. He had a rough-and-tumble youth, a youth given over to fighting and hanging around low dives, a youth which, in his words, "was retarded like the laggard waves, the backs of monsters, which the sea still keeps after a storm." Well, in this calm, tranquil, soporific dwelling he has been transformed, and in the midst of its industrous *purring* he has gradually become a different man from what he was.

From the Rue Pavée we go to Flaubert's on foot. During this long walk I talk with Daudet about the novel he is writing, in which he intends to have Morny figure in an incidental way. I urge him not to do that: the Morny whom he had the good fortune to know and to take the measure of ought, in my opinion, to be the subject of a special study where he can be put on scene as one of the figures who best represent modern times. Daudet cries out against the stupid, middle-class sides of the man's nature. I warn him to be careful not to attenuate them, since one of the characteristics of this age is the littleness of men in the midst of the greatness and torment of things, pointing out that if he tries to make an absolutely superior man of Morny, he will come out with a Maxime de Trailles or a de Marsay [in Balzac], in short, with an abstraction. He must depict the great diplomat in his sordid direction of the Ministry of the Interior, with his quality of vulgar secondhand dealer and his taste for music-hall literature. Daudet thinks my advice is good.

At Flaubert's Turgenev translates *Prometheus* for us and makes an analysis of *The Satyr*, two works of Goethe's youth, two ultra-imaginative flights. In his translation, in which Turgenev seeks to give us a sense of the vibrant young life which resides in the language, I am struck by both the familiar quality of the language and the boldness of expression. Great, original works, no matter what the tongue, have never been written in academic style.

Tuesday, March 30

Paul Lacroix confirms what Gavarni told me in confidence about Balzac's economy in spending his semen. Necking and the titillations of love just short of ejaculation, that was fine! But always short of ejaculation! To him sperm was the emission of a pure cerebral substance, and an ejaculation was like a filtration, a draining away of creativity by way of the prick. As the result of some mischance or other, when he had forgotten his theories, he once arrived at Latouche's with the outcry: "I lost a book this morning!"

However, the big fellow was sensual and dirty on occasion. His great recreation was to go hunting—yes, to go hunting! At that time he had as his mistress, or whatever you want to call her, a lady of the aristocracy, a former lady-in-waiting of Marie-Antoinette's whom Lacroix would not name, who he said was well preserved, but who could not have been less than seventy. Balzac, on all fours in the simple costume of nature, used to pursue this old doe through all the rooms of the apartment, playing the roles of both huntsman and hound at the same time.

There is a funny anecdote connected with this habit of his. The lady did not like Latouche, whom she accused of being a Mephistopheles who led her friend astray. Balzac was therefore obliged to tell her that he didn't see Latouche any more. However, he continued to see him—especially whenever he moved, since he had the greatest confidence in Latouche's taste and liked him to oversee the interior decoration. One day the latter was at Balzac's, in his role of advisor, when the lady arrived unexpectedly. Balzac was upset by the visit. Latouche told him to pull himself together, for he would pass himself off as the decorator. And there he was on a ladder. The lady, irritated at finding a man there whom she had not expected, exclaimed: "Oh, isn't your apartment finished yet?" "Oh, yes, the decorator just has to put in a nail or two and then he will be on his way." But when Latouche, overcome by curiosity, took his time about getting down from the ladder, the lady resumed: "Isn't the decorator ever going to leave?" "Yes, yes, he's going." Then that devil Latouche began to come down the ladder whistling a hunting call and as he passed in front of the astonished lady, he made her a deep bow.

Sunday, April 4

At Flaubert's today, after talking about the fornicating and copulating spread throughout Zola's book *La Faute de l'Abbé Mouret*, we turned to the amorous habits of the author himself. Zola told us that while he was a student, it happened several times that he spent a week in bed with a woman, or at any rate lived with her in his night shirt. The room "reeked of sperm"—those were his words. He confessed to us that after one of those weeks he walked along the street on legs that seemed like cotton, helping himself along the walls by grabbing hold of the supports of the shutters. Now, he said, he is much better behaved and only has sexual congress with his wife every ten days.

He told us about certain curious personal idiosyncrasies with respect to coitus. Two or three years ago, when he began the Rougon-Macquart series, the day after a conjugal discharge he did not sit down at his desk, knowing in advance that it would be impossible to form a sentence, to write a line. Now it is just the opposite: after eight or ten days of mediocre work copulation produces on the following day a slightly feverish state which is very favorable to composition.

Finally he mentioned a peculiar phenomenon which he experienced at the beginning of his career. At those times when he was having the greatest difficulty in writing it would happen, after a half hour's struggle with a sentence, that he would ejaculate without getting an erection.

Sunday, April 18

As we leave Flaubert's, Zola and I talk about our friend's situation—he has just confided to us that after a period of black melancholy he often bursts into tears. And as we talk about the literary reasons which are the cause of this state and which kill us all one after the other, we express our surprise at the lack of attention paid to this famous man. He is famous, he has talent, he is a very good fellow, and he is very hospitable. Why, then, except for Turgenev, Daudet, Zola, and me, is there no one at his Sunday afternoons which are open to everyone? Why?

Monday, May 3

Little Daudet is a strange one; there are times when he goes on sprees that take him completely outside our sober bourgeois life. Wine "priapises" him in a wild and unpredictable manner.

A few days ago he told us that he dreaded our dinners, because he got drunk at them and when he was drunk he could no longer control himself. In fact, he did not seem too unhappy over having to go to an official dinner, which prevented him from joining us. However, he was good enough to promise to drop in at ten o'clock.

He arrived completely sober but immediately ordered a champagne frappé followed by some iced champagne. Thereupon he began to get high and became overstimulated. He told us that after our last dinner he came to at six in the morning going down the Rue Durantin in the Batignolles district—full of shame and heavy-spirited as a stone. He told us of a dwarfish whore whom he had showered with his favors, of the 150 francs that he had given away or lost during the night, of grotesque occurrences, bizarre things, which he related in a charming fashion, admitting that when he is drunk he simply has to run wild like a sailor, that he is in despair over this because he adores his wife, whose indulgent forgiveness when he returns home pierces him with remorse.

And while he was talking about his remorse in drunken tones, we felt that the madness that had led him to the Rue Durantin was about to begin again.

It was amusing to watch Flaubert listen to him with an expression of stupefaction and vulgar envy. He was jealous of the sincerity of Daudet's vices.

Wednesday, May 5

I inform Flaubert of Michel Lévy's death. When he hears this news, I see his fingers replace in his buttonhole the decoration which he would not wear in plain sight after Lévy was decorated.

Sunday, May 9

What a singular street and original district is that corner of Paris where Barbey d'Aurevilly is lodged.

That Rue Rousselet, near the remotest reaches of the Rue de Sèvres, has the character of a small-town suburb, to which the nearness of the Ecole Militaire gives a somewhat soldierly touch. In doorways the concierges give a swipe to the pavement with the fatigue caps of Algerian infantrymen. In shops selling color prints all the costumes of the Army are displayed on one-penny sheets. A primitive barber shop in a hole in the wall, the nature of the premises written in ink on the plaster, solicits the chins of military gentlemen. The houses have entryways such as you see in villages; and above the high walls is spread the tightly interlaced shade of communal gardens.

In a building that looks like a cow barn—like the one inhabited by Colonel Chabert in Balzac's novel—I address myself to a sort of peasant woman, who is Barbey's concierge. First, she tells me he is not in. I know the drill. I give battle.

Finally, she decides to take up my card and indicates to me when she comes down: "First floor, Number 4 in the corridor."

A little staircase, an even smaller corridor, and a still tinier door, painted ochre, in which there is a key. I enter into a jumble and disorder in which nothing can be distinguished. Barbey d'Aurevilly receives me in shirtsleeves and pearl-grey trousers decorated with a black band, standing in front of one of those ancient dressing tables that have a big round swinging mirror. He excuses himself for receiving me in this way, explaining that he is getting dressed to go to Mass.

I find him much as I had glimpsed him to be at Roger de Beauvoir's funeral—swarthy complexion, a long lock of hair cutting across his face, an elegance diminished by his half-dressed state. But in spite of all that, I must admit, he has the politeness of a gentleman and the graces of a man of breeding, in sharp contrast with this hovel, in which articles of clothing and toiletry, books, magazines, and newspapers are all mixed up throughout the room.

I take away from this lodging on the Rue Rousselet an impression of the lair of a wellborn man of letters down on his luck.

Thursday, July 1

I lunched today at Cernuschi's. This rich collector has given his collection a setting that is at once imposing and cold like the Louvre.[12] He has not known how to give it the warm and hospitable atmosphere of a dwelling, how to recreate a little corner of a foreign land. On these bare walls against the brick-colored background favored by our museums these objects

[12] A building which was bequeathed to the city of Paris and houses the Cernuschi Museum of Oriental Art.

from the Far East seem unhappy: you might say that an evil spirit has translated them to a palace dreamed up by the taste of a shareholder of *Le Siècle*, a taste which is at once pretentious and middle-class.

The luncheon, I hasten to say, was a thousand times better than the conception of a town-house museum—a luncheon which showed the master of the house to be sensuous, discriminating, and generous.

Then we immediately began the inspection of the two thousand bronzes, faiences, and porcelains, of that whole uncountable collection of imaginative forms. Among the bronzes some marvels which seem the very ideal of what taste and knowledgeable skill might produce. There is a vase in the production of which industry ceased to be industry and became pure art. As for the porcelains, which range up to the present day, few from the great periods, few of high quality. As for the ivories, wood sculptures, and objects in wrought iron, all those small and exquisite objects by which you recognize an amateur of refined taste, nothing, nothing, nothing.

It is almost three o'clock and already my eyes are practically falling out of their sockets. But I am not yet at the end of my day. The Sichels take me along with them. . . .

We are at the Rue Pigalle to examine some objects which have just reached the warehouse from Peking, to examine the porcelains, the jades, the bronzes, the choice curiosities which are hidden away in attics, out of public view, because they are being kept for the Rothschilds, the Camondos, etc.

It is five o'clock when someone suggests that we finish the day at Bing's and look at the things that have just been unpacked there. Thereupon we all go to the Rue Chauchat, where until seven o'clock in a state of fatigue verging on collapse we touch, handle, and stroke more rare objects. A debauch of things Japanese and Chinese which in the weariness of the end of the day and the emptiness of one's stomach make one feel that he is wandering in a nightmare where all the precious materials are mixed together, where all forms blur and merge, and where one seems to be almost enmeshed in an exotic vegetation of jade, porcelain, and wrought metal. . . .

I go to bed dead beat, my head confused, in my mind a gnawing memory of having bought some thousand francs' worth of bibelots without knowing exactly how I am going to pay for them.

Sunday, August 22

Today I went in search of *human documents* in the area around the Ecole Militaire. Nobody will ever know how much the low and ugly documents from which we have made our books cost us, in view of our natural timidity, our lack of ease among common people, our horror of the vulgar. This role of conscientious policeman ferreting out materials for the novel of the people is the most abominable one that a man of aristocratic taste can perform.

But the attraction of this new world is that it has something of the allure of a region never before explored by any traveler. Rather quickly the tension of the senses, the multiplicity of observations and remarks, the effort of memory, the play of perception, the hasty, rushing labor of a mind which is "spying out" the truth—these upset the observer's composure and make him forget in a sort of fever the hard and disgusting nature of what he observes.

Saturday, November 27

Amid the general recognition of our talent one polite denial of it, veiled but nonetheless absolute, was printed the other day in *Le Temps*.

The author of the article is young France, the bookseller's son. My brother and I were always charming toward the young snot, whose childhood was one long head cold. Later on when, as Lemerre's employe, he published proper, correct little prefaces, I wrote him the most *Hugoesque* letters. Under such circumstances when I went to ask him for an article in *Le Temps*, telling him sincerely and simply of my interest in having Lemerre bring out a new printing—not for my sake but out of regard for my brother's memory—I think he should have said to me: "My dear sir, you are making a mistake. I have a different ideal from yours, and I don't like the kind of thing you write at all. The article which you ask of me would not be of any help to your works. It would be better for you to try someone else."

He has preferred to commit an act of perfidy, this very young man. Was his perfidy inspired by Leconte de Lisle, whose ass he licks? They tell me no. I am assured that he has simply acted in accordance with his nature, his temperament of republican Jesuit, wanting to gain credit with his faction for carrying out an execution of us in the name of healthy literary doctrines and revolutionary principles.

The strange thing is that the article was written by Lemerre's clerk and published by the paper that printed *Manette Salomon*.

Friday, December 24

The Barye exhibition.

Barye is a very ordinary sculptor of the human body. Under his roughing chisel a woman takes on the quality of caricature which a true antique copied by Daumier would have.

In him is evident the maker of architectural ornament in banal period style, a man born to make pretty things in base metal.

Barye is a genius only in the sculpting of animals, and only of the big wild beasts. He is the first to have rendered the incipient leap in repose, the quiet furrowing of strength and speed in the flow of muscles in the big square planes, the elastic fluidity of the body in motion under the distended skin, the bounding leap; he is the first to have rendered the bored serenity of the king of the beasts.

As watercolorist he seems to me overrated. One is too aware in his watercolors that the wild animals sketched at the Zoo have been placed in a setting of the grey rocks at Fontainebleau. However, among the watercolors there are some of boas heavily wrapped around enormous dry trees illuminated by a livid flash of lightning which prove him to be a very dramatic colorist.

Monday, December 27

I dine this evening at Hugo's.

At eight he appears in a frock coat with a velvet collar, a white scarf loosely folded around his neck. He drops onto a divan near the fireplace, talks of the role of conciliator which he wants to play henceforth at meetings, says that he is not a moderate, since the ideals of the moderates are not his, but that he is "a man at peace," a man without ambitions who has been tested by life.

Then Saint-Victor arrives and introduces Dalloz. The editor of *Le Moniteur* at once makes a profession of faith as a progressive conservative and—comparing himself to a man going forward—his rear foot being insufficiently steady, he gets pitifully bogged down in his dazzling metaphor and almost falls flat on his face. This man is like a sewer containing all the banal ideas of vulgar society and all the old clichés of the press.

We go into the dining room. The dinner is rather like one given by a village priest to his bishop. There is a fricassee of rabbit, followed by roast beef, after which a roast chicken appears. Around the table are seated Banville, his wife and son, Dalloz, Saint-Victor, Madame Juliette, Madame Charles Hugo flanked by her two children, her devilish little daughter and her sweet little boy with fine velvety eyes.

Hugo is in fine fettle. He talks in an easy, charming manner, amused at what he is telling and interrupting his account from time to time with a loud laugh, which echoes twice in his mouth. "The only true hatreds," he says, "are literary hatreds. Political hatreds are nothing. Men do not bring to ideas in that area the same faith that they give to their literary doctrines, which are both a credo based on conviction and the result of their temperament." At this point he interrupts himself to say: "Look, there are five of us here in this room who think absolutely differently. Well, I am certain that we all like each other better than Emmanuel Arago likes me!"

Then Hugo talks about the Academy. He draws a vivid and witty portrait of Royer-Collard:

"Very shrewd eyes, very cunning under their thick brows, eyes lurking in a sort of underbrush; the lower part of his face disappearing into his neckcloth, which sometimes crawled up to his nose; a big frock coat in the Directoire style buttoned up to his chin; and always his arms crossed and his head thrown back.

"He had told me that he had read my books, that some of them pleased him, others did not, but that he would not vote for me because I would bring a temperature that would change the climate of the Academy.

"I must admit to you that I liked going to the Academy. The sessions on the dictionary interested me. I am very fond of etymologies, charmed by the mystery of such terms as subjunctive and participle. I was assiduous at that table, where right across from me, as you are, M. de Goncourt, sat Royer-Collard.

"I must explain that as soon as I entered the Academy Cousin set himself up as my antagonist, I don't know why. One day we reached the word *intempéries*: 'Its etymology?' someone asked. '*Intemperies*,' another replied. 'Gentlemen,' Cousin burst out, 'we must show a certain restraint in the choice of words which we have the honor to consecrate. *Intemperies* is not Latin; it exists in no author of good Latinity; it is kitchen Latin.' Everybody was quiet; I quietly repeated the word *intemperies* and added: 'Tacitus!' 'Tacitus, but that's not Latin!' Cousin rejoined; 'it is merely Latin that's good for romanticism! Isn't that so, Patin? You know Latin; Tacitus did not write Latin?' But before Patin could speak, we heard issue from Royer-Collard's high cravate with a nasal and mocking intonation: 'Ah, gentlemen, Cousin and Patin know their Latin!' We laughed and the etymology was accepted.

"Another day some other word came up . . . unfortunately I can't remember . . . no, I no longer remember. Cousin said the word was not French. Then, a silence, in the middle of which I said: 'M. Pingard, will you go down to the library and bring me volume III of Regnard?' The volume in hand, I read the word in a sentence from *Le Voyage en Laponie*. You must not think me more learned than I am. A few days before I had by chance been looking something up in that volume for a piece that I was writing. Cousin at once exclaimed: 'Is it sufficient reason to accept a word because it is found in an obscure corner of a good author?' Out of the big cravate we heard again: 'In good authors there are no corners, no corners . . .' Ah, yes, I liked Royer-Collard; the two men I did not like were Cousin and Guizot."

In the low-ceilinged dining room there is immediately above us a gas jet hot enough to cook your brains. Madame Charles Hugo tells me that often this heat gives her son palpitations and headaches, which make him want always to be at her side. And under this head-splitting light Hugo continues to drink champagne and to talk, as if nothing which does harm to others has any power over his robust constitution.

Dalloz, with the tact that characterizes him, then begins to talk stupidly about the psychological novelties which Dumas *fils* has brought into the theatre. Banville at once gets carried away and in a sharp, strident voice asks him to mention anything at all that is not to be found in Balzac. And everybody joins Banville in falling upon the poor idiot who has been taken in by Dumas!

Mention of Dumas *fils* turns the conversation to Dumas *père*, and Hugo says that he has just read the real *Mémoires de d'Artagnan*. He adds that while it has not been his practice to take anything from others, he had never been more tempted to appropriate a story and give it artistic form than by an episode of which Dumas *père* did not make use. . . .

We leave the table. Banville and I go to smoke a cigarette on the staircase, while our host promises that there will be a smoking room in the near future. We rejoin Hugo in the dining room, standing all alone in front of the table as he prepares to read his poetry—a preparation which has something in common with the warm up exercises before an act of prestidigitation when the prestidigitator tries out his tricks in a corner.

And there is Hugo, his back to the mantel of the fireplace in the drawing room, in his hand a large sheet of paper of his "transatlantic" copy, a portion of those manuscripts bequeathed to the Bibliothèque Nationale which he says are written on linen paper so as to assure their preservation. Then he slowly puts on his glasses, which a certain vanity kept him from wearing for a long time; with, so to speak, dreamy gestures, he uses his handkerchief for a long while to wipe away the sweat which forms in drops on his turgescent forehead. At last he begins, announcing as an exordium and as if to tell us that there are still whole worlds in his head: "Gentlemen, I am seventy-four years old and I am just beginning my career." He reads to us *Le Soufflet du Père,* a continuation of *La Légende des Siècles*, in which there are some fine transcendental lines which don't mean a thing to me.

It is curious to see Hugo read! On the mantel, set up like a theatre for the reading, fourteen candles reflected in the mirror and in the Venetian sconces provide a glowing light behind him, so that his face, a face of shadow, as he would say, stands out, encircled by an aureole, a radiance running into the rough surface of his close-cropped hair and his white collar, a rosy brightness shining through his forked satyr ears.

After *Le Soufflet du Père* we have no trouble getting the great man to read us something else. The lines that he reads this time are from a new poem, which he calls "Toute la Lyre," a poem in which he wants to put everything—one which allows him to be young, he says smiling. Then he declaims an original piece. A walk by lovers through the woods in springtime. The woman talks politics, and the man talks love. When the woman seems to be softened by the amorous awakening of nature, suddenly, recalling the last war, she shows herself altogether ready to give herself to him in a frenzy, not for the sake of making love but so that from their embrace an avenger may burst out and be born.

1876

Tuesday, January 25

Coppée is Madame Doche's lover. The affair of that young man and that old woman has for me the quality of a macabre fantasy. One evening I discerned the skeletal structure of the actress through her dressing gown, and I never talk to Coppée without being disturbed by the earthy blackness in his nostrils and at the corners of his mouth, indeed by the general morbid senility of his childish face. Thus the coupling of these two beings seems to my imagination like the coupling of a skeleton with a moldy foetus.

In their life of discreet lovemaking, in which they receive scarcely anyone under their communal roof but Barbey d'Aurevilly, I think of the frightful trio of skinny ones made up of this woman, this young man, and that old satyr, whose wrinkled and weathered dryness makes me think of the dried penis of the drum major which was exhibited in the Dantan Museum.

The literature inaugurated by Flaubert and the Goncourts could, I think, be defined as follows: a rigorous study of nature in a prose speaking the language of poetry.

Friday, May 5

Our *Society of Five* took it into our heads to eat a bouillabaisse at a tavern behind the Opéra Comique. This evening we are talkative, effervescent, expansive.

"To be able to work," it is Turgenev speaking, "I must have winter, a freeze such as we have in Russia, astringent cold, trees laden with crystal. Then . . . but I work even better in autumn, you know, in that period when there is no wind, no wind at all, when the ground is elastic, and the air has a winy savor. On my estate there is a little wooden house in a garden planted with yellow acacias—we have no white acacias. In autumn the ground is completely covered with pods, which crackle when you walk on them; and the garden is full of those birds that imitate others . . . magpies, that's it. There, all alone . . ."

Turgenev does not finish his sentence, but a contraction of his hands, which he holds closed across his breast, attests to the cerebral joy and intoxication which he experiences in that little corner of old Russia.

"Yes, a typical wedding," exclaims Flaubert. "You might say I was still a child. I was eleven. But I was the one who took off the bride's garter. There was a little girl at the wedding. I went home in love with her. I wanted to 'give her my heart'—an expression I had heard. At that time there arrived every day at my father's house hampers of game, of fish, of other things to eat—sent to him by patients whom he had cured—hampers which were put in the dining room each morning. In addition, since I was always hearing operations spoken of as usual and ordinary occurrences, for a long time I thought, I thought very seriously, about asking my father to take out my heart. And I visualized my heart being taken in a hamper by a stagecoach driver, with a badge, wearing a shaggy, curly cap; I visualized my heart being set on the buffet in my little woman's dining room. And as I imagined it there was neither wound nor blood from this physical gift of my heart."

"A tawny portal between two little white thighs," Daudet murmurs.

"As for me," Zola interrupts, "I had a perverted childhood in a bad provincial school. Yes, a depraved childhood! I necked with the woman with whom I lost my virginity before I screwed her. No, no, I tell you, I have no moral sense. I have slept with the wives of my best friends. In love I have absolutely no moral sense."

"I had been called back to Russia," Turgenev continues; "I was in Naples and had only five hundred francs. There were no railroads in those days; my return was difficult and awkward, and, as you can imagine, without any expenditure for love. I was in Lucerne, looking out from the top of the bridge, next to a woman leaning on the parapet beside me, at some of those ducks which have almond-shaped markings on their heads. The evening was magnificent. We began to chat, then to stroll along together. Our walk took us into the cemetery. Do you know the cemetery, Flaubert? I don't recall ever having been hotter in my life, more excited, more insistent. The woman lay down on a big tombstone, pulling up her dress and her skirts in such a way that her buttocks rested on the bare stone. I threw myself upon her completely wild; and in my haste and awkwardness my cock got entangled in some tufts of grass full of grit and then pulled out of them. In this coupling I had the greatest pleasure that I have ever experienced."

"What does all that amount to," Flaubert exclaims, "in comparison with this," and his elbow presses against his chest, "when close to the beloved woman you press against her for an instant as you lead her to the table?"

"Oh, shit!" says Daudet, twisting about in his chair and contracting his nervous hands above his head. "That's not my style . . . you can't imagine what I'm like . . . to feel pleasure

I have to have the flesh of two women pressing against my flesh, one of them to work on and the other to bite the behind of the one I am giving it to."

"But, Daudet, I am a swine too," Flaubert says naively.

"Go on. You are a cynic with men and sentimental with women."

"By heaven, that's true," says Flaubert, laughing. "Even with women in a brothel I call them 'little angel.' "

"It's crazy, but that's the way it is," Daudet continues, as he becomes animated again. "I need an overflowing of dirty, depraved words: 'Come, let me bugger you!' And don't have any illusions about decent women! Her temples pale, the decent woman will turn over and say to you: 'By God, I have been well buggered!' "

"Yes, yes, that's right. In love women are grateful for their degradation."

"It's strange," sighs Turgenev, who is stretched out at full length on the divan and is listening to Daudet's confession with startled and almost anxious eyes; "it's strange, but I never approach a woman without a feeling of respect, of tenderness, and of surprise at my good fortune."

"All the women I have had," Daudet replies, "I have had at my first encounter with them and while saying indecent, outrageous, disgusting, priapic things to them. Notice that I don't say that I haven't had my failures, but I have had scads of women and I have treated them all like whores."

"Have you had any Russian women?"

"No."

"Too bad. You would have found them interesting," Turgenev says. "The Russian woman, now, how can I describe her to you? She is a mixture of simplicity, tenderness, and unconscious depravity."

"In Upper Egypt," (it is Flaubert's voice) "on a night dark as a furnace they lead you past low houses amid the howling of dogs which want to devour you, they lead you to a shed no higher than a young man of seventeen. Inside, all the way at the back, you find lying on the ground a woman in a chemise whose body is wound round seven or eight times by a big gold chain, a woman whose buttocks are as cold as ice and whose interior is as hot as a brazier. Then, with this woman who remains motionless in pleasure you experience infinite enjoyment, a voluptuousness that . . ."

"Come on, Flaubert, that's literature, that is!"

Let me sum up.

Turgenev is a swine whose swinishness is tinged with sentimentality.

Zola is a gross and brutish swine, whose swinishness is expended nowadays entirely on his writing.

Daudet is a morbid swine with the wild behavior of a mind into which madness might well some day come.

Flaubert is a false swine, calling himself one and pretending to be one in order to be on a par with the real and sincere swine who are his friends.

And I, I am an intermittent swine, with crises of dirtiness which come from the exasperation of flesh tormented by the spermatic animalicule.

Thursday, May 11

Photography seems to me to bring out almost exclusively the animality contained in the man or woman represented.

Don't believe people who say they love art yet who during their whole dog's life have not given ten francs for a sketch, a drawing, for no matter what in paint or crayon. It is not enough for the true lover of art to see artistic things; he feels the need to be the owner of a little piece, a little nubbin of art, whether he is rich or not.

Friday, September 1

Flaubert was telling us that during those two months he stayed shut up in his room the heat produced in him a sort of drunken frenzy of work and that he worked fifteen hours every day. He went to bed at four in the morning and sometimes surprised himself by being back at his work table at nine, a "slogging away" that was broken only by an evening swim in the Seine.

And the product of those nine hundred hours of work is a novella [*Un Coeur Simple*] thirty pages long.

Tuesday, November 7

Talking to me this evening about the money he has made this year, Daudet said that some of it went to pay for the coat and trousers he wore at his First Communion, which had never been paid for.

Sunday, December 17

Really, one shouldn't read what one has written to literary friends. I read Zola the passage about my Fille Elisa "walking her beat," and now I come across it in his book—I won't say completely plagiarized but certainly inspired by what I read. In a different setting he uses exactly the same effects of darkness, of the pitiful shadow which she leaves behind her. He even repeats: "Sir, please listen to me!"—a phrase which is to be heard in the Saint Honoré area but not on the Chaussée Clignancourt.

Saturday, December 30

This morning I finished *La Fille Elisa*. I have only to reread it. I had intended to go a little further, to spice up the manuscript with a lot of little details from the world of prostitution and prison, but that might have been too much. And also the thought that my book will be prosecuted discourages me from doing more. I lack the will to keep on working at a book which is in danger of being suppressed.

1877

Saturday [*sic*], *February 18*

It is strange, this revolution brought by Japanese art in the taste of a people who, in matters of art, are the slaves of Greek symmetry and who, suddenly, are becoming impassioned over a plate on which the flower is not set dead in the middle, over a fabric in which harmony is not achieved by a gradation of tints but by a knowledgeable juxtaposition of raw colors.

Twenty years ago who would have dared paint a woman in a yellow dress? That was not possible until after Regnault's Japanese *Salomé*. And that authoritative introduction to the eyes of Europe of the Imperial color of the Far East was a real revolution in the chromatics of painting and dress.

Monday, February 19

Always with a doffing of his hat to the man's genius, Flaubert attacks the prefaces, doctrines, and naturalist professions of faith, in short, all that bunkum somewhat in the manner of Mangin with which Zola pushes the success of his books. Zola replies more or less in these terms: "You had a small fortune which liberated you from many things. I, who have made my living exclusively by my pen, who have been obliged to do all sorts of shameful writing, even journalism, I have retained from those experiences, how shall I put it, something of the barker's mentality. Yes, it's true that like you I make fun of this word *naturalism*, and yet I shall repeat it endlessly because you have to give a name to things in order to make the public think they are something new. Look, I play two roles as a writer. There are my works, by which people will judge me and by which I want to be judged; then there are my writings in *Le Bien Public*, my articles published in Russia, my contributions as correspondent for a Marseille paper, which don't mean a thing to me and which I am sorry about; they are only so much 'patter' to call attention to my books. First, I placed a nail and with a hammer blow drove it a centimeter into the brain of the public; then with a second blow, two centimeters. Well, my hammer is the journalism that I write about my own books."

Wednesday, March 21

Today *La Fille Elisa* comes out. I am at Charpentier's to send off some copies among clerks who are constantly putting their heads through the door to shout: "X . . . , who ordered fifty, now wants a hundred. Can we let Y . . . have fifteen? Marpon insists that we make up the rest of his thousand." (If the book is confiscated, he wants to have them tucked away.) In the activity, the noise, the commotion of this feverish dispatching I write dedications, experiencing the emotions of a gambler who risks his whole fortune on one bet, wondering if the success which is foreshadowed in a fashion so unexpected, so unhoped for, is going to be suddenly destroyed by a ministerial prosecution, wondering if this startling recognition of my talent, coming before my death, is not going to be taken away by a blow of that bad luck which has pursued my brother and me all our lives. Every time a head passes, every time a letter arrives, I expect the terrible announcement: "The book has been seized!"

On my way to the train for Auteuil I have one of the childish pleasures of authorship. I see a gentleman with my book in his hand who, unable to wait until he gets home, is reading it right in the street, in the drizzle that is falling.

Friday, March 23

A bad day. I experience something of the superstitious fear that Gautier used to feel on his own account. Will it be today? That would certainly put a damper on the Charpentier dinner this evening.

Benedetti comes to see me and, with the Prudhommesque prudery of a bourgeois persisting under his ambassador's skin, he pronounces: "A very daring title!" in a tone which tells me there will be a prosecution in a few days.

When the ambassador has left, I lie down, shattered and all to pieces. Pélagie has gone out. I hear the bell ring over and over. I do not get up. Then as soon as the caller has left I am caught in a panic. I imagine that it was Charpentier who had come to tell me that the book had been seized. And I stew in this anxiety until dinner time, when I find the Charpentier household in the most tranquil state of mind.

Wednesday, April 4

I receive a note from Burty telling me that my book got a real going over at the Ministry but that "there will be no prosecution." I am only partly reassured; all it would take to change that decision is a governmental whim or an article by Wolff in *Le Figaro*.

Wednesday, April 11

I read in *Le Bien Public* this evening that *Le Tintamarre* is being prosecuted for an article with the title "La Fille Elisabeth" which is a dirty parody of *La Fille Elisa*. That's just fine, so long as no mud splashes on me!

Monday, April 16

At a very lively and cordial dinner this evening Huysmans, Céard, Hennique, Paul Alexis, Octave Mirbeau, Guy de Maupassant, the young people of realist-naturalist literature, officially consecrated Flaubert, Zola, and me as the three masters of modern literature. The new army is in process of formation.

Thursday, May 31

Last evening in a studio on the Rue de Fleurus young Maupassant put on an obscene play he has written entitled *Feuille de Rose;* it was acted by him and his friends.

It was dismal to see these young men dressed up as women, with big gaping sex organs painted on their tights. I don't know how to describe the revulsion one involuntarily feels at seeing these actors fondle each other and simulate the gymnastics of love. The opening scene shows a young seminarian washing condoms. In the middle there is a dance by Egyptian dancing girls beneath a monumental phallus in erection, and the play ends with a scene of masturbation that is almost the real thing.

I was wondering with what complete absence of natural modesty one had to be endowed to imitate all that before an audience, at the same time trying to conceal my disgust, which would have appeared out of place in the author of *La Fille Elisa.* The worst of it was that Maupassant's father was present at the performance.

Five or six women, among them blonde Valtesse, were there, laughing artificially for appearance' sake but embarrassed by the excessive dirtiness of the thing. Lagier herself did not stay to the end of the performance.

Later, Flaubert, speaking of the play with enthusiasm,

found this phrase to describe it: "Yes, it was very fresh!" "Fresh," to characterize that uncleanness, that's really brilliant.

Friday, December 28

Yesterday at Bing's Japanese shop I saw a lanky, formless woman, very pale, bundled up in an interminable waterproof, who moved everything, displaced everything, and from time to time put an object on the floor as she said: "That will be for my sister." I did not recognize the woman, but I had a vague feeling that she was someone known to me and the public. Then her male escort came toward me, holding out his hand. It was Courmont's brother-in-law, Griffon, who they say gives her 100,000 francs a year. It is strange how today in the grey and rainy twilight Sarah Bernhardt made me think of those gaunt convalescents who pass before you in a hospital corridor in the darkness of five o'clock on a winter day as they go to pray in the chapel at the end of the hall.

1878

Sunday, January 6

At the bottom of every success there is always a worm, a bit of poison. In the midst of the unprecedented success of *Le Nabab* Daudet is in danger of being beaten up. He drew the portrait of a masseur, who turns out to be the terrible Charavay—*the masked wrestler!* no less!—who could kill my fine friend with one blow. As if readying himself for slaughter, he wrote a witty and picturesque account of the blows a man receives in the street, of the scornful commiseration of the crowd, of the desire to weep which overcomes the beaten man, the arnica with which he rubs his ringing head, etc., etc.

Today Bardoux, the Minister of Public Instruction, invited

me to dinner. It is the first time this individual has entered ministerial premises. These days ministers appear to live in something resembling big furnished apartments where you feel that the inhabitants are birds of passage who don't really live there.

There I am in the Ministry drawing room, which is furnished with terrible Boule corner cupboards, chairs upholstered in imitation velvet pretending to be antique Beauvais tapestries, and copper engravings enclosed in gilt wood moldings against the white woodwork.

The choice of guests is very audacious, and the shades of all the old, stiff university dons who, until very recently, standing with their backs to the fireplace, would come forward to greet their classic guests, must shake with indignation in their oak coffins. First of all, there are Flaubert, Daudet, and I, and all the top of the barrel from the world of painters and musicians. In the midst of all these famous people is the squat, insolent back of Dumas, who takes possession of the drawing room rather in the manner of a quarryman. Everyone wears the ribbon or the rosette of officer of the Legion of Honor; only Ambroise Thomas and the democratic painter Hébert have purple cravates and enormous crosses glittering on their chests.

We go into the dining room. Bardoux seats Girardin at his right and Berthelot at his left; the putter together of *La France* is judged more important than the taker apart of simple bodies.

The servants, who are cheerless, bored, and stiff, put into their service a certain disdain for the people they serve, a disdain which pleases me as a demonstration of a reactionary spirit.

By chance I am seated next to Leconte de Lisle, the man

who tears me to pieces behind closed doors. He gives me a friendly greeting and we chat. This man, with his luminous eyes, the marble polish of his face, and his sarcastic mouth, greatly resembles a prelate of superior origin, a Roman prelate. I find him witty but spiteful. His wit is not quite that of Paris; mixed with it is a residue of the provinces. Then too his conversation keeps too close to his trade; he talks too much about versification and syntax, and reveals much too much of the junior schoolmaster.

From time to time my glance ranges further and runs over the twenty-five heads gathered around the table. It is pleasant to look at the pretty little face of an enthusiastic young man, who they tell me is Massenet. I notice the old horse's head of Bapst from *Les Débats*, the political mountebank's head of my friend d'Osmoy, the astonishingly apelike head of Girardin, who grinds his food with the melancholy movements of the mandibles of monkeys as they chew on nothing.

We are at dessert. They set before us plates on which, printed in bistre, are portraits of the great writers of the age of Louis XIV with the dates of their birth and death on the back. I have Massillon on mine. They are very typical, and when I ask:

"This must be a dinner service of Salvandy's time?"

"Yes, exactly," Bardoux replies. "There was one from M. Fontanes' time, but it is broken."

While we are having coffee, Daudet brings over to me the young man with the pretty enthusiastic face, who tells me of the pleasure he had in reading *Madame Gervaisais*, at the end informing me charmingly that in order to buy the book he went without dinner that day. Could he have been pulling my leg?

At once Daudet, who has a tendency to get slightly tipsy

wherever he dines, takes off and outlines the novel which he is writing—a very charming imaginative piece about a queen exiled in Paris—confiding to us that during the day he had got himself into the King of Hanover's house by posing as an apprentice upholsterer.

As I am about to leave, Bardoux takes my arm affectionately and says: "Come, now, don't you have something you want to ask me for . . . for someone? Don't you have a friend you want to recommend?" I leave, much touched by his friendly offer and thinking to myself how accustomed the poor man must be to requests when he is led to try to get one out of a person who doesn't ask him for anything.

Tuesday, May 21

Renan has entered the Academy, carried in by the triumph of the democratic faction. Taine will get in no doubt by the operation of a sort of revenge by the conservative faction. Then it will turn out that the democratic group will have given a seat under the dome of the Institute to a man who is at heart most reactionary, a man who most zealously preaches government by an aristocracy, a man whose dream is to put the "scientocracy" in the place of the theocracy of former times, while the reactionary faction will bring in a man who is a university liberal in the marrow of his bones, although he now has money and is afraid.

Tuesday, December 10

Heartbreaking details about poor Flaubert's situation. His ruin would appear to be complete, and the people out of affection for whom he sacrificed his fortune begrudge him the cigars he smokes. His niece is supposed to have said: "My uncle is a strange man; he doesn't know how to bear adversity!"

Thursday, December 12

Banville was saying recently that Hugo, after a hard day's work, wanted to sacrifice to Venus but found himself incapable of it. This want of vigor, which happened to that man of granite for the first time in his life, threw him into deep melancholy: he saw in it a sign of his imminent death.

1879

Saturday, January 18

Premiere of *L'Assommoir.*

A sympathetic, applauding audience with some covert hostility that dares not show itself. What changes the years bring to the generations! In sorrowing memory of my brother I cannot refrain from saying to Lafontaine, whom I meet in the corridor: "This is not the audience that greeted *Henriette Maréchal!*" Everything is accepted and applauded; there are only two or three outbursts of hissing by some concealed hecklers during the last tableau. That is the sole protest in the midst of general enthusiasm.

According to confidences from Zola's intimates he did the whole play himself, except for some comic parts which he left to Busnach. If that is so, if he really is the author of the piece, then we cannot say that Zola has yet dared to start a revolution in the theatre. For the play—if one leaves out of account the working-class milieu, which has already been seen on stage many times—is put together with all the tricks, tirades, and banal sentimentalities of the Boulevard du Temple.

As we are leaving the performance Zola asks us, his nose a question mark, his voice doleful, if the play has really been a success. He passed the whole time of the performance in Chabrillat's office, reading some novel or other that he found in the bookcase, not daring to show himself to the actors, whom, he said, his anguished face had frozen at the previous night's rehearsal.

We go together in a band, including the Daudet couple, to Brébant's, where Chabrillat has ordered supper for his and Zola's friends. There are people of all sorts there, Busnach with his calf's head, old Janvier, beneath whose youthful manner one still discerns the ambiguous appearance of a scoundrel, the oculist Magne, whom it is pleasant to see again, Blavet, and the whole phalanx of the young. And we must not forget Chabrillat, as affectionate as you would expect a man to be who would have been forced to go into bankruptcy if the play had not been a success. Among the women are old Mother Charpentier, her daughter-in-law, Madame Chabrillat, etc.

And we have supper together rather gaily, although there is an undertone of letdown and of preoccupation about the morrow as Zola and Chabrillat go out to see the journalists, who are having supper on the floor below, as someone reads parts of a major article which is to appear tomorrow, as we hear a rumor that a ticket collector sent the Prefect of Police packing.

Manet, whom I ran into in the corridor during the performance, was disturbed that the play was accepted without a battle. He thought that just too good to be true. Could he be right?

Sunday, April 13

The whole value of romanticism lay in the fact that it provided an infusion of blood, of color into the French language, which was on its way to dying of anemia. But as for the human beings it created, they are purely ornamental.

Wednesday, May 21

How many plays are there in which the denouement is not produced by the interception of a letter or the overhearing of a conversation from behind a curtain? All the innovative imagination of the modern theatre boils down to changing a letter to a telegram and replacing the curtain by something like the door to a public toilet. It is very limited, and the theatre seems to me to be, for the mind, like the tiring labor of a squirrel in a cage.

Wednesday, May 28

A steeplechase between Daudet and Zola. For a time you saw only Zola's picture in bookstore windows. More recently you begin to see Daudet's picture slip in alongside Zola's.

Zola has a tribe of young faithfuls, whose admiration, enthusiasm, and ardor that *sly* writer maintains and indeed feeds by handing out corresponding editorships abroad, by getting well-paid articles into the papers where he reigns as master, in short, by purely material services.

Sunday, June 8

Lunch tête-à-tête with Flaubert today.

He tells me that his situation is taken care of. He has received a special appointment as librarian at the Mazarin Library with a salary of 3,000 francs, which is to be increased in a few months. He adds that he has really suffered from having to accept this money and that, moreover, he has already arranged for the State to be reimbursed some day. His brother, who is very rich and who is dying, ought to leave him 3,000 francs of income. With that and what he makes from his books he will get on his feet again.

Flaubert, the enemy of illustrations, today is thinking of

illustrations for his fairy tale to be made "by painters and not by professional illustrators," he says. His face is more brick red, more the color of a Jordaens painting than ever; and a lock of the heavy hair at the back of his head, brushed up on his bare cranium, reminds you of his Redskin ancestry.

He feels that his leg is now all right. This is the first day he has not put on a bandage.

"This is just between us," he says. "Can you imagine that Pouchet, that distinguished fellow, and another doctor who was there could see nothing wrong with me? It was a neighbor, a naval surgeon, a mere health officer, who, coming to see me, raised the sheet, gave a brutal blow to the leg, and asked: 'Did you cry, did you have a chill, did you feel any disturbance inside when you fell?' 'Yes, I felt something unpleasant in the upper abdomen.' 'Well, then, that's it. The fibula is broken. Look at this raised area. That always indicates a fracture.' "

All day long we aestheticized furiously.

At five o'clock, breathless and bulging in his light-colored trousers, Zola arrived from the running of the Grand Prix, which he attended to get information about racing so as to put into *Nana* one of those set pieces which are *à la mode* in today's novels.

Thursday, October 2

While I was posing for my portrait, Bracquemond, as he drew in the outlines, told me a bit of his life history.

The son of a dressmaker, he was put to work in a riding school and was supposed to become a groom. But he happened to live in the same building as a pupil of M. Ingres, a M. Guichard, whose children he played with. M. Guichard had him draw from plaster models, but when he saw his pen and ink drawings, he had him try etching and gave him Boissieu's *Donkey* to copy.

But Bracquemond knew nothing about this process. He was then living in Passy, in a house where a descendant of Louis XV also lived. This man possessed an old encyclopedia. Bracquemond looked up the process in it and did a creditable etching of Boissieu's *Donkey*. Then, after several other plates, he did his *Owl*, *Partridges*, and *Teals*, of which he sold several proofs.

There were difficult times, hard times, periods of misery during which Delâtre, who pulled his proofs and from whom he one day asked to borrow five francs, told him he was going to sell his plates for him. He took Bracquemond to Madame Avenin, a dealer in engravings who lived on the Rue des Gravilliers. For the plates of *Owl*, *Partridges*, and *Teals* she gave him forty-five francs—money with which he went at once to eat tripe at the wineseller's next door. It was very late, and he had not eaten that day.

This evening at Burty's there was a certain César Daly, editor of *La Revue d'Architecture*, a gentleman of English origin, whose life, passed in all parts of the world, would make a very colorful novel.

He was reared in a boarding school which served Dickens as a model, a boarding school located near the Scottish border, where it snows from October on. Some of the students had only a pair of trousers, others only a jacket. Every Saturday they went on a hunt for lice, and the student who did not bring a pen holder full of vermin was punished. And there, during a visit or an inspection, half the pupils stayed in bed. A boarding school where in a single year sixty pupils died of hunger and cold and whose master and mistress just escaped hanging.

Monday, October 20

It is amazing that all the people who are reading *Nana* in installments just now are struck by only two things: the producer of the spectacle who wants his theatre to be called a brothel, not a theatre, and Judic's remark about his wife's costume: "You'll see how it will give you a hard-on." And these two things, which are set down in my *Journal*, were appropriated from my conversation by Zola.

A journalist reports a conversation with Hugo in which I find the latter very severe toward the ugly and smutty in literature. After all it is he who brought humpbacked lovers, octopuses, and the word "shit" into books.

1880

Wednesday, February 4

Yesterday Renan was telling me with scorn about the "intriguishness" of Taine since he entered the Academy, about his busyness, his backstairs plotting, his servile flattery, his passionate participation in all the low-down transactions of the great institution, the emotional speeches he makes about a word in the dictionary, and in general his ridiculous zeal. He ended by saying that as a result Taine was going to become one of the powers of the Academy, and that right now he was working to assure the election of Maxime Du Camp.

All this is going on while the newspapers eulogize his serene, proud soul of the true philosopher.

Tuesday, February 24

In an expansive moment after dinner Zola said to Daudet: "You know, when one comes down to it, I am nothing but an assimilator."

Yes, a very powerful assimilator, but not an innovator, not

an inventor, not a sou's worth of creativeness in him. He has been, so to speak, the trumpeting and betrumpeted journalist of what my brother and I found that was new in literature.

Saturday, March 20

A story that is delighting Paris. Recently at somebody's house Madame Zola, speaking of me, is supposed to have said: "Goncourt is fine for the eighteenth century, but as for naturalism, that is not for him. He does not study his subject. Take *La Fille Elisa.* These gentlemen and I, we know that that's not the way things are done in such houses."

Easter Sunday, March 28

Today Daudet, Zola, Charpentier, and I set out to dine and spend the night at Flaubert's in Croisset.

Zola is as gay as an auctioneer's clerk going off to take an inventory, Daudet as a man escaping his home to go on a spree, Charpentier as a student who looks forward to a series of beers from bar to bar, and I, I am very happy at the prospect of embracing Flaubert.

Zola's happiness is marred by a serious preoccupation; he wonders whether on this fast train he will be able to piss in Paris, at Mantes, and at Vernon. The number of times the author of *Nana* pisses or at least tries to piss surpasses the imagination.

Daudet, a little tipsy from the porter drunk at lunch, begins to talk about "Chien Vert," about his amours with that crazy, wild, erratic woman whom he inherited from Nadar—a wild love affair, steeped in absinthe and occasionally made dramatic by knife stabs, a scar from which he shows us on one of his hands. He mockingly describes to us his dreary life with that woman, whom he lacked the courage to break away from and to whom he felt somewhat bound out of pity for her vanished beauty and for the front tooth that she broke eating hard candy. When he got married and had to cut loose from her, he tells us that, on the pretext of giving her a dinner in the country, he took her to the middle of the Meudon woods because he dreaded her outcries where other people might hear her. There among the leafless trees, when he had told her it was all over, the woman rolled at his feet in the snow and mud, bellowing like a young bull and pleading: "I won't be bad any more; I'll be your servant." Then, after that, supper, at which she ate like a bricklayer, in a state of stupefaction. He breaks off this account to tell us about a love episode with a young and charming creature named Rosa, with whom he had a night of passion in a room at Orsay, a room shared with seven or eight people who the next morning somewhat cooled the transports and poetry of their love as each one pissed at length in his chamber pot, farting loudly. A love episode a bit frightening by its perniciousness and coarseness.

"Look, that's where we live, beyond the bridge." It is Zola pointing out his property at Médan. In a clearing I see a building of feudal style which seems to have been erected in a cabbage patch.

Maupassant comes to meet us in a carriage at the Rouen station, and soon we are being greeted by Flaubert in a Calabrian hat and a bulky coat with his big behind in pleated trousers, and his kind face beaming with affection.

I had not retained a very clear memory of his property, which is really very fine. The immense Seine, on which the masts of ships that you don't see pass by as though at the back of a stage set; the beautiful big trees, their shapes twisted by winds from the sea; the garden espaliered against the hill; the long terrace-walk in full sun, a peripatetic's walk—all this makes the place a real home for a man of letters, Flaubert's home, after it had been in the eighteenth century the house of a Benedictine community.

The dinner is very good. There is a turbot in cream sauce which is a marvel. We drink many wines of all sorts and pass the whole evening telling risqué stories which make Flaubert burst out in peals of childish laughter. He refuses to read from his novel; he's at the end of his rope, he's had it. And we go off to bed in rooms which are rather chilly and are inhabited by family busts.

Next morning we get up late and stay inside talking, Flaubert declaring that a walk is a waste of energy. Then we have lunch and leave.

We reach Rouen; it is two o'clock; we will be in Paris at five; the day is lost. I suggest that we remain, make the rounds of the antique shops, have a fine dinner, and not return home until evening. Everybody agrees except Daudet, who has a family dinner scheduled and who, perhaps, has noticed an interesting-looking woman in the waiting room.

We have gone no more than fifty feet when we realize that the shops are closed; we had forgotten that it was Easter Monday. At last we find a curiosity shop with the door half open: I bargain with the woman for a pair of andirons, which she lets me have for 3,000 francs.

Back on the street again we soon find ourselves so tired that we go into a café, where we play billiards for two hours and a half, sitting in turn on the corners of the table and saying: "What a fiasco!"

At last it is six-thirty! We go to the main hotel for our special dinner. "What is the fish?" "Sir, there is not a single piece of fish in all of Rouen today." And the solemn headwaiter suggests we have veal cutlets.

A bargain in andirons at 3,000 francs and a dinner consisting of a wretched roast chicken, that is what we got out of our day in Rouen; and, to top it off, the return to Paris of all the Rouennais who live in the capital made our train two hours late. Oh, provinces, I swear I'll never again look for bibelots in your shops!

Saturday, May 8

Pélagie had just finished asking me: "Are you going to M. Flaubert's tomorrow?" when her daughter laid on the table a telegram containing these two words: "Flaubert dead!"

For quite a while I was in such a state of agitation that I did not know what I was doing or in what city I was rolling along in a carriage. I felt that a bond, sometimes loose but still inextricably close, attached us secretly to each other. Today I remembered with emotion the tear trembling at the edge of his eyelashes when he embraced me as we said goodbye on his doorstep six weeks ago.

When you come down to it, we were the two old champions of the new school, and I feel very much alone today.

Tuesday, May 11

Yesterday Popelin and I left for Rouen. We were at Croisset at four, in that sad house where I could not bring myself to stay for dinner.

Madame Commanville talked to us about the dear man, about his last moments, about his book [*Bouvard et Pécuchet*], which she thinks lacks about ten pages of being finished.

Then in the middle of the conversation, which was broken and without continuity, she told of a visit she had made recently in order to get Flaubert to take a walk, a visit to a friend living across the Seine who, on that day, had set her lastborn son on the drawing room table in a charming pink bassinet. After the visit Flaubert kept repeating on the way home: "A little creature like that in the house, that's the most important thing in the world."

This morning Pouchet drew me down a secluded pathway and told me: "He did not die of a stroke; he died of an attack of epilepsy. In his youth, you know, he had several attacks. The trip to the Orient more or less cured him. He went sixteen years without having any more. But worry over his niece's business affairs brought them on again. And Saturday he died of an attack of congestive epilepsy. Yes, with all the symptoms, foaming at the mouth. Listen, his niece wanted a cast made of his hand; it was not possible because his hand was so terribly contracted. Perhaps if I had been there, by keeping him breathing for half an hour I would have been able to save him.

"It certainly was upsetting to go into his study. His handkerchief on the table next to some papers, his pipe with ash in it on the mantel, the volume of Corneille from which he had read some passages the night before carelessly replaced on the bookstand shelf."

The funeral procession gets under way; we climb up a dusty slope to a little church—the church where Madame Bovary went to confession in the spring and where one of the little monkeys scolded by Abbé Bournisien is doing acrobatics on the top of the wall around the little old cemetery.

What is exasperating at funerals like this is the presence of a crowd of reporters, carrying in the hollow of their hands their little notepads, on which they jot down the names of people and places—which they get wrong. Even more exasperating is the presence of Laffitte from *Le Voltaire*, who, with 40,000 francs in his pocket, accompanies the corpse in order to make more money. Among the journalists who arrived this morning I see Burty, who has come to insinuate himself into this funeral as he does into everything that may bring in something for him. He even managed to get hold of one of the tassels of the hearse for a few instants, grasping it with one of the black gloves he borrowed from me.

We leave the little church and set out for the monumental Rouen cemetery under the sun along an interminable road. In the carefree crowd, who find the funeral somewhat long, faces begin to smile at the thought of a little celebration. People talk of brill *à la normande*, duck *à l'orange de Mennechet*, and Burty utters the word brothel with the winks of an amorous tomcat.

We reach the cemetery, a cemetery full of the odor of hawthorn, dominating the city shrouded in violet shadow which makes it look like a city of slate.

When the holy water has been sprinkled on the coffin the whole thirsty throng flow down to the city, their faces flushed and joking. Daudet, Zola, and I leave at once, refusing to take part in the feast being prepared for the evening, and return home speaking reverently of the dead man.

A detail which describes Daudet: this morning he had scarcely taken his seat in the train when Heredia saw him gravely donning his black gloves. When he saw that he was being observed, Daudet burst out laughing: "Already? That surprises you? Well, this is how it is. To me a train means a pleasure jaunt, the joy of vacation . . . and these black gloves are to remind me of where I am going."

Friday, May 14

Oh, what a sad and heartbreaking funeral Flaubert had on Tuesday—and as for what is going to follow . . . The nephew-in-law, who caused Flaubert's ruin, is not only a dishonest man commercially speaking, but he is a petty crook—holding on to a twenty-franc piece which the dead man had told him to pay the locksmith with—and also a cardsharp. As for the niece, Flaubert's "little darling," Maupassant says he can't tell about her. She has been, is, and will be an unwitting instrument in the hands of that swine her husband, who wields over her the kind of power that scoundrels have over decent women.

Well, this is what happened after Flaubert's death. Commanville talked endlessly about the money to be made from the dead man's works, kept coming back with such odd insistence to the love letters of our poor friend that he gave the impression of being quite capable of blackmailing the surviving lovers. He made a great deal over Maupassant at the same time he was spying on him, carrying out the surveillance of a regular policeman. That went on until Monday, when, having to go to Rouen, he disappeared and left Maupassant and Pouchet to put Flaubert's already decomposing body into the coffin. On the evening of the funeral, immediately after the dinner, at which Heredia and Maupassant were present and at which, by the way, Commanville very elegantly carved himself seven slices of ham, he took Maupassant into the little garden pavilion and kept him there a good hour, holding him by the hands in a false effusion of tenderness, literally keeping him prisoner. Maupassant, who wanted to get away, shrewdly suspected that something was up. Meanwhile Madame Commanville took Heredia to one side on a garden bench and told him that Maxime Du Camp had not even sent her a telegram, that d'Osmoy was a harum-scarum, that Zola and Daudet didn't like her, and that, as for me, she thought I was a man of honor but that she didn't know me; thus what she needed in these sad circumstances was the devotion of a man of the world who would represent her and defend her against members of her family. And this woman, whom Maupassant had not once seen weep, burst into tears in a tender abandon which rather strangely brought her head close to Heredia's breast, so that the latter said he thought if he had so much as made a movement she would have thrown herself into his arms. The scene went on; the woman removed her glove and let her hand dangle over the back of the bench, so close to Heredia's mouth that it seemed to be asking for a kiss. Was this a real access of love, suddenly invading the torn and softened being of a woman, for a man whom she had had her eye on for some time? Or wasn't it rather a sort of amorous comedy forced upon the wife by her husband in order to capture an upright young man, whom the exciting prospect of physical possession might lead to complicity in the swindling of the other heirs?

Oh, my poor Flaubert! Around your body what machinations, what human documents with which you would have been able to make a fine novel of provincial life!

1881

Sunday, February 27

M. Hugo's birthday. When God is demolished then begins the worship, the belly-crawling adoration of individuals, the ass-licking of the saints of radicalism. And don't talk to me about Hugo's genius! The literary genius of the man is something they don't give a damn about. They extol only the platitudes of his courtship of the vile masses.

Wednesday, April 6

At the de Nittis' I read the beginning of *La Faustin* to the Zolas, Daudets, Heredias, Charpentiers, and the young realists. I have a surprise. The chapters based on the liveliest documentation from life don't seem to register. On the other hand, the chapters which I look down on a bit, those based on pure imagination, grip my little audience. And Zola takes the Greek Athanassiadis to be drawn directly from life.

Saturday, April 23

A strange little "croaker" that Paul Bourget, always and everywhere coming out with this remark: "I feel that I am going to die here." "Oh, not in my house, please!" Madame Ephrussi was obliged to reply.

And what a strange creature that American etcher named Whistler is, with his bare neck, his wooden laugh, his white lock in the middle of his black hair, his manner of a fantastic and macabre homosexual.

A pretty beginning for a realist novel recounted to us this evening at the de Nittis' by Manet. A model whom he has posing for him told him that when she was thirteen, her grandmother died. She was put in the only funeral carriage with an elderly relative, who deflowered her on the way to the cemetery.

Wednesday, April 26

Gérome was speaking this evening of Meissonier, who as he painted the great Emperor identified himself so completely with his model that he made studies of himself, dressed in the historic redingote or even in a state of nature, persuaded that he was of the same build and the same physical conformation.

Apropos of this, an astonishing remark he is supposed to have made to Augier one day when the latter, finding him thus—a completely naked Emperor wearing only a suspensory—said to him: "Is something wrong with you?" "Oh, no, but the Emperor wore a suspensory."

Monday, June 20

Today the Daudets, the Charpentiers, and I go to spend the day at Zola's house at Médan.

He comes to meet us at the Poissy station. He is very happy, very lively, and as soon as he has settled us in the carriage he exclaims: "I have written a dozen pages of my novel . . . a dozen pages, by golly! It will be one of the most complicated I have ever written—there are seventy characters." As he says this, he brandishes a horrible little stereotyped volume, which turns out to be a *Paul and Virginia* that he had brought along to read in the carriage.

It is wild, absurd, crazy, this property which has now cost him more than 200,000 francs in addition to the original purchase price of 7,000 francs. You go up a staircase like the ladder in a mill, and you have to make an almost horizontal jump, as in a Deburau pantomime, to get into the water closets, which have swinging doors like those of a station restaurant.

The workroom, however, is very fine. It has height and size, but is very much spoiled by horrible knickknacks. Suits of armor, all sorts of romantic trappings; in the midst of all this you read over the mantel Balzac's motto *Nulla dies sine linea,* and in a corner you see a melodeon equipped with a *vox angelica* on which the author of *L'Assommoir* makes music at nightfall.

As for the garden, it consists of two narrow little strips of ground, one of which is ten feet lower than the other; it is extended into the fields, on the other side of the railroad line, by pieces of land which apparently belong to him, and there is another fifty acres on an island in the river.

We have a gay luncheon; afterwards we go over to the island, where he is having a chalet built—the painters are still working on it. This has one large, pine-paneled room with a monumental porcelain stove of great simplicity, in excellent taste.

We go back to the house to have dinner, and as the sun goes down, there emanates from this garden without trees, this house without children, a sadness which catches hold of Daudet as well as me.

As we eat dinner the conversation turns to Vallès' book *Le Bachelier*—Zola has just written an article on it for *Le Figaro.* He apologizes with some liveliness for having written it. He says that in the book everything is bunkum and lies and that it contains no study of human nature. He repeats two or three times in a sort of comic anger: "In my opinion Vallès isn't worth any more than a grain of hempseed, yes, that's it, hempseed!"

A curious detail about Vallès and the night he spent at Zola's. He refused a night shirt and slept raw. There is something sleep-in-the-nude about that writer.

On Zola's work table I noticed a brand-new copy of *René Mauperin.* "Yes," he said, as he caught me looking at the volume, "before beginning my book [*La Joie de Vivre*] I wanted to reread everything that others have written."

Wednesday, August 17

When you come down to it, Racine and Corneille were never anything but arrangers in verse of Greek, Latin, and Spanish plays. By themselves they discovered nothing, invented nothing, created nothing. I don't think anybody has ever said this before.

Thursday, October 13

A visit by the manager of *Le Voltaire*, telling me that he is going to cover Paris with posters and that on the day the first installment of *La Faustin* appears, he will distribute in the streets of Paris 100,000 copies of a chromolithographed picture of La Faustin. Then he laments that the police do not permit sandwich men, who are one of the great means of publicity in London. But he has something else in mind. And as he goes down the stairs he can't continue to hide his idea, but turns around suddenly and, leaning on the railing, says to me: "All right, here is my idea. There are some big posts along the boulevard. Well, the idea is to get permission to attach to them some big streamers with '*La Faustin* November 1 in *Le Voltaire*' written on them. Of course, the police will intervene and have them removed, but they will last a day." I listened to him shamefacedly, but, I must admit, not sufficiently revolted by the prospect of being dishonored very shortly by this Sarah Bernhardt type of publicity.

Monday, October 31

Posters of every color, of every size, covering the walls of Paris and everywhere announcing *La Faustin* in colossal letters. At the station a painted sign forty meters high and two hundred and seventy-five meters long. One hundred and twenty thousand copies of this morning's edition of *Le Voltaire* were handed out in the streets. Also this morning 10,000 copies of a chromolithograph of a scene in the novel were distributed on the boulevards, a distribution which is to continue for a week.

Friday, November 18

Today I receive a proposal from *Le Gil Blas* which indicates that *La Faustin* is being read. The newspaper wants permission to give the novel as a premium to its subscribers.

The memoirs which Du Camp is publishing in *La Revue*

des Deux Mondes I find sadly instructive about the romantics. In their liaisons, in their friendships they are always actors and nothing but actors. There is a letter of Flaubert's about a dead friend, a cry of pain from the soul which must have cost him forty-eight hours of laborious composition—for I know how he worked. And those scenes in which Du Camp and Flaubert declaimed passages from the Bible at the bedside of a dying woman and before her corpse made invocations to Job! What mockers of real feeling, of real emotions!

1882

Thursday, January 19

Everywhere there is an excellent display of *La Faustin*. At Marpon's I see copies from the fifth thousand, and at Lefilleul's I am astonished to see my book enjoying the high distinction of "The Throne." Suddenly in the midst of my contemplation of this I hear resounding on the boulevard: "Gambetta resigns!" Am I condemned to remain all my life the man who published his first book on the day of the coup d'état?

Saturday, January 21

At the railway station I run into Guy de Maupassant, and when I ask him if the wound he inflicted on his finger while taking a revolver to pieces is better, he tells me that the bullet that grazed him was from a revolver fired by a husband. Yesterday Zola told me that he is a terrible liar.

Sunday, May 14

This evening as we came back from the Banvilles' Madame de Nittis repeated to me what Charcot had said about Daudet, that he was being badly cared for by Potain, who did not see what was the matter with him, and that Daudet was threatened with locomotor ataxia within six months. Fortunately Charcot is well known for discovering in all sick people patients who need his treatment.

Friday, July 14

Have an idea like mine for the foundation I want to set up to provide a pension of 6,000 francs a year to ten talented men of letters whom the Academy spurns.[13] For that idea sacrifice many things, the desire to marry and to have at your deathbed someone like Mademoiselle Abbatucci to surround you with her attentions and sweet company. And your reward will be an article in a little paper accusing you of being a "schemer," an article by Vallès comparing you to Fenayrou, an article by Armand Silvestre, that *novelliere* of excrement and farts, holding you up to ridicule.

Apropos of Heredia, whose terrible sonority of language issues forth with the effort of stammering, I said the other day: "He is a piece of fireworks that has been put out by the rain."

Friday, December 29

Dinner at Daudet's yesterday with the painter Beaulieu, the companion of the d'Osmoys, whose studio I described in

[13] The Académie Goncourt was established by testament in July 1874. The original list of members was frequently altered either because of death or, as in the case of Loti and Zola, by real or putative desertion to the Académie Française. Daudet died before the provisions of the will could be put into effect, leaving only J.-K. Huysmans, J. H. Rosny, Justin Rosny, Léon Hennique, Paul Margueritte, Octave Mirbeau, and Gustave Geffroy. In December 1900 they elected Léon Daudet, Elémir Bourges, and Lucien Descaves to fill up the complement of ten. The Academy still continues the award of an annual prize to a work of literature, but its income from the author's estate was insufficient to provide the annuity of 6,000 francs to each member also set down in his will.

Manette Salomon and whom I had lost sight of for at least fifteen years. He is the same as ever, though a bit more hairy and wearing glasses.

A madness, a sexual passion for things Japanese. This year I have spent 30,000 francs on them—all the money I have made—and out of all that money I have never been able to find forty francs with which to buy myself an aluminum watch.

1883

Monday, February 19

Excelsior, at the Eden, a ballet you could call the Saint Vitus dance of the ballet. Nine hundred arms and nine hundred legs continually in the air with the flash of color of Algerian whatnots, with the glass spangles of Chinese kiosks in the midst of vulgar Bengal fire. A frenzy of movement amid lights that hurt your eyes and leave you stiff as if you had been focusing your eye for three hours on a kaleidoscope that was being vigorously shaken.

Inside the theatre a more baleful prostitution than ever, the women trying to look macabre and cadaverous.

Apropos of electric lighting, it could be nicely used while making love. It might be very pleasant to enjoy the body of a woman "clair-de-luned" by it.

Tuesday, February 20

This evening after dinner, at the foot of that bed which looks like an archbishop's bed in a play on the boulevards, at the place where he serves liqueurs, Zola, as usual, starts talking about death. He says that once the light is out, it is impossible for him to stretch out between the four posts of his bed without thinking that he is in a coffin. Everybody feels that way, he assures us, but everybody is ashamed to talk about it.

The thought of death is more frequent than ever with him since his mother died. After a silence he adds that her death has undermined his negative attitude toward religious beliefs, because he finds it so horrible to think of eternal separation. He says that being obsessed by death is perhaps a development of philosophic ideas produced by the death of a dear one, and he is thinking of introducing it into a novel, to which he might give a title such as *La Douleur.*

He is actually working up this novel right now as he walks about in the streets of Paris. He hasn't yet found a plot for it, and he has to have a plot since analysis is not at all his forte.

Sunday, March 4

In writing *La Petite Fille du Maréchal* [*Chérie*] I am trying for something that no longer resembles a novel. Absence of plot is not enough for me any more. I would like the structure, the form, to be different; I would like this book to have the character of memoirs of one person written by another. Certainly the word novel no longer describes the books we are writing now. I would like a new label—which I can't seem to find—in which perhaps I would use the word *Histories* with an ad hoc epithet. But that's the rub, the epithet. No, to designate the novel of the nineteenth century we need a special word.

Thursday, April 5

I am told today that the Charpentier firm, which has been shaky for a long time, is about to be sold to Calmann-Lévy. Now that's bad news. I must say, moreover, that since I devoted myself to literature my publishers, one after the other, have had business troubles: La Librairie Nouvelle, Lacroix, Charpentier.

Tuesday, April 10

The dinners with Flaubert and Turgenev which Zola, Daudet, and I used to have resume today with Huysmans and Céard.

We talk about Veuillot, whom Zola refuses to recognize as a great writer because . . . because . . . because he will leave no disciple—no Paul Alexis! Zola is certainly too personal and too limited in discussions. Daudet, who is not enthusiastic either about Veuillot's talent, hits the nail on the head when he says: "The press has lost its writer."

Then we talk about the de luxe editions put out by Ollendorff, Havard, and others, about editions of Halévy which, it seems, run to only 350 copies. Ernest Daudet asserts that he has seen the printer's vouchers.

And, I don't know how, we start talking about the effect obscene books have on women's imaginations. Thereupon Daudet recalls that in the next alcove—we are at Foyot's—he gave a supper to N . . . and a redheaded Bretonne, who was a friend of Madame N . . . He recited to them Monnier's *The Lesbians,* which he had learned by heart for the occasion. All of a sudden the two women, pushing the serving dishes and plates to one side with their hands, devoured each other on the table.

Next we turn to Maupassant, whose new book *Une Vie* I have just seen exhibited in the show window at the Galeries de l'Odéon, a volume which is dedicated to Madame Brainne. When they hear about the dedication, Céard and Huysmans tell of a terrible scene between Madame Brainne and the author at Zola's. Maupassant arrived that day in white tie, boasting of having stood up a society woman whom he was supposed to take to the Opéra that evening so that he might take someone else instead. The door opened, and there was Madame Brainne, who had never been at Zola's before and who never came again afterwards. No sooner had she sat down than she spat out a torrent of words, and all the time she was speaking she slapped her gloved hand with the long glove she had removed from the other hand, cynically making fun of Maupassant, who was completely out of countenance, with a ferocity that was embarrassing to those who were there. "You know, she was just like Madame Plessy in *Henriette Maréchal*," said Zola. Then the woman left, after making a sign to Maupassant, who slipped away a few minutes later, furious at the witnesses to this moral thrashing and avoiding their company thereafter.

Zola's nose is a very special nose: it is a nose that questions, approves, and condemns; it is a nose that is gay, or sad; a nose in which resides the whole physiognomy of its master; a real hunting dog's nose, whose impressions, sensations, and appetencies divide the tip into two little lobes which seem at times to quiver.

Today the end of his nose does not quiver; it is melancholy and echoes what the dejected voice of its master utters in the tones of "Brother, we must die!" about the sales of our future books—"Big sales . . . our big sales are over!"

Dinner ends with a conversation about poor Turgenev, who Charcot says is finished. We speak of that original teller of tales, of his stories, whose openings seem to come out of a fog, at first arousing no interest and then, as they go along, becoming so gripping, so moving, so thrilling. You could say that they are pretty, delicate things which pass slowly from shadow into light with a gradual unfolding of their tiniest details one by one.

Saturday, April 21

The English poet Wilde was telling me this evening that today the only Englishman who has read Balzac is Swinburne. He depicts Swinburne as a boaster about his vices who has done everything possible to make his fellow citizens believe in his homosexuality and bestiality, whereas he is not a homosexual or a bestializer at all.

Wednesday, April 25

Our good old Turgenev is a real man of letters. They had just removed a tumor from his belly, and he said to Daudet, who went to see him recently: "During the operation I thought about our dinners and tried to find the words which would give you an exact impression of the steel penetrating my skin and entering into my flesh . . . just like a knife slicing a banana."

Saturday, May 5

When Thiers or Zola writes a critique of the Salon each produces the kind of copy you would expect from men without any education in the arts or any knowledge of technique. Yet Thiers has one advantage over Zola: he has been a somewhat more successful collector.

Just the same it is an odd tyranny of our times that forces a pure man of letters, in order to make a start, to glorify an art about which he knows absolutely nothing.

Thursday, May 17

Daudet tells me today that he will definitely not present himself to the Academy and, without giving me any details, he says that a host of disgusting things have already occurred in this connection. But that is the way it is in all elections, and Daudet is not so ingenuous as to be unaware of it.

Charpentier's deal with Lévy has fallen through; he will be swallowed up less nobly, by Marpon. There has been a pretty little incident in this affair. Charpentier's cashier, named Gaulet, whose mistress takes a glass of beer in company with Marpon's mistress, has completely sold out his boss and has gone over bag and baggage to the lover of his mistress's friend. One of the booksellers was so naive as to warn that dolt Charpentier about this, and the latter had Gaulet send the bookseller an abusive letter.

Thursday, May 24

I was invited to Daudet's for dinner this evening, and as I went into his study, I found Ebner, his secretary, seated facing him and addressing an envelope at Daudet's dictation: "There or at the Café de Madrid," he said. And as Ebner was leaving he added: "You understand? The two letters are to be delivered this evening." There was something serious in the way he spoke which made me ask him if anything was the matter. "No, nothing at all!" was the answer.

But when his son followed Ebner out of the room, he told me: "Yes, I am sending two seconds to Delpit, who in an article about the Academy . . . you know, it's always the same thing, a continuation of the legend which has grown up about me: I have betrayed my friends, and no one is more skillful than I at wrapping betrayal in fine phrases. Well, that word 'Carthaginian' has begun to annoy me. I am sending some friends to ask for a retraction, old friends who, I think, can bear witness that I have not betrayed them."

Sunday, May 27

When we parted on Thursday Daudet said he would write me next day. I had heard nothing and thought the Delpit affair settled, when yesterday, on my return from dinner with the de Nittis, I found this letter: "My dear Goncourt, I am writing you from the Gare de l'Ouest, swords ready, as I wait for the doctor. We are going to Le Vésinet." And he asks me "if there is an accident" to take his wife a note which he has enclosed in the letter, concluding with these tender words: "After her husband, her children, her mother and father, it is you whom she loves most."

This upsets me. I sleep badly. I am awakened this morning by a telegram: "I am back from Le Vésinet. I gave Delpit a sword thrust." At once I leap out of bed to go to embrace him. And while the door of his study is pushed open by friends who come to give him a handshake and then go on their way, this is what he recounts about his duel, in his attractive, joking Southern way, depicting his original second Gouvet and the clownish packer who provided both the case of swords and the garden of his country house, and the five unnerving hours he waited at the Gare de l'Ouest for his adversary, whom he suspected of having gone to take two or three lessons in dueling at twenty francs apiece, and his fear that the light would be gone when they fought, and the solemn departure for Le Vésinet, and their entry into the packer's garden, between two green trees which he wittily compares to the entrance to a pretty cemetery, and the donning of formidable goggles which he asks to have removed if he is wounded, and finally Delpit's frightened face, which he compares to the ridiculous face of a clown, to a fearful Auguste fighting a duel in a pantomime.

A charming family detail. On Thursday Daudet's elder son had heard, through the door, his father tell me that he had sent his seconds to Delpit. The boy let none of his anxiety appear before his mother, but on Saturday, when his father was late for dinner and they were eating without him, he suddenly burst into tears. And when his mother made fun of his foolish little boy fears, he kept on crying but said nothing about what he guessed was happening at that moment.

Wednesday, June 6

Today I am visited by a student, one of those tall fellows with a beard, each hair of which is accompanied by a pimple. He has come to tell me of his admiration and informs me that at the present time in the schools the intelligent students, the grinds, the enthusiasts for literature are divided into two camps: the future Normalians, who belong to About and Sarcey, and the others, on whom Baudelaire and I seem to be the two contemporary authors who have the most influence.

Tuesday, July 10

The Exhibition of the Hundred Masterpieces.

The first painter of these times is a landscape artist, Théodore Rousseau. I think it almost undeniable that Raphael is superior to M. Ingres and beyond doubt that Titian and Rubens are better than M. Delacroix. But it has certainly not been proved that Hobbema painted nature better than Rousseau.

Thursday, July 12

The Daudets came to lunch today with their children. I read them a few notes from my *Memoirs*; they appear to be sincerely astonished at the sense of life preserved in these pages devoted to the dead past.

During lunch Madame Daudet admitted, somewhat shamefacedly, that she has taken on a maid recommended by Madame Burty, who has already provided one for Madame Charpentier. It is really strange how that couple place their spies in the kitchens and antechambers of people's houses and seek to get a foothold by making themselves masters of domestic secrets.

Tuesday, July 17

Bing will have seen almost all the art of China and Japan pass through his hands. Of those two bodies of art representing the civilization of the Orient he will have been the sultan and dispenser, to the profit of clients whom it pleases him to favor.

Friday, September 7

Today the religious ceremony over the coffin of Turgenev brought out of Paris houses a whole little world of people of giant stature, with flat features and the beards of God-the-Father—a whole little Russia which we did not suspect inhabited the capital.

There were also many Russian women, German women, and English women, pious and faithful readers who had come to pay homage to the great and subtle novelist.

Saturday, December 1

The other day at Sichel's, About let it be known that a deal had been made between him and Dumas by which About undertook to have Dumas made commander of the Legion of Honor and Dumas to get About into the Academy.

Really, in that fellow of talent named Paul Bourget what a twisting of ideas, what a propensity for the inconsequent in analysis, what a finicky pursuit of the outré in his hypotheses!

1884

Sunday, February 10

Viaud, the author of *Le Mariage de Loti*, a short, thin man, slight, skimpy, and skinny, with the big sensual nose of a

Caragueus—the Polichinelle of the Far East—and a faint voice resembling the dying tones of a sick man. A taciturn fellow who says he is terribly shy. You have to pull words out of him. He gives us this stunning example of the usurious contracts of Calmann-Lévy, contracts by which for six years the author must divide with his publisher all that he makes from his writing for magazines and newspapers, with the result that Calmann-Lévy received half of what Viaud made from his articles on Tonkin in *Le Figaro.* Isn't that monstrous and shouldn't that legal thief be put under the ban of public opinion and deprived of the handshakes of honest men?

A little later Viaud recounts as the most ordinary thing in the world a sailor's being washed overboard during a storm and the absolution given by the chaplain from the deck to the unfortunate man abandoned on his life preserver. When Daudet asks him if he comes from a family of sailors, he answers very simply in his soft little voice: "Yes, I had an uncle who was eaten up on the *Medusa's* raft."

Monday, February 11

When you get down to it, in the novel *La Joie de Vivre* [by Zola] Pauline in her superhuman perfection is a Feuillet heroine set in filth, a Feuillet heroine who, instead of having no menstrual periods, has them continually and who, instead of doing acts of charity to the well-washed poor, does them to beings from the dungheap. There is nothing in the book that is really interesting to us except the analysis, under the name of Lazare, that Zola has made of himself, of his fear of death, of his extraordinary moral absurdity.

For in this book, as in the other books of this singular head of a school, he always presents purely imaginary characters,

characters put together in the fashion of all the authors who preceded him! Yes, I repeat again that in Zola only the *milieux* are drawn from nature, while the characters are always made up out of whole cloth. That is the way he is preparing to write his novel about the mines, by going for a week to Saint Etienne, descending the shafts, and taking notes on the coal-mining area. As for the make-up of his people, it will be done without any sense of our common humanity, without contact with individuals, without intimate knowledge of human material. That was not the way *Madame Bovary* was done; that was not our way in *Renée Mauperin*, which was composed from ten years of notes on the young girl studied; that was not our way in *Germinie Lacerteux*, made from twenty years of observation and the knowledge of the secret depths of the unfortunate woman as revealed to us by the midwife who attended her in childbirth and who happened to be my mistress at that time.

Thursday, April 10

A luncheon given by *Le Gil Blas*, which I have to attend because *Chérie* is running in that paper. More than a hundred men of letters, of whom I swear that we three, Daudet, Mendès, and I, know no more than ten.

A swarm of reporters with an expression of official seriousness and gravity on their heads, which you feel contain very small brains. And as special treats for the luncheon, old Thérésa with her thick masculine lower lip like that of a calf's head, and old Léonide Leblanc, with her pearly teeth, who still has a pretty glint of the eye in her wizened little face. As their aide-de-camp, tottery as the old lackeys at the Comédie Française, these two have ataxic Claudin, who remains always young, always the gallant, always uttering his " 'Sblood" in a senility at once macabre and comic—Claudin, whom Léonide calls "uncle."

A detestable luncheon, boringly solemn, amusing only by reason of the ferocious ogling of Daudet by Léonide Leblanc, who is seized with a desire to sleep with him because he is the star of the group. Then Thérésa sings, she sings "La Chanson," she sings "Le Conte Bleu"; and in spite of my revulsion toward that woman monster, I can't help recognizing that she is a superior artist—she is able to produce that little shiver across the back of your neck which only great actresses evoke.

This evening I have dinner at Daudet's with Mistral. A fine forehead, the limpid eyes of a child, something good, smiling, calm produced by outdoor living in the South—by good wine and the quiet creation of troubadourlike songs and poetry. That is the portrait of the Provençal poet.

Tuesday, April 29

At dinner on the Avenue de l'Observatoire, Mistral defined Daudet rather nicely: he proclaimed him a man of disillusion and illusion, one with an old man's scepticism and a child's credulity. Then he started telling us about the way he works, of the easygoing labors of a Southern poet, writing a few lines at dusk, at the hour when nature goes to sleep, because, said Mistral, morning in the fields is too full of the noisy awakening of animality.

Then all of a sudden this soft-spoken man, this enunciator of delicate thoughts is transformed into a regular town crier, into a burly vendor of patent medicine, into a Mangin selling poetry as he would sell pencils from the platform of a cabriolet, into a man who is unbearable and common, oh, so common. While he is "troubadourizing" off in his corner of the drawing room, Gille from *Le Figaro* in a harsh voice like that of a Paris street urchin likens his Provençal singsong to "distinguished Auvergnat speech."

Sunday, June 8

To render nature Gautier had recourse only to his eyes. Since then all the senses of an author have been drawn on to render a landscape in prose. Fromentin brought in hearing and wrote his fine piece on the silence of the desert. Now the nose comes into play: the smells, the odor of a locality, be it the enclosure of the Central Market or a corner of Africa, these we have with Zola and Loti. And indeed both of them have a remarkable olfactory apparatus: Loti with his nose of a sensual Polichinelle, Zola with his hunting dog's nose and its interrogations, sniffing as it points, and its little quiverings, which are something like the tickling of a membrane as a fly passes over it.

Wednesday, June 18

What a strange fellow Daudet is! He confided to me that yesterday after his surgeon told him that he would without doubt have to perform another operation, he was overcome by "venereal weakness." Yes, he went to a prostitute who had a very pretty, young face. And that was his way of saying "shit!" to future troubles. And also, he added, to some extent to find out what kind of shape he was in; and, son of a bitch, he almost became ill during the experiment.

Daudet was on the point of leaving when, followed by Heredia, Montesquiou-Fezensac came in, the man who is the model for the novel *A Rebours* [by Huysmans]. Looking at him and listening to him today with a certain deliberate curiosity, I found that he has far more human quality than Des

Esseintes, who is merely a caricature of him, only an overdrawn portrait. There is no denying that he is a highly mannered individual, but a very distinguished one, who may well have genuine literary talent.

Monday, August 25

As we were coming back from Saint Germain to Paris by train last Friday, Dumas talked to me a lot about Madame Sand, whom he depicted as a monster unaware of her whorishness, her egoism, her good-natured cruelty.

She sent for him after Manceau's death. With the dead man not yet in the ground she replied to Dumas' question as to how she felt: "I want to take a bath and afterward go for a walk in the woods, and tonight see a play!" "The play will have to wait until you get to Paris!" After she had been back in Paris for a while, the old woman took to eating late suppers, drinking champagne, and screwing, carrying on like a forty-year-old student, behavior that caused her to fall ill and send for Doctor Favre. He declared forthrightly that she had senile anemia, and, after telling her she would "croak" if she kept on that way for a few months, he prescribed living a family life in these words, which were sublimely sceptical as to her qualities of heart: "Now, you understand, you must make yourself believe that you love your grandchildren!"

Sunday, September 14

Yesterday I ran through *Les Malheurs de Justine* by Sade. The originality of this abominable work lies not in its dirtiness, not in its vileness, but in the celestial punishment of virtue, that is, in the absolute inversion of the denouements of all other novels and plays.

Thursday, December 18

Incredible, bizarre furnishings! Good heavens, the interior decoration of a whore! I am talking about Guy de Maupassant's dwelling. No, I have never seen the like. Imagine, in a man's apartment, sky-blue woodwork with maroon stripes, a mirror over the mantel that is half-veiled in fluffy material, a turquoise-blue toilet set of Sèvres porcelain mounted in copper such as you find in a secondhand store, and the upper panels of the doors made of the heads of angels in painted wood from an old church at Etretat—winged heads flying over waves of gauze! Really, it is not fair of God to have given such execrable taste to a man of talent!

Wednesday, December 24

Guy de Maupassant confides to me that Cannes is a mine of information for him. There the de Luynes, the Princess de Sagan, and the d'Orléans pass the winter; and there it is much easier to get on intimate terms with such people; they let down their guard much more quickly and readily than in Paris. And he indicates to me very perceptively and intelligently that for the novels he wants to write about society, about Parisian society and its love life, it is in such a place that he finds his types of men and women.

1885

Saturday, January 17

Today at Sichel's Cernuschi was telling us that on the day of the premiere of Théodora [by Sardou] he received a letter from Sarah Bernhardt pretty much in these terms: "I am as poor as my ancestor Job. Will you give me 3,000 francs for the tiger for which I paid 6,000 at Bing's? I need money right now. I am turning to you because my tiger is *superb and Japanese.*"

Strauss, who was there, told us that on the same day Alphonse de Rothschild received a letter from Sarah asking him to buy some miserable bronzes she owned. He sent her 10,000 francs and asked for an orchestra seat for the second performance. The fantastic creature returned 3,000 francs, informing him that 7,000 was all she needed—but she did not send him a ticket—not Sarah.

Sunday, January 25

Today Daudet and his wife come for a preview of my *Grenier.* They stay a long time, a very long time, until it is dusk. And in our tête-à-tête in the gathering shadows we chat with tender expansiveness.

Daudet tells of the first years of their marriage. He tells me that his wife did not know there was such a thing as a pawnshop, and when she learned about it, out of a certain sense of shame she would never speak of it by name but would say to him: "Have you been *there*?" The nice thing was that this young woman, brought up in such bourgeois fashion, felt not the least fright over her new existence among the horde of scroungers of a meal, borrowers of a twenty-franc piece, and filchers of a pair of pants.

"Well, just imagine," Daudet exclaims, "the dear little woman didn't spend a thing, not a thing, on herself. We still have our little account books from those days, where alongside a gold louis taken by me or someone else there is set down here and there to her account only 'omnibus, thirty centimes.' " Madame Daudet interrupts him and says ingenuously: "I don't think I was fully mature at that time; I didn't realize . . ." I would think rather that she had the faith of people who are happy and in love, the confidence that everything would come out all right.

And Daudet goes on to say that during all those years he did nothing, that all he felt was a need to live, to live actively, violently, noisily, a need to sing, to make music, to run through the woods and, tipsy after a bit of wine, to get into a fight. He admits that in those days he had no literary ambition; but there was within him an instinctive pleasure in noting everything, in writing things down, even his dreams. It was the war, he asserts, which changed him, which awakened in him the idea that he might die without having done anything, without leaving anything lasting. Only then did he set to work, and with work literary ambition was born in him.

Sunday, February 1

Today the inauguration of my *Grenier*. There were only twenty-two invitations, and fifteen or sixteen people came.[14] Gayda, who had asked permission to do an article for *Le Figaro* on this first occasion, arrived at five o'clock, saying that he had been obliged to write the article before he came —Blavet, the chief writer for the "Parisis" column, who had to dine out, in the suburbs, I think, had asked that the article be handed in by three o'clock.

We talk of Vallès, who is very ill, and talk about him leads the conversation to Séverine. She may be a victim of the University in her fashion, as Vallès is in his. It seems she is the daughter of a professor who was such a pedant that he talked

[14] The invitations read as follows: "Le *Grenier* de Goncourt ouvre des dimanches littéraires le ler février 1885. Il sera honoré de votre présence." On December 14, 1894, Goncourt sets down for posterity a thirteen-page inventory of the contents of his *Grenier*. His guests must have had claustrophobia.

Latin to her at meals. Abomination of her family reached such a point in Séverine that at the time of the big fires during the Commune, although still a little girl, as she looked out from Passy at burning Paris, she sighed: "Oh, if the fire would only burn down papa's house!"

There is mention of the fantastic Montesquiou, and someone relates the man's first amours, Baudelairian amours, an affair with a lady ventriloquist, whose voice from her belly, imitating the vinous voice of a pimp, would threaten the noble client Montesquiou while he did the labor of love.

Daudet makes an original comparison. He says that Renan's brain resembles a secularized cathedral which contains wood, piles of straw, a heap of all sorts of things enclosed within its ecclesiastical architecture. Lemaître must have based his article in *La Revue Bleue* on this witticism.

Monday, February 2

This morning I read Gayda's article in *Le Figaro*. It would seem that yesterday all Paris was at my house, and included in that "all Paris" were people who are very much at outs with each other and enemies whom one does not speak to. Poor twentieth century, what a sell if it tries to get information about the nineteenth century from the newspapers!

Sunday, February 8

Poor crippled Desprez, the author of *Autour d'un Clocher*, who goes into prison tomorrow to begin his one-month term with his crutches, his poor anemic face, his toupee askew, seems to be in flesh and blood the woodcut by Tony Johannot removed from the cover of his *Le Diable Boiteux*.

Thursday, February 12

There is really a great flurry in the press about *Henriette*

Maréchal. We shall see what effect this has on attendance at the performances.

Sunday, February 22

Caraguel said today at my Sunday at home that it would take only ten students who wanted to have some fun and raise Cain to make the play fail. In these words tossed out casually by that big Southerner I sense an echo of the temper of the Latin Quarter, the announcement of a resurrection of *Pipe-en-Bois,* a veiled warning of a second cabal.

Tuesday, March 3

When I wake up I read an article in *L'Evénement* which, beneath polite formality and even ceremonial bows, reveals a covert hostility.

Then I read an article in *Le Gaulois,* which prints at the top of the page an appeal to republicans to hiss our play again this evening—an appeal signed by Charles Dupuy, one of the signatories of the manifesto of December 7, 1865, a manifesto in which this severe man of letters expressed himself in astonishing prose. . . .

It really is funny to find this appeal by Charles Dupuy in the conservative paper par excellence, in the paper run by that Jewish man of the world Meyer! Well, it is fated that there be a battle over our name, even to the end of the surviving brother's life, and that I, deriving no consideration or benefit from my more than sixty years, cannot have a success untinged by bitterness, a success which is not a mortal blow to my moral being. The perpetuation of literary hatreds is certainly strange! They forced us out of the theatre, where, surely, we would have amounted to something and would have done something new; they killed my brother. And this hatred has not been disarmed. This hatred positively resembles the barbaric insatiability of those revolutionary hags who piss with *gaping cunts* on the corpses of the people they have slaughtered.

To be honest, the *Gaulois* article gets my wind up. For if this evening there are a few hisses, then, with all the bad feeling latent in most of my colleagues who will be present in the theatre, the venture is imperiled, it will be a *flop,* once again! The fact is that I fear what may happen this evening and I go to bed until dinner time: this is my recourse in the great troubles of life. I do not succeed in sleeping, but I do obtain a sort of numbness in the darkness of my closed bedroom so that my anxiety formulates itself to my mind in a less distinct manner, one that is vague and blurred.

It is five o'clock. I had planned to eat dinner in a restaurant on the Right Bank where I would be sure not to meet a soul I know, and then until nine o'clock roam the deserted streets in the vicinity of the Odéon. But it is raining buckets and my tête-à-tête with myself is sad and unbearable, and I need to be with people I love until curtain time.

Quickly then into a hack in the pelting rain with a limping horse and a coachman who doesn't know the way, passing through desolate streets, where I perceive above a shop as through the dirty water of an abandoned aquarium and under a gaslight which seems to be sneezing: "Maison Dieu, repair of all kinds of trusses." "Will you give me a bowl of soup?" I say to the Daudets as I go into the study. There I am in the comfort and affectionate warmth of a friendly house; and we eat dinner at the end of the table already laid for the supper in honor of the revival of *Henriette Maréchal.*

I let the Daudets go into the Odéon by themselves. I roam around the lighted building, bright as day, without daring to enter, waiting for the end of the first act, about which I am uneasy—thinking of the Princess, who, being a princess, would not be content with a first-tier box but insisted on a stage box; I imagine her abused and insulted in the bursts of noise which at times come out of the closed doors and windows of a theatre.

I finally can't stand it. After ten turns around the Odéon I decide to push through the swinging door at the stage entrance; I climb the stairway and ask Emile: "Is it a good house?" "Excellent!"

I am only halfway reassured by this reply, and I go down still panting into the wings, where the muffled bursts of applause from the auditorium at first sound to me like hissing. But that impression lasts only a second: it really and truly is applause, frenzied applause, as the curtain falls on the first act.

And in the succeeding acts the play goes admirably, with, however, just a touch of coldness in the second act, which had been the great success of the dress rehearsal, but with an enthusiastic ovation for the third.

The Princess, who had sent for me and whom I refused to go to see in the auditorium, comes with her companions to embrace me in the green room, saying to me, somewhat intoxicated herself by all the bravos: "It's superb, it's superb . . . Let me kiss you!"

And after embraces right and left we set out for Daudet's, where they put me at the head of the table. And we have supper in the midst of a delightful gaiety and a hopefulness on the part of everyone that my success will open wide the doorway to the *realistic* theatre.

When I reach home at four o'clock, Pélagie, who has gotten up to let me in, confirms the success of the evening, telling me that at one moment she and her daughter were afraid that the top galleries, full of students and young people, would fall down upon them because of the delirious stamping of feet.

Wednesday, March 4

Le Figaro is excellent. The rest of the press rather quibbling, declaring my play to be an ordinary work in which, however, are to be found a certain delicacy and a quality of style drawn from present-day plays such as everybody is writing. The critics seem to be unaware that this play brings to the theatre the real spoken language of life and a *realism*, not of situations in human life, but a *realism* of human feelings in a given situation—which, after all, is about as much as the theatre can stand of truth. . . .

This evening the Princess showers on me that amiability which is shown in society to the man who succeeds.

Sunday, March 8

Tonight the theatre is jammed with spectators; there is unending applause. Léonide, who proudly shows me her back where the skin is raw from cupping, is happy that her voice has partly come back. Chelles predicts a hundred performances. And although I have arrived in despair, I go away *rehoping*. The abominable thing about the theatre is these ups and downs, which occur without any transition.

Monday, March 9

A letter from Porel telling me that the Odéon made close to 7,000 francs yesterday, including the matinee. A letter from Debry, the agent for the Society of Dramatic Authors, informing me that Mademoiselle Favart has accepted my conditions for her tour. . . .

I read a striking advertisement for the play by my critic

Claretie: an announcement that three members of the Academy—unnamed—were present at the performance in orchestra seats.

Thursday, March 12

A Delacroix exhibition at the Beaux Arts. I have no high regard for the genius of Ingres, and, I must confess, I have scarcely more for the genius of Delacroix.

People insist that he is a colorist; I agree, but he is the most unharmonious colorist in existence. His reds are like the wax seals on the papers of bankrupt stationers; his blues have the harshness of Prussian blue; his yellows and violets are those of old European pottery—and the highlighting of parts of his nudes with cross strokes of pure white is, as I have already pointed out, utterly unbearable and cruel to the eye.

As for the movement of his figures, I never find it natural. It is epileptic, always theatrical—worse than that, caricatural! And his human figures have exactly the gesticulation of the ridiculous third-rate actors in Gavarni's lithographs.

I concede him only one quality, in which he is superior to any painter in the world: it is his ability to render the surging of a crowd in a mad rush, as in *The Massacre at Liège* and *Boissy d'Anglas,* where the exaggerated mimicry of each single figure disappears in the general movement of the group.

Basically, a true painter is never an illustrator of literature. He paints the things which come before his eyes—men, women, landscapes, textiles, what have you, even red herrings! But he rarely goes to seek the motifs for his palette in books; one might set down this axiom: a literary painter is always an incomplete painter.

Thus today this great painter strikes me as being a Beaulieu, a droll romantic of the brush.

Monday, May 4

Rehearsal of *L'Arlésienne* at the Odéon. In the orchestra dry Legouvé, thin Halévy, and big-bellied Meilhac, under whose clothing I imagine I see their anatomies as Daumier shows the fat and the thin at the swimming school.

After the rehearsal a visit to Tessandier, whom we find bare from the waist up, two terrible wads of astrakhan in her armpits, appearing before us in the murky conflict of light from the street and the gaslight in the dressing room—a dressing room filled with the rank odor of a cage of wild beasts at the Zoo.

When we leave there, Daudet, worn out and forced to lean on my arm, goes with me to order the *Henriette Maréchal* dinner, whose menu is due to a Daudet-Goncourt collaboration.

Saturday, May 16

Collapse of my hopes. Today for the performances of *Henriette Maréchal* during the month of April I receive 1,200 francs. And I gather from Charpentier's expression that my brother's *Letters* are not selling.

Sunday, May 24

At my house at the very moment we were saying that Hugo was the triumph of language, the apotheosis of the word, Zola came in and said in a hushed voice as though he were an actor: "I thought he would bury us all, yes, that's what I thought!" Having said that, he walked around my study in a state of relief as a result of this death, as though he expected to inherit the papacy of literature.

Then he declared that Hugo had exercised no influence and repeated the old cliché that his own masters "were Taine and . . ." And as he hesitated this time over the second name,

I had it on the tip of my tongue to say, "Yes, yes, Taine and Claude Bernard, they are the ones who gave you the idea for *L'Assommoir*, aren't they?"

Monday, May 25

Never in human affairs has hypocrisy been as monstrous as at this moment. The official mourners for Hugo are Sardou, who never went to his house, and Dumas, who told Lavoix that Hugo was the man he held in deepest scorn.

Boredom with the praise given Hugo in the newspapers has become so great that you can hear the author of a most flamboyant article burst out when he has to correct the proofs: "Oh, no, shit, the old hack is just too boring!"

Tuesday, June 2

It appears that the night preceding Hugo's burial—the sorrowful wake of a whole people—was celebrated by a tremendous copulation, by an erotic frenzy on the part of all the women from the brothels, who had taken the night off and screwed all comers on the grass along the Champs Elysées—republican nuptials which the good-natured police did not disturb.

Someone suggests that the President encouraged the immensity of the celebration in order to diminish Gambetta's funeral and efface the memory of it from people's minds. Then Spuller interjects with a triumphant air that the Republic now has a million spectators at its command for celebrations, about the number of pilgrims that Catholic festivities in Rome brought there in the fifteenth century. And while declaring that the Church no longer controls anything or anybody—which is very near the truth—he demands that they stop construction of the church of Sacré Coeur, because it is a monument to the civil war.

Responding to this, Renan suggests that the church be converted into a "Temple of Oblivion," where chapels would be set up to Marat, Marie-Antoinette, etc. Then after a bit he sets about immolating Lamartine to the advantage of Hugo, speaking of his closed mind, his rigid principles, and his maladroit behavior which caused him to have a bitter and solitary old age, whereas Hugo's behavior had brought him the funeral we had just witnessed. This was just the kind of sermon one might expect from Renan, the banal and servile adulator of success achieved no matter how. Oh, he is not one of those who are revolted and scandalized by the ass-lickers of the common people!

Another detail about the *fucking* funeral rites for the great man—a detail which comes from the police. For the last week all the Fantines of the big brothels have carried on their trade with their natural parts draped in a scarf of black crepe—*their cunts in mourning*.

Sunday, June 14

Today Daudet comes into my house with drawn face, dead eyes, and nervous contractions of his body, a state which leads him to say: "I am really suffering too much; there are moments when I wish for death as a deliverance!" The Sunday visitors arrive. We talk, we joke, we get excited, we get mad, and little by little Daudet begins to take part in the conversation, in the laughter or anger of our words, and blood comes back to his cheeks, there is life in his eyes, his body relaxes, and he no longer seems to be about to "croak" as he did when he arrived.

"Ah, my play *L'Oeillet Blanc!*" he says at one point. "I had just received 1,500 francs for it in those days when I didn't know what money was. Yes, I had got 1,500 francs from Peragallo, which I asked him to pay me in gold; it made a big bump there," he says, tapping his trousers pocket. "Oh, what a night! I had supper at La Maison d'Or with a prostitute, a very beautiful girl, who was as unconcerned about money as I. Our only thought was to use the money in my pocket to make the people around us happy. The next day, a beautiful rosy morning, she had a notion to do the driving—she was a coachman's daughter! And, installed on the driver's seat, she drove us all the way to the Bastille . . . at such a clip . . . such a clip!"

Thursday, July 2

Removed from the deafening sonority of Heredia's voice, from the noisy footwork of Céard and Drumont, who are practicing fencing in the billiard room, Barbey d'Aurevilly, as usual in a strange costume, the hard color which dye gives to his beard and hair making him look like a wax figure at Curtius's—Barbey d'Aurevilly tells us about his youth.

He depicts for us the severe, Jansenist atmosphere of his father's house, where he began to grow very bored at seventeen. His father, a wild-eyed legitimist, would not let him serve under Louis Philippe. He then asked permission to study law, which his father granted on condition, however, that he not do it in Paris because he would lead a profligate life there. Thus he studied law at Caen. There, when he became the lover of a married woman, his father forced him to make a choice between her and his family. He did not hesitate a moment over which to choose.

Then there began for him at seventeen a life of penury during which his father sent him not a single five-franc piece.

And it was not easy to earn a living as a writer at that time when pay was so low and when he would never agree—he burst out with pride—to delete a word from an article. "Knowing that, the editors of the newspapers took advantage of me by printing only two articles out of the four that were stipulated in my contract." He had to get into debt, with creditors of whom he spoke most glowingly. Yes, hard years during which he never received a word from his mother, who held her husband in such adoration that out of fear of angering him she showed her son no sign of life, of maternal affection, during all that long time. Reconciliation came only after the publication of *L'Ensorcelée*, his novel about the Breton royalists, which so gratified the convictions of that old royalist his father that he decided to write to his son: "Come home, sir." I don't need to add that there was about as much conventionality in this account as there was in the narrator's costume.

Tuesday, October 27

This evening at Charpentier's Zola tells us that *Germinal* [the play] has been banned. He is superb in his indignation, declaring that he will stop at nothing, that he will go all the way, that he will proclaim Goblet a fool. And as he tells the story of the interdiction, he says that after leaving Goblet's he and Busnach were on their way to see Brisson when suddenly he said to Busnach: "No, let's not go there. We would be making a mistake. You can't tell what may happen. Let's keep Brisson in reserve." And then the man who says he won't give in on anything reads us his letter to Magnard, which he interrupts to call to our attention the fact that at one point he has taken out the word "ministry" so as not to put all the ministers against him. Then he falls into a long silence, from which he emerges after a while with this remark: "If some day they give the play back to me, I shall ask the director who takes it for a ten-thousand-franc premium. It will be worth that much then, because it once was banned!" You can see all of Zola in those words: crafty in his audacities, skillful in his literary effrontery.

Thursday, November 19

I spend my afternoon at Duret's looking at old Japanese prints. Among the artists represented there is a master held in particular affection by the proprietor, one named Moronobu. He was the first to announce the act of love by a slight baring of the top of the woman's shoulder, a chaste and delicate indication of what would soon take place between the man and the woman. It is a very fine choice, this bit of shoulder on which, at the little death of coitus, the man lets fall a kiss as if in thanks for the pleasure this body has given him.

Sunday, November 29

Dinner with the Hugos, the Lockroys, the Gouziens. Lockroy, "the gentleman who has no cheeks," according to my little god-daughter's expression, has the pleasant, soft voice of a good little old man in a fairy tale. Jeanne Hugo, whom I have not seen since that day at my house when, still a little girl, she fell asleep in the middle of dinner, her cheek resting on a hand clutching a drumstick, has something of her mother in her, but gross, peasantlike. As for Gouzien, he is a fellow who brings to a dinner the noisiness of a traveling salesman filling the role of groomsman at a wedding feast.

Thursday, December 3

The critic Lemaître has a little laugh from the bottom of his throat, a laugh which is the essence of diplomacy, giving him time not to say what he is thinking but to conceal and arrange it. He speaks in hypocritical circumlocutions, behind which are concealed at no great depth the ideas of the critic Sainte-Beuve.

Wednesday, December 9

Desprez, that child, that twenty-three-year-old writer, has just died as a result of being shut up with robbers and crooks, at the good pleasure of M. Camescasse, treated like an ordinary felon! There is no instance of a murder such as this under the Ancien Régime or under the two Napoleons. Zola, who went to see him in prison only at Daudet's insistence, has just written a brutal letter to *Le Figaro*, as was right and necessary, but in it his own tremendous personality makes itself felt too much, as in everything he does. In this letter he seems to me like one of those men who parade a corpse through the streets of Paris at the beginning of a revolution without any feeling for the man but purely for the egoistic furthering of a cause.

Monday, December 14

Today I set to work on the portrait of Daudet which Koning had *Le Gaulois* commission from me. This work gives me real joy; and under the stimulus of that joy I feel almost sorry at my decision not to work any more—at least for publication during my lifetime—on things having to do with the present, the contemporary, on things from life as it is actually being lived.

Basically, for Daudet luck has been so great, publicity so tremendous, the hail of gold which falls on him so extraordinary that at times I am afraid for him, and I imagine a blow awaiting him somewhere out of sight, so that when I am outdoors with him there are times when I have a hallucinatory vision of a hand raised to strike his face.

Sunday, December 27

We were talking today about the thirty-fifth fitting of Halévy's Academy uniform, which is being made by Dusautoy.

Monday, December 28

The University provides literature with only journalists and critics—at bottom junior masters who, like Paradol, wage war with pin pricks or, like About, with childish tricks; there are loutish junior masters like Sarcey, playful ones like Lemaître. But when it comes to works of the imagination a man like About is not a novelist or romancer in the manner of writers who have never been Normalians, but always remains somewhat the journalist, somewhat the critic.

At this evening's gathering of Japanese enthusiasts at Bing's, Hayashi shows us a series of fifty-seven compositions by Hokusai executed for his *One Hundred Poets*, fifty-seven sketches that have not been included in the well-known series. According to Hayashi these drawings were bought by an Englishman for 25,000 francs.

Tuesday, December 29

A transfusion of new blood into our Magny dinner; among the newcomers is M. de Vogüé: the sloping forehead of a stubborn imbecile, the eyes of a dumb beast, of an animal, a face on which one notices nothing but a pale and bloodless animation.

1886

Tuesday, January 5

At the Spartiate dinner today Drumont officially announced the forthcoming publication of his book attacking the Jews [*La France Juive*]—that book written for the personal satisfaction of hatred by a Catholic and reactionary in the midst of the complete and insolent triumph of republican Jewry. If he is unbearable and even a little despicable sometimes because of the narrowness of his ideas on everything, at least Drumont has the valiance of spirit of a man of another age and almost an appetite for martyrdom.

Wednesday, January 20

A sample of the language and simple speech of Gounod.

Madame Bizet, then a young girl of only fifteen, was getting ready to take her first piano lesson with him when he said to her: "Arch your wrists and make a *lilac* note in which I can wash my hands."

It was Gounod also who, at a performance of *Manon*, ended his praise of a passage with this extraordinary statement: "Indeed, I find it *octagonal*." "I was about to say so myself!" Madame Bizet answered wittily.

Tuesday, February 16

I go to see Robert Caze, who was wounded in a duel yesterday. He lives on the Rue Condorcet, all the way at the end, in an area where the street takes on almost the appearance of a Parisian suburb. An apartment on the fifth floor beyond a courtyard—the lodging of a minor employe. A pale, thin young woman glimpsed in the half night of a corridor.

He is in bed, and on his fine features one discerns the worry of a wounded man without means who lives from his pen: "Ah, I was much better than he!" he tells me. "But the sword hypnotizes me . . . that happens to me even at fencing school. I hurled myself on his sword . . . It touched my liver. If peritonitis does not set in . . ." He does not finish his sentence.

Weak as he is from loss of blood and although he fought with a nobody in order to avoid fighting Champsaur, you feel in the depths of his eyes a covert determination to fight again some day with Champsaur.

Sunday, February 28

The Princess came to my Sunday gathering today to take a look at my naturalists. It was very amusing to observe her curiosity and at the same time a sort of moral apprehension of these people whom she calls "the dirty fellows."

Wednesday, March 3

Speaking at dinner tonight of the young writers whom she saw at my *Grenier*, the Princess said in a somewhat surprised tone: "You know, really they are quite nice . . . and Huysmans looks distinguished. What they need is to meet some people of quality, to go into society a bit." To which I replied: "You have only to invite them; they wouldn't ask for anything better!"

Tuesday, March 23

I was on my way to get news about Robert Caze, who Daudet told me was getting better, and I had almost arrived at the station when a young man came up to me, addressed me, and asked if I were M. de Goncourt. When I said yes, he replied: "Here is *Grand'mère*, the volume Robert Caze dedicated to you . . . He asked me to offer his excuses for not having written something in the book, but he does not have the strength." And he told me that the poor fellow is not expected to live.

Tuesday, March 30

Paschal Grousset came by yesterday to ask me, on behalf of Madame Robert Caze, to be an honorary pallbearer for her husband. . . .

. . . At the church I am somewhat astonished when my eyes encounter the face of Hennequin, his adversary's second. Such lack of tact is strange: not to understand that he doesn't belong there and that he is as out of place as the man who did the killing! And in the reverent sadness of the ceremony, I saw again the dear young fellow with his kindly plump face, his limpid child's eyes aglow with passion when one spoke of people or things he did not like—a nature somewhat gross in appearance but with curious delicacy and tenderness underneath, a writer who brought to his friends in the world of letters a complete devotion, without reserve or limitation of any kind. And my thoughts turned to my *Grenier*, to that assembly open only since last year, two of whose youngest members, Desprez and Robert Caze, are already dead.

Saturday, April 17

During the afternoon Bracquemond takes me to visit the sculptor Rodin. He has the features of a man of the people, a fleshy nose, clear eyes blinking under lids that are a sickly red, a long yellow beard, hair cut en brosse, a round head, a head expressing gentle and obstinate stubbornness—physically a man such as I imagine the disciples of Jesus Christ to have been.

We find him in his studio on the Boulevard de Vaugirard, an ordinary sculptor's studio with walls splashed with plaster, a sad little cast-iron stove, a cold humidity emanating from all those big objects made of damp clay wrapped in rags, and all those casts of heads, arms, legs—in the middle of which two emaciated cats look like effigies of fantastic gryphons. And there too I see a model with bare torso who looks like a stevedore. Rodin turns on their tables the life-size clay figures of his *Six Burghers of Calais*, which have been modeled with a powerful realist thrust and which have in human flesh those beautiful hollows which Barye put in the flanks of his animals. He shows us also a robust roughcast of a nude woman, an Italian, a short and supple creature, a panther as he puts it, which he says with regret in his voice he cannot finish because one of his pupils, a Russian, fell in love with her and married her. He is a true master of flesh, yet in the most beautiful and accurate reproduction of anatomy there is one detail of extraordinary disproportion—almost always his women's feet.

A marvel done by Rodin is a bust of Dalou executed in wax, in a transparent green wax which has the quality of jade. You can have no idea of the light touch of the sculptor in the modeling of the eyelids and the delicate flaring of the nose. The poor devil has really had bad luck with his *Burghers of Calais!* The banker who held the funds absconded, and Rodin does not know whether he will get his pay. However, he has gone so far with the work that he must finish it, and in order to finish it he will have to spend 4,500 francs on models, a studio, etc.

From his studio on the Boulevard de Vaugirard Rodin takes us to his workshop near the Ecole Militaire to see his famous doorway destined for the future Palace of Decorative Arts. On the two immense panels there is a jumble, a confusion, a tangle something like the interlacing of a mass of madrepores. Then after a few seconds the eye perceives in the apparent madrepores of its first glance the projections and recesses, the protrusions and cavities of a whole host of delicious little figures, bustling, so to speak, in an animation and movement which Rodin seeks to imitate from *The Last Judgment* of Michelangelo and certain mob scenes in Delacroix's paintings—all this in unparalleled relief, such as only he and Dalou have dared to attempt.

The studio on the Boulevard de Vaugirard is filled with

lifelike humanity; the one on the Ile des Cygnes is like the domicile of a poetic humanity. Choosing at random from a heap of casts spread out on the floor, Rodin gives us a close look at a detail of his doorway. There are admirable torsos of small women, in which he has excelled at modeling the flow of the back and, so to speak, the wing beats of the shoulders. He is also imaginative to the highest degree in reproducing the joining and intertwining of two amorous bodies clinging to one another like those leeches you see coiled one on the other in a jar. One of the most original groups represents his conception of physical love, but the concretization of his idea is not obscene. It shows a male holding against the upper part of his breast a female faun whose body is contracted and whose legs are drawn up in an astonishing similarity to the stance of a frog which is about to jump.

This man seems to me to have the hand of a genius but to lack a conception peculiar to himself, to have in his head a *mishmash* of Dante, Michelangelo, Hugo, Delacroix. He strikes me also as a man of projects, sketches, fragmenting himself in a thousand imaginings, a thousand dreams, but bringing nothing to complete realization.

Thursday, April 22

I eat dinner this evening with Drumont, who will fight a duel on Saturday with Meyer of *Le Gaulois*, Daudet and M. Albert Duruy acting as his seconds. Drumont arrives nervous, tense, yet droll and gay. "Today," he exclaims, "fifty-five people. The bell never stopped ringing. Crowds began to stop in the street in front of the house when they saw all those people entering it—coming to say to me: 'Oh, how we thank you for having said what we feel!' Some Carmelites sent word they would pray for me on Saturday . . .

and my lay sister, who has just come into my household and was told that I was a sort of lay priest . . . she doesn't know what to make of it. Yes, there's not a copy of the book left, the 2,000 are all gone. Marpon is urging me to make another printing. They are going to put eight presses to work. It's aggravating just the same. I have talked eight hours today, and my voice is gone."

Sunday, April 25

Young Lavedan, who gets around, was present when Meyer got off the train on his return from the duel. The whole boulevard in front of *Le Gaulois* was full of Jews; and broughams, such as one sees in front of the Saint Augustin church on the day of a big wedding, were pouring out a Yid a minute onto the boulevard. There were all the Dollfuses and all the Dreyfuses in creation, and Halévy and Koning and Ollendorff, with Ohnet in tow.

Finally Meyer appeared and all of Yiddom threw themselves upon him to congratulate him. "Don't compliment me, gentlemen. I acquitted myself as badly as possible in this affair. That man is a lion!"

At that point in the account Daudet comes in and says it was ferocious, that at one moment he was on the point of fighting Meyer himself, and that he certainly would have fought him in order to give him a chance to redeem himself, but he saw that the man had too ugly an expression.

Then he describes to us the place of combat, a former estate of Baron Hirsch, a broad stretch of country in which horses on the loose stupidly came up to the duelists.

Finally he fills in the details. There was a first encounter in which, when Meyer parried with his left hand, Daudet called him a scoundrel and told him he ought to have his hand tied behind his back. A second attack followed, and this time Meyer grasped the sword with his hand and wounded Drumont. And Daudet describes the scene at the entrance to the barn where he had been carried, of Drumont, his trousers already removed, slapping his bloodstained shirt tail and shouting angrily at Meyer and his seconds: "Back to the ghetto with you, you dirty Jews! You are a bunch of murderers! You are the ones who chose this house belonging to Hirsch which was bound to bring me bad luck!" Daudet adds, "Yes, indeed, that man, behaving incorrectly, that guttersnipe giving vent to a vulgar outburst, was superb, whereas Meyer, that correct Semite, looked like a haberdasher's clerk."

Caught up for a moment in his memory of the beauty of the day, the grandeur of the landscape, the serenity of the scene, Daudet says that in the midst of it all these two petty beings were altogether ridiculous in their jerky movements as they tried to kill each other.

Thursday, May 6

The real truth about the duel, as told by Daudet in confidence, is this: Meyer, who was expected to give way, to turn tail and run, conducted himself very staunchly at first and carried out the thrust which he had told his intimates about, a thrust in prime, I believe, which was to get Drumont in the belly. But when the thrust was made, and very well made, not parried at all by Drumont, and Meyer had at length withdrawn his sword—bent apparently not by a pants button but by a truss—he completely lost his head and behaved like a cad.

Sunday, June 20

De Bonnières and his young wife went to Maupassant's place at Chatou to spend a few days. Now, wasn't it odd and a bit unconventional for that young woman to sleep under the roof of a young bachelor—even in the company of her husband? And at the Cossack dinner this is what Maupassant had to say about their visit. As the group were out rowing the name of a courtesan was mentioned by chance, and Maupassant let slip the fact that he had diddled her. After making the remark he was greatly embarrassed and lowered his head between the two oars. Whereupon the young woman, stretched out by the tiller, rescued him from his embarrassment by saying kindly: "It's all right. We are all fellows here!"

Maupassant also said, in front of the twenty guests at the dinner, that his servant complained that he had never seen people get the sheets so dirty! For heaven's sake, what kind of people is good society made up of today!

Friday, September 17

Madame Daudet was talking of the people who replace each other at the Charcots', people whom you see there two or three times and never see again, such as Dalou and other artists. She has christened the house "a house where you don't last."

Saturday, December 18

A fantastic day. Yesterday I had a note from Céard asking me to go to the office of an American lawyer on the Avenue de l'Opéra. . . .

It is a matter of the purchase of the play *Renée Mauperin* by America. After a little while Samary of the Odéon and Céard come in and inform me—an incredible piece of news—that the play has been bought by the niece of the American chargé d'affaires. She arrives shortly, a charming young woman, and tells us in her stumbling French that after making a great deal of money for the poor by acting for them, she now wishes to earn some for herself by starting out with *Renée Mauperin.*

The agreement is concluded, the American society woman defending her interests like a cashier—an expression of Samary, who means a cashier at a bakery! And—something new—the contract instead of being written out is printed on a little machine with keys. The lawyer hands us 1,500 francs and helps us on with our overcoats in the anteroom.

1887

Wednesday, January 5

I have Bracquemond and the sculptor Rodin to lunch today.

Rodin, who is full of *faunishness*, asks to see my Japanese erotics, and he is full of admiration before the women's drooping heads, the broken lines of their necks, the rigid extension of arms, the contractions of feet, all the voluptuous and frenetic reality of coitus, all the sculptural twining of bodies melted and interlocked in the spasm of pleasure.

Dinner at Charpentier's, where Daudet declares there is a fine book to be written called *The Century of Offenbach*, asserting that everything in these times comes down from him, from his nonsense and his music, which basically are nothing but a parody of serious things and serious music which he has travestied. And Céard rather wittily confers on him the title of "the Scarron of music."

Saturday, January 8

Dinner at Banville's.

It is strange what influence the café-concert has at the present time and how its ditties have seized hold of people's minds. I hear Daudet humming constantly

Trois, rue du Paon
Un petit appartement
Sur le devant

breaking off suddenly, a little ashamed of this stupid obsession.

Then Coppée says that melodrama, once a mania with him, no longer has the power to amuse him; now there is only the café-concert, only Paulus to give him pleasure, that it has provided something for him to do with himself in the evening.

Thus it is that this neuro-epileptic gaiety is on the way to conquering all Paris and putting its *gaga* tunes on the lips of even the most intelligent people. It is something like the crises of hysteria that run through a hospital ward, going from bed to bed, involving everybody.

Banville, with his special brand of irony, which is charming in its good humor, tells how Sarcey during some play or other at the Odéon a few years ago took him to drink a glass of beer at a café and said to him suddenly: "You know, Hugo is a great lyric writer. Yes, not long ago a friend took me out into the country and in the armoire of my bedroom there was a repulsive-looking book, one that was all stained, *Les Feuilles d'Automne;* do you know it? Well, in it there is a piece about a beggar warming himself before a fire, the light of which passes through his coat like stars in a night sky. Now that, you know, is a great lyric!" And then he made a scene when Banville would not share his admiration!

At the end of the evening in a corner a light, mocking conversation of the kind habitual with Coppée, who confesses to me his astonishment over Taine's *gullibility*, his astonishment at that man's ability to *swallow anything*, a man who by reputation is such a great gentleman.

Sunday, January 16

Today Stéphane Mallarmé was one of my visitors. He is subtle, delicate, witty, in his conversation showing nothing of the opaqueness of his poetry. But, really, these poets have no ability at observation. The metamorphoses, the avatars that occur in the people with whom they live they do not notice at all, and Mallarmé holds for Catulle Mendès today exactly the same judgment he had of him formerly, and the same goes for Rollinat.

Saturday, April 16

Yesterday was the first performance of *Renée* [by Zola]. Not a scene where you feel life as it is really lived, and all the time the trite tirades of the old-style theatre. Indeed, since there is such a thing as *naturalism*, let us admit it, there is not a play by Dumas or Augier which is not a hundred times more naturalistic than this drama, which resembles one by Becque in his early manner.

Sunday, June 26

The last Sunday of my *Grenier*. Huysmans in a rather droll manner predicts the advent of Hervieu and de Bonnières as the Center-Left, the Louis-Philippe party of *naturalism.*

As he leaves, Rosny thanks me with affectionate warmth for having opened my house to him, for having brought him into relation with people, for having powerfully forwarded his literary career.

Tuesday, June 28

That Puvis de Chavannes! To think that there are so many fine blank spaces on our public monuments which are condemned to be dirtied by those sad tint drawings which are so badly, or worse, so stupidly drawn! Since painting began I know of no painter whose drawing was so banal.

Thursday, August 18

To my great surprise when I opened *Le Figaro* this morning I found prominently displayed a literary execution of Zola signed by the five following names: Paul Bonnetain, Rosny, Descaves, Margueritte, and Guiches. The devil of it is that four of the five are frequenters of my *Grenier*. . . .

. . . [Léon Daudet and I] take the train for Champrosay, where I have dinner. Daudet was as uninformed as I about the *Manifesto of the Five*, who carried out their misdeed in the deepest secrecy. At this time of servility toward Zola on the part of the press we find the act to be courageous, but the manifesto to be badly written with too many scientific terms and too outrageously directed at the physical being of the author.

At one point during the evening Daudet exclaims that he was really overcome with disgust for his colleague's writing one evening at Charpentier's at the time *Pot-Bouille* was being printed—an after-dinner gathering at which Madame Zola said to her husband: "Mimile, your book is *dirty*, really *dirty!*" Zola made no reply and Madame Charpentier, smiling broadly, let fall: "Come now, do you think it's all that bad?" And Charpentier, hilarious, patting his cheeks with both hands, chortled with laughter: "It will sell all the better for that!"

Sunday, August 21

Zola, who says in an interview with Xau that he wishes to make no reply to the *Manifesto of the Five*, indeed does reply, and here is the statement that concerns Daudet and me:

"What would be more interesting to know is what influence these these young people unconsciously received that led them so brusquely to break with someone who doesn't even know them. People have suggested that perhaps in their act we must discern the echo of certain criticisms emanating from people whom I hold in high literary and personal esteem, people who profess the same sentiments toward me. I refuse to credit this suggestion, whatever appearance of reality may be given it by several passages in the document, some relating to the great literary battle that still goes on, some having to do with me personally. On the contrary, I am certain that the persons to whom I refer are distressed at a published statement which received neither their inspiration nor their assent."

Isn't that like Zola? Isn't the statement characteristically Machiavellian, with perfidy cloaked in noisome good humor? Oh, the dirty Dago!

That kind of innuendo, which killed Robert Caze, has conveyed to readers of *L'Evénement* the suggestion that we might very well be the instigators of the *Manifesto*. And Rosny, who comes to see me today, tells me that in a *Réveil-Matin* article Bauër, no doubt intoxicated by the honor of having sat on Madame Zola's right at the supper after *Renée*, calls me—though not naming me—an old fakir who plotted all this behind a Japanese screen, impelled by the black envy of a man of letters whose writings have not found favor with the public.

Tonight at ten o'clock, just as I am about to go to bed, Geffroy is ushered in. Upset and pained by the savage attacks against me, he has come to read an article he has written, one which absolves us, Daudet and me, from any part in the *Manifesto*. But I ask him not to let it be published, saying that I do not want to make a reply, that I consider the accusation beneath my notice, that I knew absolutely nothing about the *Manifesto*, and that if I had felt a need to express myself in respect to Zola's writings, I would have done so openly, above my signature, since it is not in my nature to hide behind others.

Thursday, August 25

Geffroy came to have lunch with me today. He describes Céard as a police spy in Zola's pay, going to the newspapers to inspect the proofs of articles on the current literary quarrel before they appear, trying to soften the attacks and prevent them from being published, or at least learning them by heart so as to carry out his role of informer.

Thursday, September 29

Apropos of Margueritte's novel *Pascal Géfosse* Daudet was saying that at the present time, following the example of Bourget, there was a clutch of psychological novels, whose authors, imitating Stendhal, wished to set down not what the heroes of the novels were doing, but what they were thinking. Unfortunately, thoughts are boring unless they are superior or very original, whereas a mediocre action takes hold of and amuses the reader by reason of its movement. He added also that these psychologists were, willy nilly, more apt at description of externality than of internal phenomena, and that as a result of their literary training in the present day they were capable of depicting a gesture very well, and a movement of the soul rather badly.

Saturday, October 1

In the rage of aggressiveness which has taken hold of Drumont he has become a comic character. Nature is no more to him than a dueling ground. When he rented his house at Soisy, he exclaimed: "Ah, there's a fine garden in which to fight with pistols!" A certain path at Daudet's makes him say: "Oh, what a fine path for a duel with swords." And recently when marriage was being suggested to him, did he not reply: "Yes, very well, very well, that's fine, what you tell me about the young woman. But do you think she will get all upset when two gentlemen call for me some morning?"

Friday, October 7

Léon Daudet, who was with me on the train and who had been at Hugo's house on Guernsey when it was opened up, was telling me that the armoires were overflowing with condoms of gigantic size, and that it was rather embarrassing to spirit them away in Madame Charles Hugo's presence. They also discovered a series of amorous letters, addressed apparently not to Hugo but to Vacquerie, containing obscene drawings, cunt hairs, menstrual smears, letters—who would have believed it?—from Louise Michel in the days when she was a school teacher. These letters were presumably burned.

Tuesday, October 11

This evening the Théâtre Libre put on *Soeur Philomène*, an original play drawn from our novel by Jules Vidal and Arthur Byl.

I go there with Geffroy and Descaves. A most singular theatre. At the end of streets which look like suburban streets in the provinces where you seek out a brothel, there is a middle-class house and in that house a stage trodden by actors smelling of garlic as one has never been assailed by garlic on an omnibus of the Rue de Vaugirard. A strangely composed audience, quite unlike what you always find in the big theatres: some women, mistresses or wives of literary men and painters; some models—in short, what Porel calls a "studio audience." To my astonishment, the piece is well performed, and performed with all the charm of actors from good society. Antoine in the role of Barnier is marvelously natural. There is a "For God's sake!" which he does not toss out standing, but utters it as he is stretched out, half lying, on a table, and this "For God's sake!"—accentuating his defense of the saintly women—has a powerful effect. It is a success that brings down the house. The prayer scene, where the responses of the patients are interrupted by Romaine's dying song, is greeted by thunderous applause, by the emotion of an audience which has been deeply stirred. And do you know where the power of the play comes from, a power I had not anticipated on reading it? It comes from the mixing of the delicacy of feeling, style, and action with its realism of setting.

Zola, with whom I came face to face on the stage and to whom, damn it, I was anything but cordial, made two remarks that sum him up. He said to Raffaelli about my play: "Oh, right now in this theatre anything they put on would be a success!" And in my presence he said to somebody else: "As far as I am concerned, I am convinced that if a theatre director were to take this play, the censors would keep it from being performed!"

Thinking about the hostility—the literary injustice, I might say—shown by Turgenev toward Daudet and me, I find the reason for this injustice to lie in a quality shared by Daudet and my brother—irony. It is peculiar how foreigners, as well as provincials, are intimidated, embarrassed by this altogether Parisian gift and how they consciously take against people whose words conceal from them secrets and veiled mockery to which they do not possess the key. Turgenev, that subtle and distinguished intelligence, was at ease only with gross minds like those of Flaubert and Zola.

Sunday, October 30

Young Descaves confides to me that Zola passes every evening at the Théâtre Libre, that he has bought two season tickets, that he daily pays the most enormous compliments to Antoine, that he kisses the actresses in fatherly fashion, and that, in short, with the aid of his ass-licker Céard he is trying to take over the theatre. He tells me too that down inside Antoine is deeply hurt because I have not written to compliment him, and that even the actresses are a little miffed because I have never kissed them.

Thursday, December 22

I go to Didot's in the hope of receiving from Hébert some indication of satisfaction over the success of *Madame de Pompadour*. He tells me that sales are going very well but that my book has brought the Didot firm a slap from Brunetière's paw in *La Revue des Deux Mondes*. And I can see that these publishers for the Academy are upset by this attack, are almost blushing for having offered a volume on the mistress of Louis XV for the holiday gift trade. And I sense that in spite of the success of this volume they will not publish the other two in the series. I was thinking of the interesting, curious, and vengeful piece a young grind of a researcher could work up about the harm the Buloz dynasty has done to modern literature by the pens of its *hirelings*, Planche, Pontmartin, and Brunetière. Ah, that would make a fine book, without anger or insult, but full of facts—with a study in depth of the articles published by the review and of unpublished autograph correspondence, a history of the big and little infamies committed by that review against those who have ceased to belong to it—Gautier, Sand, etc.—and against all those who have refused to belong.

Thursday, December 29

After dinner I chat with Rodin, who tells me of his laborious life, rising at seven, going to his studio at eight, his work interrupted only by lunch and continuing until dark, work carried on standing or perched on a ladder, which leaves him worn out at night and ready for bed after an hour's reading.

He tells me about the illustrations for Baudelaire's poetry that he is doing for a collector, work that he would have liked to get "inside of" but was unable to, being paid too little—2,000 francs—and thus not able to give enough time to it. Moreover, for this book, which will receive no publicity and will remain shut up in the collector's cabinet, he feels no enthusiasm, none of the excitement he would have for illustrations commissioned by a publisher. And when I express the hope that he may some day illustrate *Venise la Nuit*, he points out that his forte is the nude, not clothed figures.

Next he discusses the medallion of my brother and asks me if I resemble him, saying that he would like to begin with a medallion of me; after that he would be more at ease making the medallion of my brother. And all the time that he is talking to me, I feel that he is observing me, studying me—drawing, sculpting, and etching me in his mind.

He goes on for a long time about his bust of Hugo, who did not pose but who let him come to him as often as he wished. He made a stack of rough sketches of the great poet—sixty, I think—from the right, the left, and above, but nearly all of them foreshortened, in attitudes of reading or meditation, sketches from which he was obliged to make the bust.

It is amusing to hear him recount the battles he had to fight in order to show the man as he saw him, the difficulties he encountered in getting permission from the family not to adopt their conventional idealization of the sublime writer, of his triple-domed forehead, etc., etc., in short, to be allowed to render and model his real mask and not the one which had been invented by literature.

1888

Monday, January 9

I spend the whole day supervising the planting of some forty peonies that Hayashi sent me from Japan and which, he informed me, are the most remarkable and rare species.

In the preface to his new novel [*Pierre et Jean*] Maupassant, in an attack on *artistic writing*, has singled me out without naming me. I had already discovered that his straightforwardness left something to be desired from his behavior over the Flaubert subscription and from his *Gil Blas* article. Today's attack comes at the same time as a letter in which, by mail, he expresses his admiration and devotion. All this forces me to believe that he is a Norman of Normans. Zola, indeed, had told me that he was the king of liars.

Now it may be that he is a very skillful storyteller about Normandy, in the manner of Monnier, but he is not a writer, and he has his reasons for depreciating *artistic writing*. A true writer, ever since La Bruyère, Bossuet, and Saint-Simon, coming down through Chateaubriand and ending with Flaubert, has his own signature and makes his writing recognizable to literate people without signing his name, and a man is a great writer only on this condition. Now a page of Maupassant is not signed, it is very simply just some good, ordinary copy such as anybody might write.

Last Sunday Guiches made the best assessment of the man's undeniable talent, though a talent of the second order. He said that Maupassant's books were read but not reread.

Friday, February 17

A dinner given to the sculptor Rodin by friends of his person and talent, a dinner at which I preside with a draft on my back.

Next to me is Clemenceau, with his round Kalmuk head, who tells me rather curious things about sick peasants in his provincial constituency and the open-air consultations they ask him for in the midst of his peregrinations through the department. As he was leaving one place, just as the horses of his break were about to go into a gallop, an enormous woman leaned across their croups and shouted: "Oh, sir, I suffer terribly from gas!" Whereupon the radical Deputy, whipping up his horses, shouted back: "Very well, my good woman, you must fart!"

Sunday, February 19

Today Rosny makes my flesh creep by his imaginings about books in which he will make blind men see by development of a frontal lobe, deaf men hear by means of electricity, etc., etc. A series of fantastico-scientifico-phono-literary books, somewhat derived from Poe. He certainly has a strange mind, and of all the minds of the *young* whom I know his is the most disposed and the most ready to produce something original and powerful.

Tuesday, February 21

Dinner with Loti at Daudet's.

Loti, the strange writer and the even stranger naval officer, heavily made up, his eyes embellished with the black that women use to make their eyes look velvety and dirtily sensual—a gaze which in Loti's case always turns away from you so that you never meet it, a gaze bizarrely in harmony with his toneless voice, which seems to be speaking in a room where someone is dying.

He had asked to bring his sailor friend to dinner with him, a pretty sailor who was so decolleté that, after the two men left, Madame Daudet said she was embarrassed.

Loti had no sooner come in than he declared that he was through, that perhaps he would publish a few more stories but that he would not publish any more volumes, since he felt himself completely worn out and empty. He said this in a tone of cold desperation with a melancholy and a discouragement with life so extreme that I have the presentiment that this man will have a dramatic end, perhaps suicide.

At one point he talked about the two hundred and fifty or three hundred drawings he had done for an edition of *Le Mariage de Loti* which Guillaume was to publish. Guillaume had the plates made by an imbecile engraver who turned his Tahitians into Parisian women, and he is now trying to get them done over.

Almost at once he went into a corner of the drawing room to talk to Madame Daudet about his wife, telling her that the latter, who was deaf in one ear before their marriage, became deaf in both afterwards and that he, loving above all strength, beauty, health, was very unhappy and felt something approaching aversion for his wife.

Then he left, after his sailor boy had shaken us all by the hand—damply.

What goes on in that brain, the brain of a man of talent? Where does the comedy begin? What is the truth about him? Is the homosexuality which he flaunts really sincere? Daudet sees in him the recoil and struggle of his Protestantism—he is from a Protestant family—against being caught up in infamous vices and low immorality.

Friday, April 6

Yesterday Léon Daudet described the domestic interior of Fournier, the son-in-law and successor of Ricord, a house always full of gaiety where at parties and dinners, they talk only about men's and women's natural parts and where, at balls, young girls can read titles such as *On Chancres* on books left wide open on the tables.

Antoine has dinner at Daudet's this evening. He is a slight, frail, nervous fellow with a rather debauched-looking nose and soft, velvety, altogether seductive eyes.

He tells me about his plans for the future. He wants two more full years devoted to productions like those he is now doing, two years during which he will thoroughly learn his craft and the business of running a theatre.

After that he is confident that he will get a theatre subsidized by the government; hoping to have at that point 600 subscribers, that is, an income of 60,000 francs, and with 100,000 francs, counting in a rent-free theatre, and the support of actors whom he will discover and pay modestly, he sees himself as director of a theatre where they will put on 120 acts a year. They will "spill out" on the boards everything that is at all dramatic from the portfolios of young writers. However successful a play may be, his idea is to put it on for only two weeks, after which the author will be free to take it to another theatre.

For his part, he would continue to act and would ask for a salary of only 12,000 francs, jealously keeping literary control of the theatre but giving over financial control to a committee.

And he joked about how a subscriber who contributed 100

francs might get a dividend of 200 to 300 francs if the venture had a little luck.

In this conception there is truly a new and original idea which could be very helpful to dramatic production, an idea worthy of the government's encouragement.

It is a real pleasure to listen to this young Antoine, who admits with a certain modesty that there is a lot of infatuation felt for him. You feel from his brilliant hallucinated eyes that he believes in his work, and there is something of the proselytizer in this actor, who already has completely won over his father, an old employe of the gas company, where the son also worked—a father who in the beginning was altogether hostile toward his dramatic efforts.

Friday, April 20

I was very happy over the announcement made in *Le Matin* that Réjane had been engaged for *Germinie Lacerteux*, but Porel informs me that this has not been settled. Charpentier tells me that Zola is furious because he has only a box and and eight seats for *Germinal*, that the director sold out the theatre for the day of the premiere for 30,000 francs, a sum representing roughly half the expenses he has incurred, and that as a result of this sale the authors risk having a half-empty house or an audience absolutely furious over the price they have had to pay for their seats.

Poetry, we must not forget, was in former days entirely a matter of the invention, the creation, the imagining of past times. Today there are still versifiers, but no more poets, for all the invention, all the creation, all the imagination of the present day is in its prose.

Monday, April 23

First a session at the Musée Carnavalet to prepare the illustrations for *La Société Française pendant la Révolution*, which the Quantin firm is definitely putting out for the centennial of 1789. Then from the Rue Sévigné to the Quai Malaquais and the Exposition of Caricature at the Beaux Arts.

The first person whom I run into is Pierre Gavarni, as upset and angry as I at the injustice toward his father's talent committed by the entire press. And he has to agree that I predicted everything that is happening now and that I vigorously urged him to set up an exhibition of his father's work alone, and not with Daumier. For I had no doubt that with Daumier, the pure, the republican, they would belabor Gavarni, the corrupt, the reactionary. But indeed the poleaxing has gone even further than I expected. The man who made the *Vireloque* drawings has been called an illustrator for confectioners. Oh, our contemporary art criticism!

Tuesday, May 8

La Revue Indépendante gives a passage from George Moore's *Confessions* in which, reporting the scurrilous remarks at the Café de la Nouvelle Athènes, or rather remarks by Degas, he asserts that I am not an artist.

Oh, those fine Impressionists! Nobody else is an artist! Funny artists, who have never been able to *realize* anything. Now the difficult thing in art is realization: a work pushed to that degree of finish which takes it beyond the rough sketch and turns it into a picture. Yes, makers of outlines, of blobs—and blobs, moreover, which are not their invention but are stolen from Goya, from the Japanese. And the pretentiousness of these Impressionists! How amusing it is to hear a Degas declare that all current literature is inspired by painting, Degas, whose success was based on his laundresses and dancers during those years when I was suggesting to genre painters, in *Manette Salomon*, these two categories of women as vehicles for the nude and creamy white. Degas, that constipated painter, that man of meannesses labored over and worked out during nights when he cannot sleep because of his failures. Degas, the scrounger, the poor bugger whom I have described in his relations with the de Nittis!

Indeed it is too stupid. I am not an artist! Then among modern writers who is?

Friday, May 25

Ah, if I still had a few years left to live I would like to write a book on Japanese art of the sort that I did on eighteenth-century art, one which would be less documentary than the latter, one going further in a penetrating and revelatory description of things. This book would be made up of four studies: one on Hokusai, the modern renewer of ancient Japanese art; one on Utamaro, their Watteau; one on Korin and another on Ritsono, two celebrated painters and lacquerists. To these four studies I might join a fifth on Gakutei, the great artist of *surimonos,* a man who in his delicate color prints has succeeded in joining the charm of Persian miniatures with that of European miniatures of the Middle Ages.

Sunday, June 3

As Bonnetain comes in he asks me: "Have you seen this morning's *L'Evénement*?" "No." "Well, it is shameful! There is an article on Madame Daudet which states that she has no talent, that she dyes her hair, and that the only reason she is friendly toward you is her hope of an inheritance." "Is it signed?" " 'Vertuchou.' " "Could that be Vignier?"

And then comes Ajalbert, who, speaking of his duel, says that he had to wait for Vignier at the dueling ground for an hour and a quarter and that his seconds refused to accept this hour of nervous waiting on his account. And he tells amusingly about this duel which did not come off and cost him 250 francs. His landau cost him sixty francs, since the duel took place on the day of the Flower Festival. Then going to pick up Fleury, who was to be present as a doctor, he came to Sainte Périne, also in the middle of the festival, the mangy and infirm denizens of the place all decked in flowers.

We come back to the *Evénement* article and the responsibility which should fall on that purveyor of scandalous articles, and I think, without saying it out loud, that Léon Daudet should give Magnier a beating with a lead-weighted cane and challenge him to a duel, and after that seek out the author of the article and put a bullet or two in his carcass without doing him the honor of any further ceremony. Yes, there ought to be the kind of execution carried out here of a mad dog, and in America of a *blackmailing* journalist.

What court would dare condemn a son who would cleanse his mother of such odious calumnies by means of blood—the decent and excellent woman that Madame Daudet is?

Wednesday, June 6

I am getting ready to leave for Champrosay, in a state of anxiety as to whether they know about the article in *L'Evénement*. I hear the rumble of a carriage; it is Léon Daudet, who is coming to pick me up. The Daudets do know about the article; Lorrain has stupidly and tactlessly sent them a copy of the paper with a note saying he is not the author. Madame Daudet is in a terrible state, and Léon adds: "It's on that account that this morning I did two hours of fencing and target practice." And he speaks of his desire to kill one of those swine, though he is prevented for the moment by his father's age. But he hopes "soon and under any pretext at all to finish one of them off!"

I find Madame Daudet a figure of desolation. She leads me down a path and says with a feverish excitement which verges on madness: "It's incredible that they don't defend my honor, for I am a decent woman. It is strange that Alphonse, who is always so prickly on his own account, is not sensitive over the insult to me!" And, her husband appearing, she accuses him of being the cause of the attack on her by reason of his aggressive novels. Then she begins to rave like a poor creature that has been mortally wounded and demands that an article be written reestablishing the truth about her.

I point out to her that an article answering the one in *L'Evénement* would only serve to publicize the insults directed at her, that her honorableness, her respectability ought to make her disdain these low calumnies, and that the article arises above all from the fact that she has talent. But I sense that she is not listening to me, that my words do not get through to her.

Thursday, June 7

This morning Daudet comes into my room and says:

"After carefully thinking it over, I have come to a decision. I must act. In the beginning my first instinct was to do nothing, but in the face of the deep grief that my wife feels, I believe that I owe vengeance for her pain. Frantz Jourdain is coming this morning. I will ask him to be my second. I shall take Gouvet, of whom I am sure. I also have Drumont available, but he is too much a bringer of bad luck. Obviously I cannot fight with a sword; I would be ridiculous; I would fall down. With swords people would pity me as an old man. I will fight with pistols, and my conditions are these: at fifteen paces—I think that is all I can get—and the pistols to be reloaded until one of us falls."

In reply to my observation that this really makes no sense, for a man of his worth to fight a Magnier, he replies: "No, I have completely made up my mind. I am going to see Frantz Jourdain, who ought to be downstairs with the workmen. Now, get dressed; in an hour we are going to buy some fish in Corbeil."

I find Daudet in the garden with Frantz Jourdain, and Jourdain and I ask him to consider it sufficient satisfaction if Magnier consents to condemn the author of the article. Madame Daudet then appears, and her husband tells her that he will definitely write the article she asked him for last night and that he will be going to Paris tomorrow.

We set out for Corbeil, and on the way, after a silence, he says to me: "As for me, with my novels, it is natural that all sorts of misadventures should happen to me, but she has done nothing to deserve such an outrage. You know she has spent two nights in tears. And then, you know, my life, stricken as I am, I enjoy so few things!" After which he becomes once more the gay, waggish, amusing Daudet of ordinary days, with a relaxed air that is not put on, preoccupied only about how he will be able to return to Paris on the day of the duel without upsetting his wife or having his son guess. He ends by saying: "Bah, I'll tell them I am going to correct the proofs of my article!"

After lunch, in a final effort to prevent the duel, I address myself to Madame Daudet, who is somewhat more calm and has recovered some of her equanimity by reason of my presence, and I say to her: "Come, now, Madame Daudet, now that the painful crisis is over you ought to try to get your husband to give up his article." And in fact she does what I ask. But when I go out, Daudet tells her that he now believes the appearance of that article to be absolutely necessary.

Daudet has stayed at Champrosay today because it is the day of their at home. As we are getting ready to go to meet the people coming by train, poor Madame Daudet confesses to us that she had thought of going to Paris in order to avoid seeing anyone, because of the shame she feels over the attack made upon her. We tease her, and she decides to come with us. But on reaching the gate to the park she refuses to go out and awaits her guests seated on a bench in the shade.

The first arrivals are Léon and Geffroy, then another train brings us Bonnetain and Rosny, soon followed by Drumont, whom Léon and Geffroy had tried to pick up at home. And all during dinner Daudet is the man of daring and lively wit of ordinary days. After dinner there is a spirited discussion about a pictorial feeling for landscapes, which Rosny and I say was not evidenced in antiquity. Daudet cites Vergil in opposition to our claim; and the evening ends in a battle about Rousseau's talent.

At night when Daudet in his nice way comes up to my room to see me into bed as is his custom, in answer to my remarks about his wife's calming down, to my urging that he give up this encounter which he did not at first intend and to which he had been spurred by his wife's anger and grief, he replies: "No, my dear friend, it would just start up all over again."

Friday, June 8

Daudet has left, and in the tranquil silence of the house you hear only the weak cries of fledgling birds and Edmée's little stumbling steps on the gravel of the garden paths. And while my thoughts are on Daudet's arrival in Paris, his meeting with his seconds, and the conditions set for this duel to the death, Madame Daudet, with smiling face, comes up to me and says that she is glad she followed my advice and that certainly it will be supported by Gille, whom her husband has gone to consult, and when he gives up his idea of a letter to *Le Figaro*, we will have no further complications to fear.

At lunch Edmée keeps repeating: "Papa not here?" while Madame Daudet, with complete serenity, explains to me that if Daudet is lunching at Gille's it may be that he will not return by the four o'clock train but rather by the one at six.

And at six there is Daudet getting off the train, red in the face, walking very badly, and speaking with a jerky voice. To begin with, he is furious at Brinn' Gaubast, his son's tutor, who, without informing Daudet, and passing himself off as the latter's secretary, took the liberty of asking Magnier to reply to the *Evénement* article. . . .

Up in my room he tells me that his seconds have seen Magnier, who wished to get out of it and push it off on the author of the article. But Gouvet cut him off short and said: "You are well aware that M. Alphonse Daudet cannot have M. 'Vertuchou,' 'Vertugadin,' 'Vertu-what-ever-you-call-him' as his adversary." Then Magnier arranged for Scholl and Henry Houssaye to be his seconds. "The annoying thing," he bursts out, "is that I had to come back without knowing how the discussion among the seconds came out. Tomorrow I shall arrive in Paris not knowing whether I am to receive satisfaction or whether I am to fight."

And we have dinner to the gay sallies of the elder son, who had lunched at Bonnetain's and who, knowing nothing of what has occurred, tosses out to his father: "Papa, did you have champagne at lunch today?"

At that moment they bring in a telegram. I am all eyes as I watch Daudet read it and then toss it onto the table as he says to his wife: "Yes, you will get it, the article that you have asked for!" I cannot help getting up from the table and going over to embrace him. Madame Daudet looks at me in astonishment.

"Yes," I say to the people at the table, who are all looking at me. "Yes, indeed, I have had a bad night and a bad day. He didn't go to Paris about an article, but about a duel!"

"What? And that story about lunch at Gille's was not true?" Madame Daudet exclaims.

"That was the bad part of my situation," Daudet answers. "For the rest . . . but all those lies, that was hateful."

And Léon cannot refrain from exclaiming: "It's all right for you to have deceived Mama. But me! you certainly pulled the wool over my eyes!"

What odd, bizarre creatures women are! After such a happy ending one would have thought there would be a joyful, tender evening. Not at all. Surprise and emotion about what could have happened put Madame Daudet in such a nervous state that, when we begin talking about the *Evénement* article again and Daudet makes the mistake of saying that he did not think the article merited a duel and that he was impelled to demand satisfaction only when he saw the extent of her unhappiness, Madame Daudet, getting more and more excited and not realizing what she is saying—words she would take back a few minutes later—goes so far as to declare that it was worth the death of a man. When we all protest, and Daudet asserts that in their interpretation of some things respectable women are imbeciles, Madame Daudet gets up and leaves, after having thrown out at me, in reference to a statement of mine in support of her husband: "All right, you may as well bludgeon me too!" She comes back a few instants later but does not say a word to me for the rest of the evening.

As I was beginning to undress she came up to my room with

her husband and, all in tears, with suffering in her soft eyes, asked me to pardon her for having hurt me.

Sunday, June 10

A walk with Daudet this morning in the Forest of Sénart.

"Yes, it's only my cock that makes me do things that are not nice . . . and then too the pleasure of being immoral. Oh, I am vicious!" And he tells me how he screwed a young cousin at the very moment her mother was on the point of death from an overdose of laudanum.

And we talk of the incitation to screwing brought about by great emotions, even painful ones. In this connection he cites the story of Madame X . . ., who, knowing her son saved, began to squeeze him, Daudet, in her arms, began to kiss him, and, throwing herself down before him on a chaise longue, stretched out full length with her skirts pulled up. Then Naquet came to call and the lady was obliged to see him, but her hands were patting Daudet's hands for the whole time of the visit.

Saturday, June 23

The Daudets are concerned about the existence of a love affair between Jeanne Hugo and Léon, and are even a little upset about the place their son has in the affections of Jeanne's mother and brother. They said to me very sincerely this evening: "Yes, if this marriage took place, we would be afraid for our child's future, and we would rather see him marry a young girl like Mademoiselle Pillaut, who would bring him a dowry of a hundred thousand francs. For Léon has a future as a great doctor," Daudet adds. "Do you know how Potain introduced him to the Hugos' family doctor, who considered him a mere youngster? 'Here is the doctor who is going to replace us, the doctor of tomorrow.' "

Saturday, July 28

In the world of letters "Troublot" [Paul Alexis] is truly about the only defender of real talent and things literarily clean. His intimacy with Zola has never prevented him from tooting Daudet's horn and mine whenever he found an occasion to do so, and his intimacy with Zola has not prevented him from directly reproaching the latter, reproaching him really harshly for his apostasy. What a shame that in his prose this fine, upright man, who is so enamored of justice, seems to feel the need to use the slang of criminals, which is not at all necessary to the success of his literary supplement pieces!

Friday, September 7

The current success of the Russian novel is due to the irritation felt by right-thinking literary people over the success of the French *naturist* novel. They have cast about for something with which to counter this success. Yet, without doubt, it is the same kind of literature: the reality of things human seen from a sad, human, nonpoetic point of view.

And neither Tolstoy nor Dostoevsky nor the others invented this literature! They took it from Flaubert, from me, from Zola, with a vigorous crossbreeding from Poe. Oh, if one of those Dostoevsky novels which they admire so much, toward whose *gloom* they are so indulgent, were signed Goncourt, what a crushing attack there would be right down the line! Now the man who has devised this skillful diversionary tactic, who has so unpatriotically enlisted sympathy for a foreign literature—yes, robbing us of the admiration which is our due—that man is M. de Vogüé.[15] So he has deserved

[15] Vicomte E.-M. de Vogüé, whose *Le Roman Russe*, 1886, introduced Gogol, Turgenev, Tolstoy, and Dostoevsky to French and European readers. He was elected to the Academy in 1889.

well of the Academy, which will shortly take him to its bosom!

Friday, September 21

For three days running all the paper has been removed from the toilet and all I can find to use is the same four "Sonnets Insolents" by Brinn' Gaubast as published in *Le Décadent*. That gentleman is so complicated that I am convinced that it is a device he has thought up to make me read his poems!

Tuesday, December 4

Now the attack on my play [*Germinie Lacerteux*] is getting under way and the newspapers are already encouraging hissing. Today *L'Echo de Paris* describes in advance the affront to the modesty of actresses who have to play Germinie and indicates that Réjane has to pronounce the word "whore." When I think of Zola's bad faith in choosing this moment to sing the praises of journalism. Indeed, if the proprietors of the cafés in the Latin Quarter take sides with the journalists, poor *Germinie Lacerteux* will have the fate of *Henriette Maréchal*. Yes, the café owners of the area are furious because there is only one intermission—something which I want to introduce into the theatre—which reduces to one the five glasses of beer consumed when there are five acts and five [sic] intermissions.

Porel announces today that *Germinie* is to have its first performance on December 15.

Friday, December 7

There is a delay in the rehearsal today. I go to look at the sketch for my portrait by Bracquemond in the new Luxembourg Museum. And when, because of my interest in two or three paintings there, I buy the catalogue, I am astonished to see that my portrait is merely entitled "Portrait," no more. Emmanuel Arago is director of the museum, and we once had a little sparring match over *Henriette Maréchal* and the old gentleman at the Opéra ball disrespectfully compared to Lafayette's white horse. Is this a petty vengeance by the former writer for *Le Siècle*?

Porel was summoned by the censors today. He had to leave the rehearsal and asked me to wait for him in order to know the outcome. After the rehearsal it got later and later. I left Réjane, who insisted on waiting for him, in his office and went on my way, wishing to spare myself an angry night. Tomorrow we shall see what happened.

Saturday, December 8

I take the censor's manuscript home with me from the theatre so that I can make a copy. Could anyone imagine that on the eve of the hundredth anniversary of 1789 a theatre director would have to do battle with the censorship commission for a good quarter of an hour in order to keep in this sentence: "My baby is about to come"!

Tuesday, December 18

This morning a bitter-sweet note in *L'Echo de Paris*. Yesterday at the Odéon Gouzien had already told me about the bad feelings among the journalists caused by the cancellation of the dress rehearsal.

All day spent coughing and working on my piece against censorship.

This evening I receive a letter from Magnard, who was to have printed the preface to my play in *Le Figaro* tomorrow, saying that he can't do it because a part of it appeared in *L'Evénement* this morning.

Wednesday, December 19

I certainly fear that with the cancellation of the dress rehearsal and *Le Figaro's* refusal of the preface to my play the game is off to a bad start.

All morning and afternoon I labor to finish my petition to the Chamber of Deputies, a piece that I have written with my nerves and which I consider one of the best things I have done.

Really, for a man who is approaching sixty-seven, it's not bad, the amount of energy I put out! But I have a presentiment that after the performance I shall collapse all of a sudden.

Fine! when I leave my house there is a fog which makes me fear that carriages will be unable to circulate this evening.

To kill time before dinner, I go to Bing's, where I cannot keep my eyes on the prints that Lévy is showing me or refrain from pacing the room as I talk about this evening.

At six-thirty—today is Madame Daudet's at home—I find there Madame de Bonnières, who had already called on me last Sunday. She shows that she would very much like to be invited to the supper which the Daudets are giving this evening in honor of *Germinie*. But she is not invited because then it would be necessary to invite Magnard, and Daudet and I think that we should not appear to be trying to influence the reviews by inviting journalists to this supper.

Dinner over, there I am with the Daudets in Porel's stage box, away in the back and invisible to such a degree that Scholl, who comes to chat with Daudet, does not see me as he leans against the edge of the box.

"The Odéon has never had such a firstnight audience," Porel says to me.

The play begins. There are two expressions in the first tableau which I had counted on to reveal the audience's attitude. They are "an old bag like me" and "the kids whose behinds one has wiped." They get by, and I conclude that the audience is well disposed.

During the second tableau some hissing and the beginning of a feeling of outraged modesty on the part of the audience. "Now we get a whiff of gun powder. I like that!" Porel says in a tone which is not really very enthusiastic about gun powder.

Daudet goes out in order to calm down his son, whom he sees seated in the orchestra ready to do battle, and returns shortly with an angry face and with Léon, who says that his father was so belligerent in the corridors that he was afraid he would get into a fight. Really deeply touched, I look at father and son, each preaching moderation to the other and each one equally furious inside.

The battle between the hissers and the applauders, among whom I see some ministers and their wives, continues during the tableau at the Boule Noire dance hall and the tableau at Jupillon's glove shop. Finally we reach the tableau of the dinner for the little girls.

There, I confess, I thought I was safe. But there the hissing redoubles. They don't want to listen to Madame Crosnier's lines; they shout: "Beddy-bye, kids!" And for a moment I have the painful expectation that they will not allow the play to finish. Oh, how hard that was to take! For, as I had told my friends, while I did not know what the fate of my play would be, what I wanted, all I asked, was to give battle, and I was afraid that it would not go all the way to the end. Finally Réjane imposes silence with the scene of the borrowing of the forty francs.

I slip backstage for a moment, and I see two of my little actresses, so cruelly buffeted by this pitiless audience, weeping against a flat.

In the midst of all that uproar and determination not to listen, Réjane, to whom perhaps I owe having been able to see the end of my play, manages to make herself heard and applauded in the scene where the money is brought to save Jupillon from conscription.

During the tableaus that follow it becomes a real battle, in the midst of which—when Mademoiselle de Varandeuil says: "Oh, if I had only known, I would have buried you in rags, you trollop!"—a woman's outraged voice is raised and evokes a hubbub of indignation. And the voice is that of Marie Colombier, a notorious and well-known whore.

For that matter, the indignation of the men at this premiere is of pretty much the same quality. There is Vitu, who is in his box with his mistress and son. There is Fouquier, whom everyone supposes to be his wife's daughter's lover. There is Koning, who started out by being the Jupillon of sixty-year-old Déjazet, of Page, and of I don't know what other old women. There is Blavet, Blavet the lowest of the low.

At the end when Dumény wishes to speak my name, the audience refuses absolutely to let it be uttered, as though it dishonored French literature, and Dumény has to wait a long time, a very long time; he has to take advantage of a lull in the hissing to toss out my name, and I must say he tosses it out defiantly, as a man might flip his calling card at someone who had insulted him.

I remained clear to the end, in the back of my box, without showing any signs of weakness but thinking sadly that my brother and I were not born under an auspicious star. I was astonished and touched at the fall of the curtain by the handshake of a man who had been hostile toward me, a strong and comforting handshake by Bauër.

The people lost in the fog are reunited around the tables

at Daudet's supper party, tables on which have been placed the four pheasants with magnificent plumage sent to me by Comtesse Greffulhe "because of their Japanese nuances."

To my astonishment, Lockroy, who is not staying for supper, comes over for a moment to congratulate me on the play.

Everybody is gay. We do not feel that the battle has been completely lost. And I forget the evening's setback in my satisfaction at having seen the piece played through to the end. Supper goes on for a long time, as we discuss the evening's incidents.

Mariéton, who paid twenty-five francs for a parterre seat, saw someone pay 190 francs apiece for the last two seats in the orchestra.

Somebody heard an imbecile partisan of noble prose exclaim in the corridors: "Ah, if the Germans were to see this play!"

Wolff, who sat behind young Hugo, punched him in the back with his cane in friendly fashion and said: "It's a shame for Hugo's grandson to applaud this!" He received a reply something like this: "I beg your pardon, sir; we do not know each other well enough for you to speak to me so familiarly."

They say that the poet Haraucourt lambasted the play out loud all the time; moreover, when it was over, as he paused by the ticket gate, he said to I don't know who: "Oh, you are having supper with Daudet? If it is as amusing as the play, it won't be much fun!" Whereupon Geffroy relates that one time when Haraucourt was staying at Rollinat's country place, it was his habit to loll around completely naked in his room all day long, which caused Rollinat's mother to send him away.

In the midst of the conversation, which becomes very noisy, suddenly Zola's voice can be heard as he says: "To Edmond de Goncourt and to the memory of Jules de Goncourt!" I am deeply touched, and I thank Zola with feeling as, looking at Daudet, I think I divine from his expression that he too perceives a good deal of suppressed emotion in this toast.

Friday, December 21

I connect an anonymous letter I have just received telling me how Dumas, Sardou, and Halévy made fun of my lack of success with what Pélagie told me yesterday morning. She was right at the top of the Odéon, sitting next to a young couple who spent all their time saying that the play was a horror, at best suitable to be put on in Belleville. At one point the woman asked Pélagie if she knew Dumas and if she saw him in the audience. Then the husband went down to see if he could find him, and on his return his wife asked him if he had succeeded. He answered yes, but since the woman had seen Pélagie and her daughter applauding, she gestured to her husband to keep his voice down, and Pélagie did not hear the rest of the conversation. That's odd, that couple going to get their orders from Dumas!

A note from Daudet informing me that at last night's performance they shouted: "Down with Vitu!"

A friendly visit by Réjane, smiling and happy, who is sorry I did not attend the performance last night, a second performance at which the play picked up completely. She is kind enough to say that if she has had a success she owes it in part to the prose which underlies her role, her lines.

She tells me that Derenbourg, the director of Les Menus-Plaisirs, confided to her that on the eve of the opening he was dining at a house he did not want to name, where they said: "The play must not be allowed to close tomorrow!"

Coming back to yesterday's applause and curtain calls, she confides to me that in the feverish happiness she and Porel felt they went out to supper like two school kids and that in the cab Porel did not stop repeating: "Two thousand five hundred francs of box-office receipts today . . . after this morning's press . . . I was not mistaken . . . I am not a doddering fool!"

Monday, December 24

After telling me that Sunday night was good, Porel informs me that Charcot hissed from his stage box. Charcot, in the important position he occupies, can you imagine him hissing? Does he hold it against me that ever since I became a writer I have worked with nervous disorders? Would he like to be the only man in the world to stake out a claim to this subject? When you get down to it, he is a man of low origins who will always be a student and will never be able to rise to the level of gentleman.

Porel adds, with an astonishment he cannot conceal, that *Le Figaro,* in the battle to the death it is waging against me, will not even accept paid advertisements announcing the receipts of *Germinie Lacerteux,* and that it is the same for *Le Temps* and *Le Petit Journal.*

Someone from Bing's who was present at the premiere tells me that in front of him was a row of old and young men belonging to a Catholic club, who, by the way, had paid twelve francs for their seats; they argued about the novel and hissed the play. It is odd that there should be this hostility of the clerical world toward a play which contains a fine passage in honor of the priest, who is the only person to listen to the sorrows of the woman of the people.

Sunday [*sic*], *December 26*

I read in an evening paper about a session of the Senate at which the Right, the whole Right, demanded that my play be closed.

Monday, December 31

All my intimate friends are busy taking candy to Réjane and the other actresses and to the eight little girls who are in my play.

Marpon, whom I run into at the entrance to his shop on the Boulevard des Italiens, informs me that the matinee of *Germinie Lacerteux* was canceled by order of the Ministry and that most of the people who had bought tickets asked for their money back when they were offered *Le Lion Amoureux* [by Ponsard] instead of *Germinie.*

1889

Sunday, January 13

This evening Porel comes into the box where Daudet and his wife are with me since they wanted to see the play again. He tells us that there are things going on such as we could not imagine, about which he will tell us at length some day. Moreover, he says that he received on Saturday, only on Saturday, a telegram informing him that as the result of a decision made by the Council of Ministers the next day's matinee, announced several days earlier, was canceled. He at once went to the Ministry and demanded that he be permitted to put "By Order" on a poster. But the Ministry did not have the courage to acknowledge the decision which Carnot had imposed upon it and refused permission for "By Order."

An incontestable proof of Carnot's hostility toward the play is this. He went to the opening of *Henri III* [by Dumas *père*], as a gesture of protest against my play at the Odéon, and there in his box at the Comédie Française he summoned the director of Beaux Arts and, in front of the people present, said it was shameful to have allowed *Germinie Lacerteux* to be put on.

This week Porel has again asked permission to give *Germinie* at matinees, but Lockroy has refused, begging him not to insist and telling him he cannot imagine all the difficulties the Minister has had over this play.

Finally, it is definite that the Ministry has sent its agents to the performances to study the audience and find out by its attitude if the play could be suppressed.

Thursday, February 21

Back on good terms with Anatole France, who, in answer to a remark I make about the article he wrote in *Le Temps* after my brother's death, tells me that he is sorry about that "stupid article" and that he is very happy about our reconciliation, adding as a postscript to the conversation that he "admires me."

Tuesday, March 12

The Eiffel Tower makes me conclude that monuments built of iron are not *human* monuments, or at any rate not monuments of the old humanity, which for the construction of its dwellings knew only stone and wood. Then too in iron monuments the flat parts are always frightfully ugly. When one looks at the first platform of the Eiffel Tower with that row of double sentry boxes, there is nothing one can imagine more ugly to the eye of a man of the old civilization, and the iron monument is bearable only in those openwork parts which look like rope netting.

Monday, April 1

There is no doubt about it, and I may as well admit it. At the revival of *Henriette Maréchal* all the young were with me. I hold them still, but not all of them.[16] The Decadents, al-

[16] One of those whom he still held was Romain Rolland, whose undated letter he quotes on December 25, 1888. Rolland states that he and

though they owe something to my style, have turned against me. Then also in today's youth there is a curious side that differentiates them from the youth of other epochs. They do not wish to recognize fathers and progenitors, and by the time they are twenty, in the first stammering expression of their talent, they consider themselves the *discoverers* of everything. This is youth in the image of the Republic; they wipe out the past.

Monday, June 10

All this hurried rolling of wheels, all this congestion of carriages on the public streets leading to the Exposition; this seems to me like a nightmare of activity.

I stop in at Stevens' panorama; he has asked my consent to retouch my scraggly moustache. Indicating the dominant place he has given me in the naturalist group, he says: "That will annoy people, but I wanted you placed there as the *papa*!" However, if I had known that he would separate me from my brother, I would not have lent him my head.

Saturday, June 15

Then Mirbeau turns the conversation to Bourget, who aspires to the Academy—as everybody knows—but who aspires even more to belong to the Jockey Club. He tells us that Bourget has a very special physiological peculiarity, that he has a little duct in his liver which permits him to throw up basins of bile. Taking me to one side and alluding to the letter he received from Bourget after his ferocious article in

---

other students had come to the play as a gesture of protest against the miserable cabal which was attacking Goncourt "in order to force the respect due to your talent. We did not come to applaud. But your play gripped us, stood us on our heads, aroused our enthusiasm."

Le Figaro, Mirbeau says to me: "I will show the letter to you, because you know that I like women, but I would not dare show it to others. One could believe from the tenderness of his reproaches that we had had homosexual relations." Oh, what a gentle fellow he is, and what a miserable character Bourget is!

Sunday, June 23

Many people at my house. Madame Pardo-Bazán, in better health and more resounding than ever, tells me that she has definitely found a publisher for her translation of *Les Frères Zemganno*, which will be illustrated by the most celebrated Spanish black-and-white artist of the moment.

With regard to the joint exhibition of works of Rodin and Monet, it appears that some terrible scenes have occurred in which gentle Rodin, suddenly exhibiting a Rodin unknown to his friends, shouted: "I don't give a damn about Monet; I don't give a damn about anybody; I care only about myself!"

Friday, September 20

This evening during dinner Drumont, asking each of us for three francs for his enterprise of "rendering the fat out of finance," bursts out:

"Oh, if someone would only subscribe 50,000 francs . . ."

"Well, then, what would you buy with it?"

"An uprising against the Jews. Yes, after a few days of warming up the populace, when things had reached a fever pitch, a rendezvous at the Place de la Concorde. And from there to the Rue Saint Honoré, shattering windows and breaking in doors, and if an Alphonse de Rothschild happened to be caught . . . you get it!"

And Drumont spends the rest of the evening naively asking

Daudet and his wife for information about bird calls so as to put a bit of nature in his next book.

Sunday, October 20

This morning a visit by the Danish critic Brandes, who tells me of my popularity in his country and in Russia. He expresses his astonishment at the *snobbism* he has observed in Taine and Bourget.

Thursday, November 21

Today Paul Alexis, who has come along with Oscar Méténier to submit to me the first act of *Charles Demailly*, confirms with certainty that Zola has a *petit ménage*. The latter apparently told him that his wife had fine qualities as a housekeeper but was *refrigerating* in other respects, which had caused him to seek a little *warmth* elsewhere. And Alexis speaks of the resurgence of youth, the rage for enjoyment of all sorts and for satisfaction of worldly vanities occurring in this old writer, who recently asked Céard whether in twelve lessons he would be able to learn how to ride horseback well enough to take a turn through the Bois. Oh, an equestrian Zola, that I cannot see!

Thursday, December 12

Loti, who has come to town to make his Academy visits, dines with me. He has seen twenty members of the Academy, all of whom were "very nice" to him, Doucet as well as the others, but the latter reproached him for a *tendency toward originality*.

Sunday, December 15

Prosecution of Descaves at the instigation of the Minister of War has been announced. Soon, therefore, because of a novel attacking the corporation of bailiffs an author will be haled into court at the demand of the Minister of Justice, and because of a novel attacking embassy attachés an author will be prosecuted by the Minister of Foreign Affairs; for a novel lambasting schoolmasters there will be prosecution by the Minister of Public Instruction, etc., etc. That's the way it will be for any novel showing up the swinishness of any group, for all the corporative bodies of the State come under some ministry.

In any event, Descaves owes me a fine candle for having forced him to change the name of his book and for giving him the title *Sous-Offs* in place of *Les Culs Rouges*, which was the original title! Such a title killed all possibility of discussion, all polemics, since it made any mention of the book impossible.

Sunday, December 29

Descaves, whom I have not seen since the appearance of his book, comes to my *Grenier* today. He still has the rough, growling manner of a young drummer boy, but today it is tinged with melancholy. He has received his summons to appear before the examining magistrate on a Monday; and a policeman, upsetting his family, has come to get his pay-book to bring it up-to-date—that is, to have him stricken from the rolls. He tells us that swine Quesnay de Beaurepaire himself took the novel to Sarrut, who is the most considerable and the most respected lawyer at the Palais de Justice, asking the latter to read the book and to report next day whether he was ready to prosecute "with the greatest energy," and that Sarrut replied in the affirmative. The latter's acceptance is a very bad augury for him. He asserts rather forlornly that sales, which have now reached 14,000, are not in proportion to the uproar about the book and adds bitterly that in more than two hundred articles about it there are not thirty lines which discuss the literary quality of the work.

He has been wise enough to withdraw his play *L'Envers du Galon* from the Théâtre Libre; this act evoked a bitter-sweet letter from Antoine, who wrote that it was a retreat, and one which appeared to justify the prosecution.

1890

Sunday, February 16

Léon Daudet, who has come to take me to dinner, tells me in the brougham as we are riding along about young Hugo's extravagant escapades with women, about the heritage of eroticism which he has from his grandfather and father, and about the terrific debts he is contracting and the fantastic IOU's he signs after a bottle of champagne, in short, about the imminent dissipation of his fortune. In this connection, he tells me there is a "black band" associated with the great courtesans, made up of men who are at one and the same time the business agents of these women and lenders of money at usurious rates to the young men who keep the women.

Monday, February 24

It appears that young Hugo's excesses are abominable! How much he has eaten up of his personal fortune and the fortunes of his mother and sister nobody knows. It is impossible to get to the bottom of his affairs, and there have been distraints on the whole Hugo group, including the salary of Lockroy's deputy, who has nothing else to live on. With the blindness of maternal love, Lockroy's wife kept all this secret as long as she could; and when Lockroy sent the police into this den of usury, into whose hands almost the whole of the four millions left by Father Hugo has disappeared, it was already too late. Moreover, it has been discovered that among the "black band" of usurers there are some big decorators, some formidable jewelers from the boulevards, in short, important businessmen whom the government is afraid to prosecute.

In the midst of this distress, this ruin of a family, his sister, sweet Jeanne, accepts no invitations to balls because she has nothing with which to buy dresses, and he without enjoyment continues his senseless life and melancholy debauches. Thursday he did not come to dinner at the Daudets' because he was dining with la Brandès, whom he was going to sleep with.

Wednesday, March 5

Descaves accompanied by his wife comes to see me today. He is afraid that things are going badly for him. It has got back to him that since there is no certainty of a conviction for his attack on the Army, the prosecution is going to place its whole emphasis on outrage to public morals. And when one of his lawyers asked him how long a prison term he expected and he replied, "Three months," the lawyer said: "Triple that at least. You will get a year!" He is at once very sad and very much annoyed, declaring that the injustice of it is exasperating and that there is no reason for him to be condemned when Méténier and Mendès are not prosecuted for their latest novels.

Wednesday, March 12

"What are you doing now, Zola?" I asked the author of *La Bête Humaine*, who had just sat down beside me in the course of the evening.

"Well, nothing. I simply cannot get down to it. *L'Argent* is so vast that I don't know where to take hold of it. And I am embarrassed, more than ever before, about how to find the documents for this book, where to strike out for them. Oh, I would like to be done with these last three books. After *L'Argent* will come *La Guerre*; it will not be a novel but a promenade by a man through the Siege and the Commune, without any plot. But really the book which draws me, which attracts me, is the last one, in which I shall place a scientist on stage. I would like to draw this scientist after Claude Bernard and make use of his papers and letters. It will be fun. I shall portray a scientist with a bigoted and reactionary wife, who will destroy his work as fast as he finishes it."

"And after that what will you do?"

"Afterward it would be more sensible not to write any more books, to give up literature, to move on to another life, considering the first one finished."

"But one never has the courage?"

"That is very likely."

Thursday, March 13

The admiration expressed in all the papers for Mademoiselle Cassatt's etchings is enough to make you die of laughter! Etchings in which there is one little corner that is well done, one small part out of a whole in which the drawing is heavily stupid and the acid bite clumsy. Oh, really, this age makes a religion out of *failures*; its grand pontiff is Degas, and Mademoiselle Cassatt is his choirboy.

Sunday, March 16

Everyone at my house today is full of joy and surprise over the acquittal of Descaves, for the jury was almost entirely made up of old greybeards, of men who had been soldiers in the days when you could buy your way out. Fortunately the prosecution was less able than expected, and Tézénas was very skillful. Poor Geffroy was among those applauding the verdict who might have got two years in prison for contempt of court.

My *Grenier* is doing rather well! It is beginning to attract the attention of Paris—with Hennique's play at the Odéon, and the play by Alexis and Méténier at Les Variétés, and Descaves' book and his acquittal.

This evening Ajalbert talked about Clemenceau's despotism over people, whom he does not pay, and his insistence on having around him the court of his editorial staff. When he comes in from the Opéra at midnight, a gardenia in his buttonhole, he stretches out at full length on the table covered with bottles and, leaning on his elbow like a Roman on a *triclinium*, wide awake and ready for pleasure, he presides over people who would like to go to bed.

Sunday, May 18

I am convinced that, like a lightning rod that attracts the lightning, the Eiffel Tower causes all the storms that formerly passed safely overhead to fall on Paris now . . . and that some day they will have to tear the building down. This is in a sense a revenge of nature against science, which annoys it, worries it, and tries to penetrate its impenetrable secrets.

Thursday, July 4

In a letter pulsing with feverish maternal pride Madame Daudet informs me of the imminent engagement of her son Léon and the young Hugo girl.

Wednesday, July 16

A visit by Cousin Ambroy, who is bequeathing to Léon

Daudet the property at Fontvieille where the father wrote *Lettres de mon Moulin.*

An amusing detail of Jeanne's and Léon's love for each other. Jeanne has made him swear that he will not eat carp, because carp contain many bones, one of which might cause her to lose her future husband.

Apropos of this marriage, Lockroy told Léon that he ought to be glad that old Hugo was dead, that he had no idea of the speeches, the pontifications, the embarrassments he would have had to endure!

Sunday, November 9

This veneration on the part of some, indeed most, of the young men of letters for literature which draws its characters and setting from the past, this veneration which leads them to admire *Salammbô* more than *Madame Bovary*, to me seems somewhat like the respectful admiration of people in the second gallery for plays with characters and settings drawn from the old monarchy.

No, it cannot be ignored that with the apologues of Renan and the imaginative works of his two acolytes, tales in the manner of Anatole France's *Thaïs* and certain stories by Lemaître, there is currently an offensive against reality and truth, a reaction which will certainly increase in the next few years. But one can feel easy about it, the stupid stuffed or mummified humanity that these gentlemen put into their archaic lucubrations cannot have a long existence!

1891

Thursday, February 12

Reading the papers this morning, I feel there is really too much publicity about this marriage! After the detailed list of the gifts put on view, which appeared in *Le Figaro* yesterday, today there is the special list of the gifts made by the twelve-year-old brother and the five-year-old sister, along with a lyrical statement about the writings of the grandfather and grandmother. Oh, doesn't Daudet realize he is drawing down the lightning on the heads of the young married couple?

They are still talking about the flowers provided by the City, about the Lamoureux Orchestra, etc., etc. My thought is that the unique character of a secular wedding is the simplicity and uniformity of the ceremony for the union of all, great or little, of the earth.

At half-past five the Montéguts and Nicolle come to get me in the official wedding landau and take me to Avenue Victor Hugo.

There I find Daudet, all atwitter, tense, highly nervous, with a trace of frenzy in his eyes. He tells me that he was so tormented during the night by the recollection of the fire at the Schwarzenberg ball [17] that this morning he sent a telegram to Lockroy asking him to have the lighting checked in the Salle des Fêtes, where the marriage is to take place, and then sent Ebner to the Prefecture of Police to ask for more policemen. He is morbidly disturbed about the rush of the crowd, about the danger that the little flower girl Mémette could run in that huge gathering; he is anxious about how he is going to get up the grand staircase through that multitude with four thousand eyes fixed on him. On top of that there

[17] The reference is to a ball given by the Austrian Ambassador on July 1, 1810, as part of the festivities for the marriage of Napoleon and Marie-Louise of Austria. A curtain accidentally caught fire from a candle and several persons were burned to death or trampled by the crowd. Daudet by this reference manifests a certain *folie de grandeur*.

are family worries: his sister has decided to come, but has persisted in refusing to let her daughter be a flower girl and keeps herself apart with her colorless husband in a corner of the drawing room as though keeping her distance from her brother and the Lockroys.

As for Mémette, whose charming little face disappears under a white hat as big as a box kite, she is fully occupied with a little boy of her age on whose chest she dandles her head as she sings and whom from time to time she kisses full on the mouth, while the poor little boy is very embarrassed, very much put to shame by all this attention. A sight which makes Daudet and me remark that the little girl is responding to a natural law, one which has been changed by civilization, since in the childhood of the world it was the woman who courted the man, and not the man the woman.

The procession is organized, then placed in carriages, and I find myself with Daudet, his wife, and his son, who is as nervous as his father and who, when the coachman goes to the wrong entrance, says to the policeman: "I am the one who is getting married, for heaven's sake!"

In spite of a light drizzle, a crowd surrounding the municipal offices as on a day of riot. And, oh, the terrible endless stairway on which, through an overflowing crowd, barely able to make my way, I mount, virtually carrying poor Daudet along on my arms; in him I feel how the fear of not being able to get to the top accelerates the beating of his heart, fills his mouth with unuttered words of despair, and causes him to beat the bottom of my legs with the spasms of his inert feet, in which the little life still left seems to be in rebellion.

Finally, thank God, we are at the top of the stairway, and,

having gone across the room, we are on the platform where, at the end of his strength and will, Daudet sinks into an armchair.

The number of people in the room is frightening; it is everybody from the world of politics, the world of letters, the world of elegance, in a word, from all the worlds of Paris. For a moment there is a ground swell of movement and of murmurs a bit disturbing to the ceremony, as a deputation penetrating the hall by force attempts to take a bouquet trimmed with tricolor ribbons to the bride. A moment in which I murmur jokingly in Daudet's ear: "Is it going to be as it was in *Thermidor* [by Sardou, first performed January 24, 1891]? Are they going to forbid the marriage?" But he doesn't let me finish, and with a gesture of fright almost closes my mouth by a movement of his hand, pushing back my words. But there is only a moment of disturbance, in the midst of which we see Commissaire Céard multiply himself with a swollen sense of official importance. Soon all is quiet, everything calms down, the civil marriage ceremony begins, followed by a speech by Marmottan, the most monotone orator I have ever heard.

After Marmottan Jules Simon makes an address to the bride, an address which is really very charming, the truly apt familial allocution of a civil marriage. Oh, what a delightful actor Jules Simon is, not a ham actor but a delicate society actor.

Then I stand in the receiving line for an hour, where, exhausted and a bit nauseated by the heat and the scent of white lilacs, half concealed behind the Allards and the Ernest Daudets, from time to time I shake the hand of a man or a woman who spies me out behind the others.

At last on the stroke of eight the people who are dining at the Lockroys' are back at Avenue Victor Hugo. Dr. Potain,

Léon's second witness, has come back with us, but in spite of everybody's urging he refuses to stay for dinner and leaves, since he holds to the principle that if he dined out once he would be obliged to do so on other occasions and his evening's work would be completely lost. He is very much an individual, this doctor, whose face does not seem to be completely finished, not yet to have achieved the solidification of a face—it is one I would compare to an uncooked egg on a plate, but it is a face on which, I recognize, there is great goodness and tender humanity.

Those at dinner are Schoelcher, the Jules Simons, the Ernest Daudets and their daughter, the two Montégut brothers, and Nicolle.

Schoelcher—with a nutcracker head, not the bad nutcracker but the good kind. A gold chain hanging out of his waistcoat makes us ask him what it is. For a moment he refuses to say, complaining of the fact that today he had worn a waistcoat which revealed it; then he admits that it is the chain of a locket containing some of his father's hair; and at the end of the dinner I hear him arguing with Daudet and maintaining that man today is better than man two hundred years ago.

Jules Simon, whom I meet for the first time and of whom I had a very low opinion based on the stories of others, has an agreeable expression, an intelligent forehead, seductive eyes, with at times a worried look, a discontented expression at the corners of his mouth under his little wine merchant's twisted moustaches. His wife is ugly but not unpleasantly so; she has the ugliness of an intelligent she-monkey.

The dinner is cordial without being particularly lively, except for a bit of boisterousness between young Hugo and the Montégut from *L'Intransigeant.*

The bride is so happy that it is a pleasure to look at her, with a pretty gay smile on her half-opened lips, a smile that is modestly sensual.

As for the groom, who this evening is now assured that "they will never take her away from him, that she belongs to him"—the groom, who all day has been in a state of nervous abstraction, when I indicate to him my astonishment at several very exact observations he made at the municipal offices, tells me that the little that he perceived during the day had taken on for him an altogether strange intensity.

Exactly at eleven we embrace each other and leave. One of the Montéguts and Nicolle insist on accompanying me home.

Thursday, April 2

Dinner at Zola's, a dinner which he is giving in celebration of his birthday—he is fifty-one today—and which brings the Daudets and me to his table after three or four years of coolness and estrangement.

In his house the showy furniture of the parvenu, furniture of a gross Italian richness—there are chairs with gilt backs seven feet high; you see yourself reflected in mirrors with frames made of gold and silver chasubles; you see the Paris street through the archaic coloration of stained glass; you evoke a picture of the couple sleeping in an alleylike area fenced in by a wrought-iron grille—a piece of furniture which looks a bit like something Zola might have inherited from a Venetian Cardinal. But all that *cathedrallike* hand-me-down stuff provides a very unlikely setting for the author of *L'Assommoir* and *Nana.*

The dinner is not very relaxed. Before starting out Daudet and I had told each other that we must watch what we said in this house. Besides I am embarrassed by the slyly hostile attitude of our old friend Céard, who, when I say something that makes others laugh, pulls a straight face, like a donkey drinking out of a bucket, or turns to his neighbor with a private comment.

We talk about that poor devil Antoine, and I am a bit surprised to hear Céard openly drop him. Then he begins to talk with an artificial enthusiasm about Ibsen's originality in *The Wild Duck*, giving vent to the great bursts of laughter of a man from the Wine Market as he talks about the extraordinary character of the dismissed gamekeeper who on some days felt a compulsion to wear his uniform cap indoors.

For a moment Daudet was in fine form, saying what a remarkable "purveyor of happiness" he would make since he would know exactly what kind of happiness each person should have after questioning him as to his temperament, his tastes, his background, etc.

As he saw me out, Zola revealed his wish to renew relations with us and spoke about reunions during the coming winter when his house would be entirely in order, the furnishing complete.

Saturday, April 4

From the Rue de Berri I go to Bing's shop, from which I carry away enough Japanese prints to load a horse, taking them on the run to Hayashi's so that he may interpret them to me then and there, until seven o'clock, when I have promised to return them to Bing's.

I really believe that when you know how to look at a picture, how to discover all there is in it, you do not have to visit the country it depicts. Thus today, having under my eyes a picture by Toyokuni representing the office of a Green House, a house of prostitution, and being given a Japanese explanation of all the large and small objects adorning the office, I was convinced that by my description I could give the reader a feeling for the place with as much photographic accuracy as one of Loti's descriptions made on the spot.

Monday, April 20

Even intelligent Japanese have not the least feeling for the construction, the composition of a historical study. Thus in preparing my study of Utamaro, when I first asked Hayashi: "Is there a portrait of Utamaro?" he said no. It was only when I asked the question again that he said: "But I think I have seen one at your house in a collection of yours." And that is how I found out about that strange portrait of the artist authenticated by his name on his gown and by the inscription on the post against which he is leaning which bears the words: "On request Utamaro has painted his own elegant face."

In the book on the Green Houses I saw a plate representing the women of Yoshiwara looking at the moon on a beautiful summer night, and the author asserted that these women had remarkable poetic feeling. This statement led me to ask Hayashi if by chance there existed in print any poetry by these women. He replied that certainly there was a big and very well-known collection, and at my request he translated four or five typical poems—which he would never have thought of doing if he had been making the study I am engaged in—and that's the way it goes generally.

Monday, April 27

Ibsen's *The Wild Duck* at the Théâtre Libre this evening. Really, distance gives foreigners too much advantage. How fine it is to be a Scandinavian! If the play were by a Parisian . . . yes, I know, a bourgeois drama which is not bad, but its wit is imitated from French wit, fabricated under the North Pole, in a spoken language which is essentially bookish, especially when it becomes a bit heightened.

Monday, May 4

At Daudet's yesterday we were talking about Rodenbach's wife:

"She acts like a woman whose home life is unhappy!" Daudet's mother-in-law said. "She acts like a neurotic!" was my reply.

Aren't these the judgments of romanticism and naturalism, judgments which represent the intellectual approaches of two different periods, two different attitudes of mind, two people judging in completely different ways?

Thursday, May 21

I open *La France*, which has just come off the press. Loti has been elected to the Academy. It is funny, just the same, this election which is the consequence of a sort of joke by Daudet and me. Yes, I believe I have told how on the day of the premiere of *La Lutte pour la Vie* Loti was dining at Daudet's. While he went out to put on some new epaulettes, which were very stiff, we had the idea of presenting him to the Academy, and Daudet spent part of the evening, shut up as he was in Koning's office, writing a letter of candidacy for Loti, which the latter had only to copy.

Monday, June 1

In the interview I gave Huret [18] I might have made this

[18] Jules Huret, a journalist, presented statements of leading writers about the current state of literature in *L'Echo de Paris* from March 3 to July 5, 1891. Later that year these comments were published as a book under the title *Enquête sur l'Evolution Littéraire*. The consensus was that naturalism was dead.

fundamental statement: "I provided the complete formula for naturalism in *Germinie Lacerteux*, and *L'Assommoir* was made absolutely according to the method shown in the former. Now I have been the first one to emerge from naturalism—and not the way Zola did it in servile imitation, when the success of *L'Abbé Constantin* caused him to write *Le Rêve*—but because I found the genre in its original form worn out. Yes, I was the first to move out of it by using the new materials with which the young of today wish to replace it—by *dreams*, *symbolism*, *satanism*, etc., etc.—by writing *Les Frères Zemganno* and *La Faustin*. I, the inventor of naturalism, sought to dematerialize it before anyone else thought of doing so."

Thursday, July 16

Halperin-Kaminsky, the Russian translator of his compatriots into French, informs us that Dostoevsky was an epileptic, just like Flaubert. And when I speak to him of the religious reverence of the Russians for their authors, he tells us that at Dostoevsky's burial, noticing the reverent hush of the crowd, a muzhik asked: "Was he an apostle?"

Friday, September 11

No one has said during the current literary battle what I think I said apropos of Flaubert, that great talent in literature consists in creating, on paper, beings who occupy a place in the memory of the world, like the beings created by God who have had a real life on earth. It is this kind of creation that confers immortality on an ancient or modern book. Now the Decadents, the Symbolists, and the others may have put sonority into their little volumes, but never, absolutely never, have they created in them the kind of being of which I speak—not even one of second or third order.

This evening around the Opéra silhouettes of embattled curiosity standing in front of the posters announcing that *Lohengrin* has been postponed. I hear a policeman say to one of his comrades: "How many of us are there? Fifty at the most!" To the street vendors whom the police forbid to hawk *La Patrie en Danger*, the first issue of a paper inciting to riot, one vendor says: "Say what I do: 'I am selling a piece of paper for ten centimes . . .' " I go on past the detachment of police. I should be very much surprised if there were not a disturbance on Monday, an anti-German demonstration, and it is not in the least inconceivable that prevention of the performance by the Parisian populace might bring on the war which is ready to burst out over the slightest incident.[19]

Saturday, November 7

Before the innovations made by the Impressionists all the European schools of painting were dark, except for the French school of the eighteenth century. I am convinced that this painting owed its milky color to tapestry, to the insistence on color made by that industrial art, for it was the habit of our painters of that day to work more than half the time for the establishments at Beauvais and at Sèvres.

Wednesday, December 9

Maupassant appears to be suffering from delusions of grandeur, believing that he has been made a count and insisting that he be addressed as "M. le Comte." Popelin, though forewarned that there was an onset of stammering in Maupassant's speech, did not notice it at Saint Gratien this summer but was struck by the incredible exaggeration of his stories.

[19] The opera was produced on September 16. There was renewed trouble on the following day, and on September 19 riots in the area around the Opéra forced the cavalry and police to charge the crowd.

Maupassant told about a visit he made to Duperré of the Mediterranean Squadron and the number of cannon shots fired in his honor and for his pleasure, cannon shots costing hundreds of thousands of francs, with the result that Popelin could not refrain from pointing out to him the hugeness of the sum. The extraordinary thing about this account is that Duperré, some time later, told Popelin that he had not seen Maupassant at all!

Wednesday, December 23

Rodin has hair on his chin but none on his ass. If he had, he would not submit to all the humiliations he has been made to suffer with respect to his *Hugo*! Decidedly the spine of a sculptor is even more flexible, more *collapsible*, than that of a painter.

1892

Tuesday, January 5

A surprising letter from Magnard, the editor of *Le Figaro*, who has always been so hostile toward me. In this very gracious letter Magnard offers to let me succeed Wolff as editor in the field of art, with all the independence and freedom of ideas that I wish. I refuse. But I can't help thinking of all the people whom my acceptance would have put at my feet, of the respect I would have won in the Princess's household, and not least of the ease with which I would have found publishers for illustrated editions of *La Maison d'un Artiste*, *Madame Gervaisais*, etc.

Wednesday, February 17

As we were leafing through the big plates of *Fujiyama* by Hokusai, Manzi said to me: "Look, here are Monet's great yellow areas." And he was right. People are not sufficiently aware of how much our contemporary landscape artists have borrowed from those pictures, especially Monet, whom I often encounter at Bing's in the little attic where Lévy is in charge of the Japanese prints.

Sunday, March 6

A few minutes later Zola tells me of his fatigue as he is finishing *La Débâcle*, of the enormous bulk of the book, which will have 600 pages, saying that the manuscript will run to a thousand pages of thirty-five lines—the usual small pages of his copy written on sheets of foolscap cut in four.

When someone asks what he will do after the Rougon-Macquart novels, after *Le Docteur Pascal*, he hesitates a moment, then says that the theatre, which had always attracted him greatly, does not appeal to him so much any more, now that he is nearing the time when he can work at it, adding that every time he has gone into a theatre where a play of his was being put on, he felt disgust for the piece presented. He recalls in this connection that having gone in to see *L'Assommoir* at about the tenth performance, he saw Dailly, intoxicated by success, overacting in a hateful way and adding words to the text, with the result that for a moment Zola was tempted to take legal action against him for his additions and changes in the role and to forbid them under threat of a subpoena.

Then he interrupts himself to say that he has been in Lourdes and was struck, stupefied, by the spectacle of its hallucinated believers; he feels there would be some fine things to write about this recrudescence of faith which, as he sees it, has brought mysticism into literature and other areas in the present day. As I listen to him I think of the literary canniness which has led him, feeling naturalism to be in low esteem, to see the good springboard in this material and to turn mystic with a big sale, so that the anti-Academy man has become an aspirant to the Academy.

Then, passing on from Lourdes but still talking about his future writing, he admits that he would be glad to do a column in *Le Figaro* for a year, that he has some ideas to express about M. de Vogüé and others, but that he wanted 50,000 francs, a thousand francs per article—he was willing to make the paper a gift of two articles—and Magnard only wanted to pay him 34,000 francs. And undecided as to the theatre, Lourdes, or *Le Figaro*, he trails off in the ramblings of diffuse thought which are generally the end of his conversations about himself, in which his ideas, instead of becoming clearer, become roiled up in the flow of devouring ambitions at war within his brain.

Thursday, March 17

A conversation on the influence of the dining room of Madame de Loynes, the former la Tourbey, that dining room where Rochefort on his return from Nouméa had his first dinner of reentry into society, where Taine, where Renan, where men of all political opinions and of all schools of literature have their places set. Grosclaude describes Renan's jubilant enjoyment of his food at that house, which makes me say: "Yes, Renan thinks he is dining with Aspasia!"

A chat with old Stevens, who is a veritable storehouse of anecdotes about his world and, what is better, has an extraordinary memory for the typical phrases of painters of his acquaintance, past and present, phrases which define a moral nature, a character, a talent better than twenty pages of criticism.

He says Diaz was a dazzling conversationalist who defined Delacroix's painting in these terms: "A bouquet of flowers in stagnant water!"

Diaz is also the one who in reply to Couture—who jokingly advised him to stick to painting his forest since he did not know how to put a mouth under a nose and made a Turk when he tried to paint a Virgin—said that yes, perhaps he didn't know how to place a mouth under a nose but sometimes he was lucky enough to put real flesh around the mouth and nose that didn't belong together, and not pasteboard like Couture.

Then Stevens talks to me enthusiastically about Millet, saying that he has a portrait of a woman done by the latter, done before he went to Barbizon, which is one of the most marvelous pieces of flesh he has ever seen. And when he had his son take it to show it to Bonnat, the latter, who has his share of naughtiness, exclaimed: "You must take that canvas to Henner so that he will get his face slapped!"

He attests to Rousseau's respect for Millet, who at first felt that he had no talent, which, according to Stevens, made Rousseau decide to go to live in Barbizon, in order to convince him, and after a certain time such a communion of spirit was established between the two painters that Millet went back on his original judgment.

Stevens is surprised at the complete absence of a feeling for art among most of the great writers, saying that it is not that way with respect to literature among painters of talent, even among those who have not studied the humanities, and asserting that you would never find them reading a book by a mediocre writer. And he repeats—in the hiatus of his wide open mouth, in the middle of "hon, hon," appearing to demand the approbation of his auditor at the end of every phrase—he repeats several times that Millet, Rousseau, and the others were men of *high taste*, which is not common in this low world.

Sunday, April 3

Loti, who is to make his speech at the Academy on Thursday, dines with his wife at Daudet's this evening. By extraordinary exception he wears no make-up and, I believe, the devil take me if I am wrong, does not wear in his shoes the mechanism which raises him several inches, making him walk continually on the tip of his toes. Indeed, his face is pale, his nose is red; he says he is sick, with the grippe; and he is very uneasy about the quality of his voice at Thursday's session.

Loti asserts that Camille Doucet—the man with a wolf's head, he calls him—put forward infamous things about him to prevent his election, but that Doucet, while he is still furious over Loti's admittance, now shows him all the graceful attentions possible and has just told him that he fully expects that it will be at his house, to the exclusion of anybody else, that Loti will come for a cup of tea when he leaves the session.

"Don't pay any attention to him," Daudet interjects. "There is one thing that poisons his life. He is afraid that when he is buried, people will think of Loisillon's funeral [in Daudet's *L'Immortel*]!"

We sit down at the table. Nothing is so painful as the way Loti's young wife leans forward in an attempt to hear what Daudet is saying. For she is as deaf as a post and tries to catch what is said by raising her eyelids, by the tension of her little nose, by pulling back her upper lip, and in addition she has the sad voice of a sick bird, a voice which does not have the timbre of a human voice.

Even though on the most intimate terms with Daudet, Loti,

who is a complicated being par excellence, had written him that he did not wish to tire his host, that he would leave at nine-thirty, my time—which has never been my time—that he would have his niece come to get him. Well, at nine-thirty the door of the study opens and in file Loti's sister, brother-in-law, and niece, followed by Frère Yves' successor, whose eyes are like brilliant enamel and whose hips fill out an elegant bourgeois frock coat.

After this varied group is introduced and installed, Loti in spite of his grippe goes into the drawing room and sings until midnight, accompanied by Madame Daudet at the piano; showing off his thighs in the rococo manner, he sings Breton songs that sound like the *Dies Irae* on Breton bagpipes.

Thursday, April 7

That Loti is certainly a snake in the grass! Out of respect for the imbecile antipathies of the Academy he has gone in for ass-licking exceeding anything one could imagine.

How? This man, whose anti-Academic talent belongs completely in our camp by reason of his methods of observation and his style, in order to please the Academy has cheerfully made himself the servile lambaster of all the men of talent who are his fathers and brothers!

Ah, I thought, if I had been in his place, what a fine speech I could have made glorifying Balzac, Flaubert, and our friends. They would not have allowed such a speech to be given? Well, I would have had it printed and would have threatened the Academy with my resignation, proclaiming proudly that since it had made me a member it did not have the right to impose on me ideas that were not my own. And I am sure that there would have been such a hue and cry in the press and public opinion that the Academy, which like all established bodies is cowardly by nature, would have been forced to let me give my speech.

But that was really not to be expected of this flunkey of Queens of Romania and *La Revue Nouvelle*.

And what about this author's aspiration to the *moral ideal*, an author in whose first novel the beloved was a man and who throughout his works has done nothing but glorify the prostitutes who walk their beats under the coconut palms.

Therefore I am in a fury when I go into Daudet's after reading a resumé of his speech in the evening paper. When I express myself with a bit of indignation, Madame Daudet from her high level of universal forgiveness says that he is a child, that he is unaware of what he is doing, and I answer that a fine action may be spontaneous and therefore unconscious, but that a scoundrelly one is always premeditated.

Saturday, May 7

"Yes, Corot never used green. He got his greens by a mixture of yellow and Prussian blue, mineral blue . . . and I am going to give you irrefutable proof of that."

It is the old painter Decau, a friend of Corot, who lives in Gavarni's building and who comes down again a few minutes later with the smock that Corot wore while painting, a smock which is a combination of two kitchen aprons of faded blue having in the rear a new piece of bright blue, replacing the lower part of the smock, which had been burned against a stove. In fact, the smock is all sprinkled with pale stains, among which green is absent.

Along with the smock Decau has brought down a sketch in which he has pictured Father Corot painting in the country and wearing this smock—a sketch in which, with the rebellious white hair of his bare head, his complexion of a man who lives outdoors, his briar pipe hanging out of his mouth, Corot looks exactly like an old Norman peasant.

And Decau gives us Father Corot's formula for making masterpieces straight from nature:

"Sit down in a good place," as his master Bertin taught; "put in the main lines and get your values, and," touching in turn his head and his heart, "put on canvas what you have there and there."

Decau adds: "He was a morning painter, not an afternoon one; he did not paint when there was full sun, saying: 'I am not a colorist but a harmonist!'

"Imagine," Decau continues, "until he was forty-five Corot remained like a little child in the house of his father, who had not the least faith in his talent. It happened that one day when Français had dined with Corot's father and was about to leave, the father said he would accompany him; when the son showed signs of wanting to go along, the father told him to stay behind. Then in the street he asked: 'Monsieur Français, does my son really have talent?' 'What do you mean?' replied Français. 'Why, he is my teacher!' "

Friday, May 13

Lunch with Hayashi, who leaves tonight for Japan.

The tendency to human caricature in Hokusai, Hokkei, Hiroshige, indeed, almost all Japanese artists, informs intelligent people even before they meet the natives of the Land of the Rising Sun that they have an ironic, joking spirit.

At the Salon in the Champ de Mars.

Under the stimulus of Japanese art of domestic life, French industrial art is on its way to killing great art. The tin pitcher by Baffier, the pottery vases with cupids and mythological women in relief by Joseph Chéret, the commode decorated with Montesquiou-Fezensac's hydrangeas—they are the truly original art of the exposition.

Monday, June 13

Durand-Ruel's house is an odd dwelling for a dealer in nineteenth-century pictures. An immense apartment on the Rue de Rome filled with paintings by Renoir, Monet, Degas, etc.; a bedroom with a crucifix over the bed, and a dining room with a table set for eighteen people, each guest having at his place a Pan's pipe of six glasses. Geffroy tells me that this table of Impressionist painting is set like that every day.

Friday, July 1

Dinner of Japanese enthusiasts at Véfour's. Bing talks today of the craze for Japanese prints among various American amateurs. He tells of selling a little packet of such prints for 30,000 francs to the wife of one of the richest Yankees, who in her small drawing room has an Utamaro facing the most beautiful Gainsborough in existence. And we admit to each other that the Americans, who are in process of acquiring taste, will, when they have acquired it, leave no art object for sale in Europe but will buy up everything.

Wednesday, October 5

We must put an end to all this humbug about the great man Renan. Don't people really believe that Flaubert is more deserving of the honors given to the former and that the literary legacy of the novelist enriches France to a much greater degree than that of the quibbling philosopher, whose fame twenty years from now seems to me very doubtful?

1893

Wednesday, January 4

Robert de Montesquiou, who visited me today to thank me

for a letter I wrote Comtesse Greffulhe about him, soon became expansive and told me with retrospective horror about his childhood spent at the Jesuits' school in the Rue de Vaugirard. He said that in his early years he needed the soft envelopment of women's skirts instead of the dirty soutanes of those priests; he told me that at fourteen, already writing amorous verses about the moon, one day when he went into the refectory, where they ate such bad veal, the big Jesuit who led them tossed out to him with asthmatic irony: "Dreamy, pale light of the moon!"—part of a poem of his which the spy system of the place had discovered while ferreting in his desk—and the scornful hiss of irony by the big Jesuit made him withdraw into himself and close up his soul, carefully concealing his tenderness and exaltation.

Montesquiou told me about his next volume of poems, which will be entirely given over to flowers, and about a pious poetic monument he wishes to raise to Desbordes-Valmore.

This evening Yriarte's conversation was very instructive about the way art is controlled at the present time. He declared that when it came to making decisions everything was arranged in advance so that there was no chance for experiment or innovation—everything having been settled by the biumvirate of Clemenceau and Proust.

Tuesday, January 31

Now, with regard to the *idolatry* of foreign literature by the public as well as by the press, I asked Bauër if in *The Power of Darkness*—a play which I find altogether remarkable—when Nikita, seated on the bench, crushes the child's bones and you hear the wail of the little victim, I asked whether the play would have been able to go to such an extreme if Tolstoy had been a Frenchman. And I asked him also whether the play *Miss Julie*, with its audacious brutality, would have had its three acts put on if M. Strindberg had been French.

And when Bauër, echoing the little reviews, repeated that the naturalistic theatre was dead because of its representation of exceptional beings, I humbly called it to his attention that in literature all the works that are reputed masterpieces, *Don Quixote*, *Werther*, *Le Neveu de Rameau*, *Les Liaisons Dangereuses* with Valmont, the Marquise de Merteuil, Cécile de Volanges, all such works contain exceptional beings, who, created by authors of genius, find at the end of fifty years scholiasts to demonstrate their universality—and I asked him if he thought that in Norway today Ibsen's women were considered to be general types of Norwegian women.

Then he, who is the only defender of revolutionary efforts in the theatre, ought to have admitted that everything which is permitted to foreigners is denied us by the critics, who prevent us from having a superior theatre, one that is literary, philosophical, original, one that goes beyond the intelligence and taste of Sarcey, which are confined to bourgeois events of contemporary married life—a subject which is finished and completely worn out.

Thursday, February 16

When I talk to Carrière about the *pointillage* of the painting of Pissarro and others, he says to me: "That is painting at long range, painting that you must look at from fifty feet away!"

These days the Jews, even the Protestants, trample on the poor Catholics! The painter Renoir recently was in a Protestant house where something or other led him to mention the Valois kings and Charles IX; the master of the house interrupted him to say: "We don't talk about those people here!"

This evening with regard to Heredia's *Les Trophées* Daudet said: "Among the rest of us it is the idea which summons up the word; for Heredia it is the word which gives birth to the idea." One could make an interesting article about that.

Thursday, February 23

When with all sorts of circumlocutions Alphonse Daudet asks Mallarmé if he is not presently working to be more hermetic, more abstruse than in his earlier works, the poet in his light, wheedling voice which someone has said goes into an ironically minor key on occasion—after many confused statements such as "You don't write with white"—ends his hazy amplification by admitting that at the present time he looks upon a poem as a *mystery* for which the reader must seek the key.

Then we talk of Villiers de l'Isle-Adam, for whom Mallarmé expresses a rather excessive admiration, and someone points out the Mephisto role that Catulle Mendès played toward him and his remark a few days before his death: "I am dying of Catulle Mendès!"

Sunday, March 5

A visit by Heredia, who talks about Taine, whom he is going to see when he leaves me.

After recovering from a cerebral embolism Taine now appears to have a pulmonary embolism and to be in a desperate state. . . .

Heredia admits to me that he published his book at the urging of Leconte de Lisle and of Coppée, who promised him the Academy prize of 8,000 francs. But as soon as he got wind of this de Bonnières took his *Contes* to Pingard; then it appears there is a poetess who is Dumas' protégée. However, Heredia still hopes to get 6,000 francs of the prize.

This evening I receive a telegram from Toudouze, who tells me that I have been named president of the Société des Romanciers with sixty-nine votes out of seventy. Can it be that Toudouze has rigged, falsified, faked the vote? I have sixty-nine out of seventy votes, I who am so hated by my colleagues, go on!

Zola has worked hard to get me elected. What a joker. Some day he will be able to say: "People used to say loudly that Goncourt had none of the bourgeois ambitions that I have. However, you see how readily he accepted being president of the Romanciers, and deep down, if he were sure of being elected, he would be glad to be president of the Société des Gens de Lettres, a member of the Academy, etc., etc.

Monday, March 6

Oh, how my contemporaries are passing away! Yesterday while Heredia was telling me of his last visit to Taine—his cab waiting at my door to take him there again—Taine was dying.

Wednesday, March 22

Today Alidor Delzant comes to see me. Naturally the conversation is about Ozy, the actress, from whom he has just inherited 50,000 francs, with which—there is nothing else he can do—he intends to give three pensions to three men of letters. He inherits her papers also, among which are amorous letters from Gautier, Saint-Victor, Doré, and in particular a big packet of letters from About, which he says are utterly charming in their passion and wit.

Delzant tells me that Ozy's large fortune was not the result of the gifts, though they were considerable, made by her lovers, but rather of the investment of those gifts that she had her lovers make, nearly all of them being men from the

Bourse. Besides she did not press her lovers to prodigality in stupid things, like jewels, diamonds; she was all for serious things. Thus from M. . . . , who founded the Magasins du Louvre and who was her titular entreteneur for fifteen years, Ozy invariably asked for ten, twenty, thirty shares of Lyon—a railway stock—in place of whatever he had decided to give her.[20]

Delzant is responsible for her tomb, a monumental tomb, but very proud though he is at having been chosen for the artistic supervision, he is annoyed that the deceased demands that a Doré sculpture be placed on it. To which I cannot help saying: "But that gives you a chance to set up Doré's *The Bottle* in gigantic dimensions as a monument to the woman who was accused of getting tipsy on occasion!"

Whereupon Delzant, half laughing, half indignant, gets up and says to me from the door: "That's abominable, abominable!"

Bracquemond, whom I have not seen for ages, follows Delzant. He enters with a dragging step, drops into an armchair, and in a voice that lacks its usual warm, muted tension, complains of an abdominal trouble that has made him lose fifteen pounds in six weeks, raising his vest and showing me his vanished belly. When I say that he works too hard, he answers: "That's true, but what can I do? For me work is now a real mania. When I don't work, I walk back and forth in my studio, moving my arms and legs like an epileptic."

Wednesday, April 5

Montesquiou-Fezensac drops in to see how I am and at the same time to pick up his copy of *Les Chauves-Souris* in order

[20] In an early entry dated June 12, 1861, Ozy was characterized by the witty Saint-Victor as "a stockbroker with tits."

to have it illustrated by Whistler's portrait of him. And we talk about Whistler, whose genius he says is one of contradiction, of petty bickering. He asserts that he is sure that if he asked him to show his portrait, the artist would oppose it, and if he asked him the contrary, if he showed a desire to keep it hidden away from everybody, Whistler would insist on his showing it.

Montesquiou tells me that he has gathered a great many notes and bits of information about Whistler and that some day he wants to write a study of him. He shows his admiration for this man who, he says, has ordered his life in such a way as to obtain in his lifetime victories which for others are usually posthumous, and he cites the painter's suit against the English journalist who had written of the "impertinence" of asking a thousand guineas for "throwing a pot of color at the public's face." Whistler's reply was really fine when someone asked him how much time he had spent on painting a picture and he tossed out scornfully: "One or two sittings!" and in response to the outbursts of "Oh!" added: "Yes, I only took a couple of mornings to execute it, but the canvas was painted with a lifetime's experience!"

Whistler is living just now on the Rue du Bac in a house facing the garden of the Foreign Missions. Montesquiou, who was invited to dinner there not long ago, was present at a spectacle which made a very great impression on him: as night was falling a chorus of men, a chorus of male voices rose up, singing the *Laudate* in the garden of the Foreign Missions. Montesquiou imagines this going on in front of bad paintings representing the frightful sufferings of their predecessors in exotic countries, their voices rising in exaltation before those images of martyrdom, as if the singers in the garden were eager to become bloody additions to their band.

Sunday, April 30

Hearing the name of Oscar Wilde, Henri de Régnier, who is at my *Grenier,* begins to smile. I ask him why. "Oh, don't you know? Besides, he doesn't hide it. Yes, he admits he is a homosexual. He himself said one day: 'I have had three marriages in my life, one with a woman and two with men!' You know, don't you, that after the success of his play in London he left his wife and their three children and settled in a London hotel, where he lived on a marital basis with a young English lord. One of my friends who went to see him described the room, where there was only one bed with two pillows, and while he was there, the wife, who brought the mail every morning, came in crying."

And when I remark that in a man as much given to literary plagiarism as Wilde his homosexuality must be a plagiarism of Verlaine, de Régnier agrees, saying that praise of Verlaine is always on the tongue of the English author.

Sunday, May 14

Morel was saying at my house today that at the Bibliothèque Nationale requests for books used not to go above two or three hundred a year, but that in the last ten years they have risen to 1,700.

This evening at Daudet's we were talking about poor Madame Zola's sadly taking the two children her husband had by her chambermaid out for a walk.

It would seem that she had another chambermaid to whom good old Zola made advances. That one was dismissed and stupidly replaced by another, a very beautiful girl, whom she kept for some time in spite of Madame Charpentier's warnings at her imprudence. It apparently is this one whom Zola has made his concubine in a sort of second marriage.

Then Daudet speaks of the coolness toward Zola that has developed in Céard on account of this mistress. With Zola at Médan, the mother of his two children was installed in the neighborhood and Céard was the messenger who took letters to the sweetheart, letters in which for one reason or another Zola, with his Italian duplicity, vigorously made fun of his messenger. And one day out of irritation over Céard's role, Madame Zola, ridiculing the confidence that Céard had in Zola's friendship, told him the jokes the latter made in letters which she had got hold of, I don't know how.

A scene between the two friends has changed them almost into enemies. One evening at Médan after a violent quarrel between husband and wife, Madame Zola was packing her bags preparatory to leaving Médan at once and forever, and Zola, having withdrawn to his room, was letting her go. With praiseworthy indignation Céard, who happened to be at Médan, cast off his diplomatic reserve and told Zola he would be a swine, a scoundrel, if he let her go, the woman who had shared the poverty of his bad years but whom he was throwing out the door without pity in this time of good fortune.

Saturday, July 1

A curse on Verlaine, on that drunkard, that pederast, that assassin, that coward, tormented from time to time by fears of Hell which make him shit his pants, a curse on that great perverter who, by his talent, has created among the youngsters of letters a school of all evil appetites, of all antinatural tastes, of all that is disgusting and horrible!

Saturday, July 8

Maupassant's funeral in that church at Chaillot where I attended the wedding of Louise Lerch, whom I once thought of marrying.

Madame Commanville, whom I run into, tells me that she will leave tomorrow for Nice in the pious desire to visit and comfort Maupassant's mother, who is in an alarming state of grief.

Rodin, next to whom I am seated, tells me that my letter to Poincaré, the letter urging Geffroy's nomination to the Legion of Honor, has had an excellent effect and that if he is not decorated this July 14, he will be next year.

Friday, December 8

Yesterday I finally received the famous letter of *anathema* by the ladies of the League for Emancipation, a letter signed by Madame Potonié! It is a polite letter, but I shall not answer it, for if I did I would say baldly that I believe that, if there were an autopsy made of women of original talent, like Madame Sand, Madame Viardot, etc., their genitals would be found similar to those of a man, their clitorises somewhat like our penises.

1894

Saturday, February 17

I really don't know whether M. Brunetière has a feeling for the beautiful in ancient literature, given the *gibberish* with which he talks about it. But what I can guarantee—and the future will prove it—is that he does not have the least knowledge of what is good or bad in modern literature. Now true connoisseurs of painting have a taste for beautiful modern things as well as for beautiful ancient things, and I think that taste for universal beauty is shared by true connoisseurs of literature.

Friday, February 23

During the entr'acte a visit by yesterday's new Academician, a visit by Heredia, who tells us that he frustrated all

Camille Doucet's intrigues and that young Houssaye was not elected because of a coalition organized against him for Zola's advantage, which at the next meeting of the Academy is supposed to bring about the latter's election—a maneuver by which the support of this group was clumsily swung from one seat to the other.

Heredia asserts, however, that Zola does not have a chance, that the Duc de Broglie has told him Zola will never be elected, at least while the Duke is alive; abroad there is a tendency to look upon France as a rotten country and if the Academy were to elect him it would be tantamount to approval of his past and future uncleanness. But alongside these feelings of repulsion there exist some extraordinary feelings of sympathy: the sympathy of Dumas, for example, who, according to what his daughters told the Princess, would never vote for Zola but who, at this last election, made a scene with Leconte de Lisle, saying "You are the one who has brought in this dirty foreigner [i.e., Heredia]!"

Thursday, April 19

Tonight everybody is at Verdi's *Falstaff*. Mariéton, who tends to echo general opinion, asserts that it is no longer Italian music but German music, and that it completely lacks the originality of the early compositions by the master.

Thursday, April 26

As he is leaving, Hayashi murmurs that in Japan they are trying to think up a decoration for me, and in response to my gesture of indifference, he adds: "But you deserve it, for it is you above all who are responsible for our no longer being considered Annamites, exotics without art or literature!"

Friday, June 8

The whole battle between Bauër and Antoine arises from the fact that Dorsy, Antoine's mistress, left the director of the Théâtre Libre because of some brutality on his part and took Bauër out of revenge, even though she did not feel the least love for the critic. Dorsy is a frail, nervous woman whose inner nature is full of resentment. She has exercised great influence on that big baby Bauër and now is in absolute control of his criticism, although she won't live with him, saying that he has a lot of prostitutes come to him and she has no desire to play the role of a Pompadour.

Sunday, June 10

The subject of Antoine's discomfiture and his relinquishment of the Théâtre Libre comes up, and the odious attitude of the press toward him is also discussed. Lecomte, who is altogether of my opinion, declares that Antoine was deflected from his past disinterested attitude and his absolute devotion to the revolution in art when he began his high life on the boulevards and his dinners at the Café Américain, venturing into the company and ideas of a society which was not that of his origins. . . .

Apropos of *La Maison Tellier*, the enormous success of which had just evoked Rodenbach's astonishment, Toudouze said that he happened to be in the same carriage as Hector Malot at Maupassant's funeral. Malot told him that he had provided the episode on which Maupassant based his story, but that the latter had spoiled it by ending it with a party, whereas the madam had actually said to her girls: "And tonight *you'll sleep alone.*"

Friday, June 29

Today, always apropos of the publication of my *Journal*,

I received by way of *L'Echo de Paris* an envelope filled with soiled toilet paper—anonymous shit.

Sunday, November 11

Primoli arrives and takes a snapshot of Lorrain and me. Then he chats about Duse, with whom he has just spent a week in Venice, Duse, the Italian actress who has been suggested to me to play La Faustin in London or in Germany. He says she is a woman who in many respects is deficient as an actress but who, in spite of that, is a very great artist. He describes her as an actress of great independence in the theatre, making an effort only in the scenes that appeal to her talent, and in the others which do not please her mouthing her words or becoming abstracted over anything at all. In a play in which she had to tell a daughter who had behaved badly that she "no longer had a daughter," he saw her suddenly, without regard for the audience, make the sign of the cross at her waist and send out a kiss toward the wings—a kiss for her real daughter, whom she adores.

Sunday [sic], *December 22*

We talk inevitably about the traitor Dreyfus, and wonder if the dramatic scene that is being reported really took place: General Boisdeffre giving him the treasonable letter to copy and Dreyfus, who had begun to copy it, breaking down at the second line.

Amid the regret expressed by everybody at not having the scoundrel shot out of hand, Hennique arrives and hands me a letter. "Daudet not coming?" I ask. "No, you'll see why!"

After I have read the letter, which tells me they have had a misfortune and need to see my dear face, Hennique explains in a low voice: "Madame Léon Daudet has left the conjugal residence!"

By heaven, this outcome was desirable when one thinks of the cruel life the husband has endured for months. The mother and father have kept me informed of the heart-breaking details of that existence from day to day, but I did not want to say a word about it in my *Journal* lest, in case of a reconciliation, revelations about the bad times in their marriage bring the accusation that I had been deficient in the discretion I owed to friendship. But today, now that the scandal is about to become public knowledge . . .

Sunday, December 30

I have dinner this evening with the poor fellow, who has the red eyes of a man who has been crying. Georges Hugo is also there, absolutely on Léon Daudet's side against Lockroy, to whom he has written a very harsh letter, reproaching him for his brutal treatment of his mother, his disrespectful hardness toward old Hugo, setting down in detail the whole story of his hatred for Léon Daudet, and ending with this sentence: "It is you whom I accuse." The amazing thing about it is that Georges had this letter delivered personally by his coachman, a letter that Lockroy said was intercepted by his wife. Thereupon he sent a second copy which Lockroy, in a reply in which he addressed Georges affectionately, said he had not yet read at his wife's request. What an old Tartuffe Lockroy is!

It would appear that beyond her own income Jeanne has put out some 210,000 francs on frivolous expenditures, for which her husband is liable.

1895

Sunday, January 6

Mentioning my play *La Patrie en Danger*, Carrière, who was part of the crowd at the ceremony of Dreyfus's military degradation, said he wished that I, who had depicted so well the feverish activity in the streets during the Revolution, had been present, for certainly I would have caught something of the intense emotion of the crowd.

He saw nothing of what took place in the courtyard of the Ecole Militaire, receiving only the echo of the crowd's emotion from youngsters who had climbed up in the trees and who shouted when Dreyfus arrived, walking stiffly erect: "The scum!" and a few minutes later, when he bowed his head, "The coward!"

I took the occasion to declare, in regard to that miserable man—of whose treason I am not convinced, however—that the judgments of journalists are the judgments of gamins in the trees and that in such circumstances it is really very difficult to establish the guilt or innocence of the accused from an examination of his bearing.

Sunday, February 10

At the very end of the evening Daudet says to me from the armchair where he is writing: "At the Fasquelle dinner last Friday did the Charpentiers say anything to you?"

"No."

"You're sure? They didn't tell you anything?"

"No, on my honor!"

Then Daudet comes over to sit beside me and speaks almost in a whisper:

"I shouldn't be telling you this, but since Zola has not kept the secret from Madame Charpentier in spite of our promise that we would not talk about it to anybody, I can tell you. Well, here it is! The President of the Republic, in exchange for two chevalier's crosses, has obtained an officer's cross for you, and Poincaré has asked to preside at the banquet in order to present it to you. It must be said that Zola has behaved himself very well, has put a great deal of enthusiasm into pulling this off. He even proposed going to see the Minister by himself, but I did not want him to and we went together."

Then a comical account of Zola's and Daudet's call on the Minister, Zola wanting to carry Daudet's hat so that the latter might be supported by his cane and Zola's arm; Zola making his speech holding two hats in his hands.

Daudet continues: "And do you know what happened to Zola because of you? As a result of my handshake which conveyed how moved I was by what he had done for you he was suddenly overcome by a return of friendship and confided to me what a horror his life is, telling me that for two years he has feared that he might be spattered by the blood of his children, the blood of his mistress, assassinated by his wife, has feared that he might be disfigured by that Fury, whose shrieks have forced him to shut himself up in his room at night in order not to hear her." And Zola told Daudet these things in a sort of hysterical outburst with tears running down his cheeks.

Friday, March 1

A charming bit of attention by Madame Rodenbach. This morning she sent me a big bouquet of roses, brought by her blond baby who was carried in his nurse's arms, with this kind note from his father: "Constantin Rodenbach brings to M. de Goncourt the respect and admiration of the next century, to which they will both belong."

After the baby leaves I open *La Libre Parole* and am pleasantly surprised to find in it an article like those of the days when Drumont and I were on terms of sympathy, one in which he associates himself with the people who are feting me. I thank him in a note in which, mentioning Daudet's warm memories of him, which he must reciprocate after so many years of friendship and close association, I say that neither of them should allow himself to continue into his old age an animosity that is unworthy of two noble natures.

Then I pass the endless hours of a day at the end of which something very exciting is to occur, feeling it impossible to remain at home and needing to go out for a walk though my eyes see nothing and my legs are unaware of where they are going.

An interminable lineup at the door and admission so badly organized that after waiting forty minutes on the staircase, Scholl loses courage and gives up the banquet. At last, in spite of a waiter who refuses to let me enter, I manage to slip into the reception room upstairs, whereas Daudet goes immediately to sit down at the banquet table downstairs.

Warm, enthusiastic handshakes greet me. One of those hands is that of Lafontaine, offering me a little bouquet of violets with a card on which his wife has written "Henriette Maréchal"—the role she played in 1865.

We go down to dinner. Since I am one of the last to descend, from the top of the curving staircase I am struck by the handsome and impressive appearance of this dining room two stories high, as brightly lighted as if it were day, with its pleasant arrangement of tables for 310 places, and by the friendly commotion and joyous mood of the guests as they take their seats.

Daudet is on my left and the Minister on my right. The latter, who still has the grippe, tells me flatteringly that the evening before he refused an invitation to the residence of the President of the Republic because he wished to save his strength for my banquet.

We reach dessert. Frantz Jourdain rises and reads missives from Belgium, from Holland, from the Goncourtists of Italy, Cameroni and Vittorio Pica, from Germany, among them two lines from Georg Brandes: "All the writers of Scandinavia will join me when I shout: 'Glory to the initiating master!' "

Among these messages one of homage from a Haarlem flower-grower who wants to name a hyacinth after me.

And there are other letters and messages from literary friends in France who have not been able to attend the banquet: letters and messages from Sully-Prudhomme, Claretie, Philippe Gille, Déroulède, Margueritte, Henri Lavedan, Theuriet, Larroumet, Marcel Prévost, Laurent Thailhade, Curel, Puvis de Chavannes, Alfred Stevens, Helleu, Alfred Bruneau, Gallé de Nancy, Colombey, Mévisto.

Then the Minister begins to speak, a discourse such as has never before been given by a minister decorating a man of letters, apologizing for being there as a minister and asking almost humbly on the part of the government that I accord the favor of allowing myself to be decorated.

And, leaving myself out of account, I should state here that before this, men of government have seemed to condescend to decorate writers and artists, and that this is the first time that they appear to honor themselves in so doing.

Moreover, it would be impossible to put more delicate praise and respectfully affectionate friendliness into this speech of a true man of letters, which, I must admit, brought tears to my eyes for a moment. I cannot resist the desire to write down part of the speech here:

The time has passed for the imposition of theories, obligatory aesthetic principles and State literatures. In a democracy which lives in liberty and fosters a variety of individual inspirations, the government has no edicts to give, no directives to make; it has only to fill, if it can and as it can, the discreet role of perceptive amateur, respectful of sincere talents, fine passions, and generous wills.

Now it appears to me difficult to find a prouder talent than yours, passions more ardent than those that you have nourished, a will more sovereign than that which you have applied to your researches into art and your labor over style; and it is truly a life of a writer par excellence, unswerving and full, that you two began together side by side in the joyfulness of your twinned hearts, and which you took up again with unshakable valor in the melancholy of your solitude.

You have lived only for things of the mind; and not content to seek out in the observation of our corner of nature and humanity material with which to give body to your studies and to satisfy the curiosity of your tastes, you have enlarged the contemporary horizon, you have brought to life again the charm of a vanished age, you have made familiar the imagination and mystery of distant arts.

You have had no dearer ambition than to know and to see; you have known no more exquisite pleasures than those of ideas, lines, and colors; and the sensations which you have loved you have sought to render with the effort of new signs and the vibrancy of personal notations. You have made your language flexible in order to meet the complex task of depicting observed reality, the changing necessities of transcribing the inner being, even the caprice of the most fugitive impressions. You have brought into your style the play of light, the shimmering of the open air, the coloration and the life of the external world. You have also put there the internal shocks, the subtle emotions, the secret turmoil of the moral being, and, desirous of preserving in your phrases something of that which shines and vibrates, of that which loves or suffers, you have called upon the richness and diversity of the forms of art for the faithful expression of nature's infinite multiplicity.

The government owed it to itself, dear master, to give obeisance to your being and your works, and however indifferent you may be to official recognition, it has thought that you would not refuse a mark of distinction that you have never sought except for others. The President of the Republic is very happy, upon my recommendation, to confer upon you the grade of officer of the Legion of Honor, and I trust you will permit me cordially to bestow its emblems upon you.

The emotion that I felt at that moment was shared by the assemblage, whose applause was frantic. "No," people who had attended many banquets said to me, "no, we have never witnessed such complete solidarity of feeling at a testimonial dinner!"

Then there was a toast by Heredia celebrating the golden anniversary of my wedding with literature.

Then the expected discourse by Clemenceau, saying that I, Marie-Antoinette's knight-at-arms, had come by way of love of beauty and truth to be the apologist of a Germinie Lacerteux and a Fille Elisa, who might have been women of the mob who accompanied her to the scaffold. A comparison rather dragged in by the hair in a speech that went on too long, causing Daudet, who was beginning to tire, to whisper to me: "A sermon, a sermon!"

Then a completely reconciled Céard sentimentalizing about the old days of our literary relationship.

Then Henri de Régnier with a delicate literary tribute.

Zola follows Henri de Régnier, admitting frankly that his work owes something to mine, and he, who is getting ready to write *Rome*, is kind enough to mention *Madame Gervaisais*.

After Zola Daudet makes the speech of an intimate friend, one full of tender affection:

"We have drunk to the famous man, to Goncourt novelist, historian, dramatist, and writer on art. I should like to drink to my friend, a faithful and tender companion, one who has been very good to me during some very bad times. To drink to the intimate Goncourt whom some of us know, a man cordial and sweet, indulgent and naive—a naif with sharp eyes —incapable of a low thought or of a lie even in anger."

And Daudet ends with these words: "To the writer who, since Jean-Jacques Rousseau, has most passionately loved and sought the truth!"

Then I rise and say these few words:

"Gentlemen and dear colleagues from art and literature. I am incapable of saying ten words to ten people. And you are much more numerous, gentlemen. I can thus only thank you, in a few brief words, for your affectionate sympathy and say to you that this evening which I owe to you repays me for many of the hard passages and sufferings of my literary career.

"I thank you once again!"

We go upstairs to have coffee and liqueurs. There are embraces, people whose names and faces I have forgotten recalling themselves to my memory, the introduction of Italians, Russians, Japanese; lamentations by the sculptor Rodin, who complains of being tired and says he needs to rest; a request by Albert Carré for an appointment to talk about putting on *Manette Salomon;* thanks from Gung'l, Lagier's son, for the few lines in my *Journal* about his mother; some words in my ear by Antoine, who will come soon to tell me things, fantastic things, about the goings on at the Vaudeville and the Gymnase. That great fool Darzens, who dedicated a volume to me but never sent me a copy, kisses my hand.

In the midst of all this as I catch sight of myself in a mirror I seem to see on my face a gentle stupefaction, something of the beatitude of a Buddha.

Eleven o'clock strikes. I am dying of hunger, having eaten absolutely nothing. I know that the Daudet brothers are to have supper with Barrès and the young Hugo couple, but I am afraid my old face will put a damper on these turbulent youths' enjoyment. I hope there will be something left of the chocolate I told my servants to make for themselves while they are waiting up for me. When I get home, no chocolate, no cakes, everything has been eaten.

I come home with a superb basket of flowers in my hands, a basket placed before me during the meal which, in my state of emotion, I did not examine closely, being aware only of the card from Madame Mirbeau, who had sent the basket. At home when I handle it and look at it, I see that there is a pile of little boutonnieres intended for the members of the committee. How stupid I am, how very stupid!

Wednesday, March 20

The Princess really surprises me this evening. She, who has never mentioned my decoration—who kept obstinately silent when Madame Daudet exclaimed: "Did you read in the paper about the beautiful party they gave to M. de Goncourt?"—she says to me: "As you are usually the first to arrive, I have come down to the drawing room earlier than usual to tell you that I have ordered a cross in diamonds for you."

Sunday, April 14

Duret says that in London it was impossible to have anything to do with Oscar Wilde, that one dared not be seen with him in a restaurant or café. Thereupon de Régnier affirms that one of his friends who had seen Oscar Wilde in London, before renewing relations with him in Paris, asked him what sort of friends he had there. Oscar Wilde replied bluntly: "I don't have friends. I have lovers!"

Sunday, June 16

The American painter La Farge is brought to my *Grenier* by Raffaelli. He has done watercolors of India and Japan, where he passed six months, and says some interesting things in the somewhat singsong voice of the English. He speaks briefly of the importance that written characters have in Japan and the scorn that painters of the Kano school feel for the characters by painters of the vulgar school, for those of Hokusai, whom they accuse of having his drawings almost always signed for him by his literate friends.

Wednesday, August 7

That glory before which the young generation prostrates itself on all fours, that glory based solely on *L'Après-Midi d'un Faune*, the meaning of which is not yet established by the critics after twenty years, a meaning which that wily sphinx its author refuses to divulge, is it not a leg-pulling that has gone on too long? Oh, these times, what insane enthusiasms that make Mallarmé, Villiers de l'Isle-Adam, the heroes of the young!

Monday, September 9

I find that the literary youth of today, with their disdain for the nagging torment of the flesh and their cult for things of the mind, for a beauty which forbids them to celebrate *brutal nature* and *sensual love*, show something of the hypocrisy of the Protestant religion.

Thursday, December 26

In this volume, the last to be printed during my lifetime, I do not want to bring the Goncourt *Journal* to an end without giving the history of our collaboration, without relating its origins, describing its phases, and indicating in this work in common, year after year, now the predominance of the elder brother over the younger, now the predominance of the younger over the elder.

First of all, two absolutely different temperaments; my brother, a gay, exuberant, expansive nature; I, a melancholy, dreamy, introverted one, yet—what is odd—two minds receiving identical impressions from contact with the external world.

Now at the time when, having both done painting, we turned to literature, my brother, I must admit, was a more developed stylist, more the master of turns of phrase, in short, more of a writer than I, who, at that time, had scarcely any advantage over him other than being the better *seer* into things around us and into the essential nature of beings and things not yet brought into view which could become the material of literature, of novels, short stories, and plays.

There at the beginning of our careers, my brother was under the influence of Jules Janin, and I under that of Théophile Gautier; and one can detect in *En 18* . . those two ill-matched inspirations which gave to our first book the character of a work produced by two voices, two pens. . . .

Biographies of art and historical works succeeded one another, written somewhat under my pressure and the natural predilection of my mind for the truth of the past and present —works to which I brought perhaps somewhat more than my brother. But as these works appeared one after the other there was a fusion, an amalgam of our two styles, which united in the creation of a single style, one that was very personal, very Goncourt.

In this brotherly rivalry over writing well it came about that my brother and I sought to rid ourselves of what we owed to our elders, my brother to reject the glitter of Janin's style, I the materiality of Gautier's. We were in search of a style which, while it would be altogether modern, would be masculine, concrete, concise, in its underlying Latinity coming close to the language of Tacitus, whom we were reading a great deal at that time. Above all we came to hold in horror the high coloring to which I had inclined too much, and we sought in the depiction of material things to spiritualize them by means of moral details. . . .

It gradually came about in the making of our volumes that my brother took over more specifically the direction of style and I the overall plan and content of the book. He came to feel a somewhat disdainful laziness about seeking, finding, inventing supportive data—even though he could imagine more striking details than I when he wanted to take the trouble. . . .

But while he turned over to me the workmanlike construction of the book, my brother remained passionate over style; and I have told, in a letter to Zola written shortly after his death, of the loving care he put into elaboration of form, the chiseling of phrase, the choice of words, of the way in which he would take up again passages which we had written in common and with which we had at first been satisfied, in order to rework them for hours, for half days, with an almost angry stubbornness, changing an epithet here, giving a more rhythmic cadence there, further along refashioning an expression, tiring and wearing out his brain in the pursuit of that perfection of style which is so difficult, sometimes impossible, for the French language when it comes to expression of modern sensations, and, after this labor, remaining for long moments worn out on a sofa, silent in the smoke of a cigar mixed with opium.

Afterword

Writings of the Goncourts

Biographical Notes

Index

Afterword on Japanese Art and Influence

by Hedley H. Rhys

In the time span covered by the Goncourt *Journal*, French painting was completely transformed. At mid-century, when the *Journal* begins, Courbet's realism was rudely challenging the decorum of academic art. By 1896, when the *Journal* closes, the realist movement in painting was already history, Impressionism was past its prime, the restless Art Nouveau style was approaching its brief ascendancy, and a few Cézanne paintings shown in Paris that year presaged yet another formal revolution in modern art. Though the Goncourts were part of the literary avant-garde and themselves created the word "modernism," the entries in their *Journal* show scant sympathy for modernism in painting: Courbet barely merits mention; there is qualified praise for the legendary Delacroix, but none for Manet and Monet when Impressionism was most innovative. Yet, despite this lack of enthusiasm, Edmond, almost involuntarily, just by exercising his exemplary artistic taste, helped give direction to the changes taking place in painting.

As collectors, connoisseurs, critics, and historians of the visual arts, the Goncourts made contributions to aesthetic sensibility. They first collaborated as critics in 1852 with an essay on the Paris Salon of that year. They are best known as art historians for their thorough research into French eighteenth-century painting, which led to the publication between 1859 and 1875 of the series of monographs, *L'Art du XVIIIe Siècle.* Their appreciation of Dutch and Italian painting is less well remembered. As collectors they showed a special sensitivity to the qualities of eighteenth-century French drawings; drawings by Watteau, Lancret, Pater, and Boucher were the glories of their collection. Theirs was a distinctly aristocratic taste and one that opposed the taste of the time. Contemporary art dealing with contemporary life rarely impressed them. They did, however, publish a monograph on Gavarni, that somewhat misanthropic artist and caricaturist who, despite his scorn for the democratic mystique, or because of it, depicted the Parisian scene with unvarnished realism. Perhaps his attitude was what appealed to the Goncourts.

How the brothers felt about the contemporary condition of art is succinctly expressed in their short brochure published in 1854 entitled *The Revolution in Customs.* Its opening sentence is alarming: "Industry will kill art." In explaining this fatal conflict they go on to say that "industry is the bread of the people" and art "is the egotistic adornment of aristocracies." No reconciliation seemed to them possible. And then in 1856 Bracquemond, who eventually was to paint a portrait of Edmond, discovered a little volume of prints by Hokusai, which he carried about everywhere and showed to everyone. Many years later Edmond was to publish his own studies and appreciation of Japanese art.

The Japanese print was a vigorous, popular art form that dealt with the "floating world" of actors and courtesans, of theatres and entertainments, with famous landmarks and with incidents of travel along the Tokaido road. These subjects were quite unlike the formalized subjects of European academic art. Moreover, they were not presented in a literal, descriptive manner, but were transformed into stylized, sophisticated designs. They must have been a revelation to the Goncourts. Here was a popular art that satisfied an aristocratic taste. At the time the Goncourts discovered the prints, however, they probably did not know what the American painter John La Farge, on his return from the Orient nearly forty years later, was to tell Edmond: the Kano school of painters in Japan had always had a very low opinion of the print makers. But no matter! By 1891 Edmond had come to the conclusion that under the stimulus of Japanese art French industrial art was destroying the fine arts! His avid but chilly sensibility was indeed hard to please.

In the decades between discovery and disillusionment, Japanese prints had helped to re-form French painting. The precise date of the discovery is not known: it is said that such prints were found in Paris among packing paper in barrels of imported porcelains—probably in the 1850's, just when Bracquemond found his Hokusais. Monet was attracted to them in Le Havre at about the same time. They are first mentioned in the *Journal* on June 8, 1861, and the Goncourts acquired an album of them, a pornographic collection, in 1863. However uncertain the date of their discovery, the prints appeared at a critical moment in the development of French art. Manet, quite independently of them, was at the time painting a Parisian "floating world" of entertainment: dancers, singers, people listening to music in the public gardens. In 1863 his great courtesan *Olympia* was created; she made her sensational public appearance in 1865. Manet approached these subjects just as coolly and unemotionally as the Japanese print makers approached theirs, but from quite different predispositions; he was concentrating on one vivid aspect of optical experience, the print makers on their own conventions of line and pattern. Because of its rather flat, clearly defined areas of color, the critic Castagnary called *Olympia* a playing card. He could have described a Japanese print in the same way. This similarity of effect, if not of intent, may have encouraged the progressive painters to use Japanese prints as a source of compositional ideas. In any case, they did so and thereby changed radically the course of European art.

The American Whistler was the first painter to leave a record in painting of his enthusiasm for things specifically Japanese. He had found La Porte Chinoise, a little shop under the arcades of the Rue de Rivoli, opened in 1862 by a Madame Saye, who had lived in Japan. It was there that he started to acquire Ming blue and white and to buy Japanese costumes. In 1865 Fantin-Latour painted the group portrait, *Hommage à la Vérité (Le Toast)*. It included among others Bracquemond, Manet, and Whistler, who is shown wearing a kimono. That same year Whistler exhibited his *Princesse du Pays de Porcelaine*. It shows his beautiful red-haired model Jo Heffernan magnificently clad in Oriental silks and surrounded by Chinese and Japanese bric-a-brac. But already the Oriental craze was spreading. Prints and porcelains, fans and kimonos, and even bronzes were making their way from La Porte Chinoise to the studios of many young artists as well as to the collections of Baudelaire and the Goncourts. Manet in 1868 included two Japanese prints in the background of his portrait of Zola. The extent of their influence is strikingly apparent in the composition of the portrait as a whole. Whistler's taste for Oriental artifacts remained with him throughout his career and influenced all his work. It reached its fullest expression in the Peacock Room, designed in 1873 for the house of a wealthy shipowner in Princess Gate, London, and now installed in the Freer Gallery in Washington, D.C.

Japanese art and artifacts as such are rarely represented in the works of the Impressionists in the seventies, but their influence, particularly that of the prints, is pervasive. It is manifested in the high vantage points that Manet and Pissarro, and even Renoir, selected for their paintings of the boulevards. Such vantage points, probably high balconies, produced the effects of diagonal projection and diffuse surface pattern so characteristic of Japanese panoramic prints without doing violence to the conventions of European perspective. Monet must have stood upon the Japanese footbridge that appears in his very late paintings of his garden at Giverny when he looked down at the water-lily pads floating on the surface of his pond above the reflections of the clouds. When looking at his *Water-lilies* in the Museum of Modern Art we experience a space above and below evoked only by a shimmering surface and feel no longer earth-bound, we are enjoying an augmented legacy. Monet has transmitted it to us from suggestions made by the advent of the Japanese print in Paris over a hundred years ago. He painted this picture in 1920, twenty-four years after the death of Edmond de Goncourt.

The Impressionists were great colorists; Edgar Degas was a great draughtsman, a worthy follower of Ingres. Perhaps for this reason he understood Japanese uses of line and space more profoundly than did any of his contemporaries. He achieved in his art a seamless fusion of East and West, a perfect welding of the momentary view and the decorative arrangement. His "floating world" subject matter could have had an eastern origin, but Edmond de Goncourt claims his own novel *Manette Salomon* as the source of Degas' ballet rats and laundresses. Be that as it may, Degas' placing of them in space to create asymmetrical balances of extraordinary subtlety goes to the core of the Japanese aesthetic.

What direct effect Japanese prints had upon the subject matter of nineteenth-century French painting is a moot point. Although they are not as widely known as his ballet pictures, Degas did a series of drawings in the *maisons closes* of Montmartre. It has been suggested that some decorous-seeming seventeenth-century pictures of Dutch interiors are actually brothel scenes, but brothels are not a common subject in European art. Toulouse-Lautrec's well-known pictures of these houses are, however, totally unambiguous. They could be an inevitable extension of his artistic interest in the night life of Paris, yet they do form a striking parallel to Toyokuni's series of prints depicting the poetry-writing prostitutes of the Green Houses of Edo. This series was known in Paris, very probably to Lautrec, certainly to Goncourt.

By the 1890's, the Japanese influence, and indeed exotic influences in general, had become fairly widespread. All the visual arts were affected, from architecture to the minor arts. A few major painters, moreover, still mined this vein. Van Gogh worked at it when he first came to Paris; his painting *Rain*, done in 1887, is almost a copy of a print by Hiroshige. The Nabis, especially Bonnard and Vuillard, in the work they did for *La Revue Blanche* and in their colored lithographs, show an unmistakable dependence on Japanese design principles, even if arrived at by way of Degas. Toulouse, when he incorporated lettering, sometimes vertically disposed as though it were Oriental calligraphy, into the pictorial design of posters, at once gave these broadsides the status of a fine art and assured the diffusion and even the popularization of the exotic style. In 1899 Bonnard used a Japanese-type paper screen to sum up and domesticate these influences. With a decorative asymmetry worthy of Ogata Korin himself, he distributed over the four panels the eccentric silhouettes of women and children wearing turn-of-the-century fashions. Across the top he placed a row of identical hansom cabs. The effect is unmistakably Parisian.

Despite Bracquemond's discovery of Hokusai in 1856, the Japanese influence became effective a little later in France than in England. S. Tschudi Madsen, in his book *Art Nouveau*, summarizes the events that encouraged the taste for Oriental art. In 1862, Japan for the first time after the opening up of the country participated in an international trade fair, the World Exhibition in London. When it closed, the Japanese exhibit was sold at auction. That same year the British architect Edward William Goodwin furnished his house in Japanese style and had Japanese prints on his walls. The following year, 1863, Whistler came to London, bringing his Ming blue and white and probably much more, including his kimono, all bought at Madame Saye's La Porte Chinoise. He infected Dante Gabriel Rossetti, among others, with an enthusiasm for these things. The publication dates of books assist in charting the spread of the mania: Owen Jones' *Examples of Chinese Ornament* appeared in 1867 and R. Alcock's *Art and Industries of Japan* in 1878. Several other titles appeared in England before L. Gonse's *L'Art Japonais* came out in France in 1883, more than a decade after the response of the Impressionist painters to the Japanese print.

There is little doubt that the Goncourts were among the earliest collectors of Far Eastern art. The American painter Mary Cassatt, whom Edmond with more wit than justice described as Degas' choirboy, also started early and concentrated on Japanese prints. However, not all the collectors were artists and men of letters. Henri Cernuschi, an Italian politician and economist, had been a supporter of Garibaldi and had led a revolt in Milan in 1848 before he came to Paris in 1850 to be a director of the Banque de France. He too started to collect early in the craze. His house and very rich collection, which includes a wealth of Southeastern Asian material, became the Cernuschi Museum in 1895. The London merchant Arthur Lasenby Liberty, whose East India House in Regent Street eventually became Liberty and Company, had been in charge of the sale of the Japanese exhibit after the World Exhibition in 1862. He became an active promoter of the orientalizing taste.

The most immediately influential of the collector-merchants was Samuel Bing of the House of Art Nouveau Bing. He started to collect and sell Japanese art in the 1870's; Goncourt frequently bought from him. In the 1880's he began to give exhibitions of Japanese art works and to write catalogues for them. The last of these was a comprehensive print exhibition in 1903. His own private collection was sold in 1906. The firm that bore his name commissioned and sold luxury objects that reflected an aristocratic taste in decorative design. The designers based their work on nature, animals, and Japanese art. Among them was Louis C. Tiffany, whose glass after a few decades of neglect is today again much sought after. In 1900, following the Paris Exposition Universelle, Samuel Bing received the cross of the Legion of Honor for his contribution to the renaissance of decorative design. Nine years earlier, when Edmond de Goncourt lamented in his *Journal* the destruction of the fine arts by the combination of Japanese art with French industrial art, did he have in mind Samuel Bing and his Art Nouveau? It was indeed achievement in the decorative arts that was being honored. And what would Edmond think now in the 1970's when Art Nouveau itself is enjoying a renaissance? Would he regret his early seminal enthusiasm for Japanese prints? He was always hard to please.

Writings of the Goncourts

by Edmond and Jules de Goncourt

En 18 . . ., 1851.
La Lorette, 1853.
La Révolution dans les moeurs, 1854.
L'Histoire de la société française pendant la Révolution, 1854.
L'Histoire de la société française pendant le Directoire, 1855.
La Peinture à l'exposition de 1855, 1855.
L'Italie d'hier, notes de voyage, 1855–1856.
Sophie Arnould, 1857.
Venise la nuit, 1857.
Les Portraits intimes du XVIIIe siècle, in two volumes, 1857–1858.
L'Histoire de Marie-Antoinette, 1858.
L'Art du dix-huitième siècle, in twelve brochures, 1859–1875.
Les Maîtresses de Louis XV, in two volumes, 1860.
Les Hommes de lettres, 1860, reissued as *Charles Demailly* in 1868.
Soeur Philomène, 1861.
La Femme au dix-huitième siècle, 1862.
Renée Mauperin, 1864.
Germinie Lacerteux, 1864–1865.
Idées et Sensations [Selections from the *Journal*], 1866.
Manette Salomon, 1867.
Madame Gervaisais, 1869.
Gavarni, l'homme et l'oeuvre, 1873.
L'Amour au XVIIIe siècle, 1875.

Journal des Goncourt, in nine volumes, 1887–1896.
Préfaces et Manifestes littéraires, 1888.

by Edmond de Goncourt alone

La Fille Elisa, 1877.
Les Frères Zemganno, 1879.
La Maison d'un artiste, 1881.
La Saint-Huberty, 1882.
La Faustin, 1882.
Chérie, 1884.
Mademoiselle Clairon, d'après ses correspondances et les rapports de police du temps, 1890.
Outamaro, 1891.
A bas le progrès! Bouffonnerie satirique en 1 acte, 1893.
Hokousai, 1896.

*Biographical Notes**

Abbatucci, Marie, daughter of Jean-Charles Abbatucci, 1816–1885, maid of honor of Princess Mathilde.

About, Edmond, 1828–1885, novelist and journalist, author of *Le Roi des Montagnes.*

Achard, Amédée, 1814–1875, cloak-and-sword novelist.

Ajalbert, Jean, 1863–1947, lawyer and writer, member of the Académie Goncourt.

Alexis, Paul, 1847–1901, novelist, disciple and biographer of Zola.

Allan, Madame, née Louise Despréaux, 1810–1856, actress, leading interpreter of Musset's plays.

Allard, Jules, d. 1889, and his wife Léonide, 1822–1909, parents of Madame Alphonse Daudet, owners of the villa at Champrosay.

Ambroy, Timoléon, d. 1896, friend of Alphonse Daudet, owner of the mill at Fontvieille.

Antoine, André, 1857–1943, founder of the Théâtre Libre in 1887, director of the Odéon, 1906–1913.

Arago, François, 1786–1853, celebrated physicist and astronomer.

Arago, Emmanuel, 1812–1896, son of the above, journalist and politician.

Arago, Etienne, 1802–1892, brother of the above, curator of the Luxembourg Museum, 1879.

Aubryet, Xavier Aubriet, known as Aubryet, 1827–1880, editor

*A listing of *contemporary* figures whom it is possible to identify beyond the information provided in the text.

of *L'Artiste*, on staff of *Le Corsaire*, *L'Evénement*, *Le Moniteur du Soir.*

Augier, Emile, 1820–1889, playwright.

Autran, Joseph, 1813–1877, Marseillais poet.

Baffier, Jean, 1851–1920, sculptor.

Balzac, Honoré de, 1799–1850, celebrated novelist of the *Comédie Humaine* series.

Banville, Théodore de, 1823–1891, poet, author of *Odes Funambulesques.*

Bapst, Germain, 1853–1921, historian of the crown jewels, editor of Canrobert's letters.

Barbey d'Aurevilly, Jules, 1808–1889, author, chiefly of short stories.

Barbier, Auguste, 1805–1882, poet.

Bardoux, Agénor, 1829–1897, Deputy, Minister of Public Instruction, 1877–1879.

Barrès, Maurice, 1862–1923, writer of novels and essays, anti-naturalist.

Barrière, Théodore, 1823–1877, journalist and playwright, author of the play *La Vie de Bohème.*

Barye, Louis-Antoine, 1796–1875, the famous sculptor of animals.

Baudelaire, Charles, 1821–1867, poet, author of *Les Fleurs du Mal.*

Bauër, Henry, 1851–1915, journalist deported after the Commune, later dramatic critic for *L'Echo de Paris.*

Beaulieu, Anatole-Henri de, 1819–1894, painter, pupil of Delacroix.

Beauvoir, Edouard Roger de Bully, called Roger de Beauvoir, 1809–1866, author and man about town.

Becque, Henry, 1837–1899, dramatist, author of *Les Corbeaux.*

Béhague, Octave, Comte de, 1827–1879, collector of rare books and prints.

Bellanger, Justine Leboeuf, known as Marguerite Bellanger, 1838–1886, actress at the Folies-Dramatiques, celebrated for liaison with Napoleon III.

Benedetti, Vincent, Comte, 1817–1900, diplomat, member of Princess Mathilde's circle.

Béranger, Pierre-Jean de, 1780–1857, patriotic poet and song writer.

Bernard, Dr. Claude, 1813–1878, famous physiologist, author of *L'Introduction à l'Etude de la Médecine Expérimentale*, which strongly influenced Zola's theories.

Bernhardt, Sarah, 1844–1923, celebrated actress.

Berthelot, Marcelin, 1827–1907, distinguished chemist.

Bertin, Jean-Victor, 1775–1842, painter of historical landscapes.

Berton, Charles-Francisque Montan, known as Berton, 1829–1872, noted actor at the Odéon, Vaudeville, and Gymnase.

Bescherelle, Louis-Nicolas, 1802–1884, grammarian, author of *Le Dictionnaire National.*

Bing, Siegfried, known as Samuel, 1838–1905, proprietor of a gallery specializing in Oriental objets d'art.

Bizet, Madame Georges, née Geneviève Halévy, d. 1926, widowed in 1875, married the lawyer Emile Straus, famous for her salon.

Blanc, Charles, 1813–1882, art historian, brother of Louis Blanc.

Blavet, Emile, 1838–1924, novelist and journalist, editor of *Le Gaulois*, writer of feature signed "Parisis" in *Le Figaro.*

Boisdeffre, Raoul-Charles Le Mouton de, 1839–1919, general, chief of staff, 1893, resigned after the Dreyfus affair.

Boitelle (or Boittelle), Edouard-Charles-Joseph, b. 1816, Prefect of Police under the Empire.

Bonheur, Rosa, 1822–1899, the well-known painter.

Bonnat, Joseph-Léon, 1833–1922, portrait painter.

Bonnetain, Paul, 1858–1899, novelist, colonial functionary, prosecuted for *Charlot s'Amuse.*

Bonnières, Robert de, 1850–1905, on staff of *Le Figaro* and *Le Gaulois,* a novelist.

Borel, Pierre-Joseph Borel d'Hauterive, known as Pétrus, 1809–1859, romantic poet befriended by Gautier.

Bouilhet, Louis, 1822–1869, poet and playwright, friend of Flaubert.

Bourget, Paul, 1852–1935, novelist and literary critic.

Bracquemond, Félix, 1833–1914, engraver, painter, lithographer, and designer.

Brainne, Madame Charles, née Léonie Rivoire, "femme du monde."

Brandes, Georg, 1842–1927, Danish literary critic, author of *Main Currents of Nineteenth-Century Literature.*

Brandès, Marthe Brunschwig, known as Brandès, 1862–1930, actress at the Vaudeville and the Comédie Française.

Brébant, Paul, proprietor of a restaurant which succeeded the Magny restaurant as the site of the Goncourt group dinners.

Bressant, Jean-Baptiste, 1815–1886, a very popular actor; the actresses Croizette and Samary his pupils.

Brindeau, Louis-Paul-Edouard, 1814–1882, actor at the Comédie Française, known as interpreter of Musset.

Brisson, Eugène-Henri, 1835–1912, politician, several times a minister.

Broglie, Victor, Duc de, 1785–1870, married Madame de Staël's daughter.

Broglie, Albert, Duc de, 1821–1901, son of the above, politician, member of the Académie Française.

Bruneau, Alfred, 1857–1934, composer of light operas.

Brunetière, Ferdinand, 1849–1906, literary critic opposing the naturalists.

Buloz, François, 1804–1877, founder of *La Revue des Deux Mondes.*

Burty, Philippe, 1830–1890, art critic and connoisseur of Japanese art.

Busnach, William, 1832–1907, founder of Athénée Theatre, adapter of Zola's novels for the stage.

Busquet, Alfred, 1820–1883, journalist and author.

Byl, Arthur, dramatic author, one of the adapters of *Soeur Philomène* for the stage.

Calamatta, Anne-Joséphine, wife of Luigi Calamatta, 1801–1869, an engraver and pupil of Ingres. Their daughter married Maurice Sand.

Calmann-Lévy, 1819–1891, brother, associate, and successor to Michel Lévy.

Camescasse, Jean-Louis-Ernest, 1838–1897, lawyer, Prefect of Police, Senator.

Camondo, Isaac de, 1851–1911, banker, collector of Impressionist and Oriental art, collection now in the Louvre.

Canrobert, Certain, 1809–1895, Marshal of France, aide-de-camp of Louis-Napoleon, active in the December 2 coup d'état.

Caraguel, Clément, 1819–1882, journalist on *Le Charivari*, successor to Janin as dramatic critic on *Le Journal des Débats*.

Carnot, Sadi, 1837–1894, President of the Republic, died by assassination.

Carré, Albert, 1852–1938, playwright, director of the Vaudeville, the Gymnase, and later the Opéra Comique.

Carrière, Eugène, 1849–1906, painter, *Le Baiser Maternel*.

Cassatt, Mary, 1845–1926, American painter of the Impressionist group.

Caze, Robert, 1853–1886, novelist and journalist, died after a duel with Charles Vignier.

Céard, Henry, 1851–1924, novelist and playwright, member of the naturalist group and the Académie Goncourt.

Cernuschi, Enrico, 1821–1896, Italian political refugee, collector of Oriental art, founder of the museum bearing his name.

Chabrillat, Henri, 1842–1895, journalist, playwright, director of the Ambigu Theatre, which he ceded to Sarah Bernhardt.

Champagny, Frantz, Comte de Cadore, 1804–1882, political writer, opponent of Littré.

Champfleury, Jules Husson, known as Champfleury (also as Fleury), 1821–1889, a novelist of the early realist school.

Champsaur, Félicien, 1858–1934, journalist and novelist.

Charcot, Dr. Jean-Martin, 1825–1893, celebrated neurologist at La Salpétrière Hospital.

Charles Edmond, (Charles-Edmond Chojecki), 1822–1899, Polish refugee and man of letters.

Charpentier, Georges, 1846–1905, principal publisher of the naturalists.

Chennevières-Pointel, Charles-Philippe, Marquis de, 1820–1899, director of Beaux Arts, curator at the Louvre and Luxembourg museums.

Chéret, Jules, 1836–1932, lithographer, celebrated for his colored posters.

"Chien Vert," Marie Rieu, d. 1867, Daudet's mistress, inspirer of *Sapho.*

Claretie, Jules, 1840–1913, novelist and playwright, director of the Comédie Française, 1885–1913.

Claudin, Gustave, 1823–1896, secretary to Lamartine, on staff of *Le Figaro.*

Claye, Jules, 1806–1888, printer and engraver.

Clemenceau, Georges, 1841–1929, celebrated statesman.

Colet, Louise, 1810–1876, romantic woman of letters, mistress of various important writers, including Flaubert and Musset.

Colombey, Charles-Hippolyte Tardiveau, known as Colombey, b. 1852, comic actor at the Nouveautés.

Colombier, Marie, 1841–1910, courtesan and actress.

Commanville, Ernest, married Caroline Hamard, 1864; his financial disasters ruined Flaubert.

Commanville, Madame Ernest, née Caroline Hamard, b. 1846, niece of Flaubert.

Commerson, Jean, 1802–1879, humorist, founder of *Le Tintamarre.*

Coppée, François, 1842–1908, poet.

Corot, Camille, 1796–1875, celebrated landscape painter.

Courbet, Gustave, 1819–1877, the champion of realism in painting.

Courmont, Alphonse Le Bas de, 1834–1880, a Goncourt cousin.

Cousin, Victor, 1792–1867, philosopher and politician.

Couture, Thomas, 1815–1879, painter of antiquity.

Crémieux, Hector, 1828–1892, the librettist of *Orphée aux Enfers.*

Croizette (or Croisette), Sophie, 1848–1901, beautiful and popular actress.

Crosnier, Irma, 1820–1907, actress in *Germinie Lacerteux.*

Curel, François de, 1854–1928, playwright whose reputation was established in the twentieth century.

Dailly, Joseph-François, 1839–1897, actor in *L'Assommoir.*

Dalloz, Paul, 1829–1887, editor of *Le Moniteur.*

Dalou, Jules, 1838–1902, sculptor.

Daly, César, 1811–1894, architect and archeologist, restorer of the cathedral of Albi.

Darzens, Rodolphe, 1865–1938, poet and journalist.

Daudet, Alphonse, 1840–1897, the celebrated author of novels and plays.

Daudet, Madame Alphonse, née Julia Allard, 1844–1940, author of essays and poems.

Daudet, Edmée, 1886–1937, daughter of the above, god-daughter of Edmond de Goncourt.

Daudet, Ernest, 1837–1921, older brother of Alphonse, author, editor, Senator.

Daudet, Léon, 1868–1942, elder son of Alphonse Daudet, writer, rightist political figure, founded *L'Action Française*, 1907.

Daudet, Lucien, b. 1879, second son of Alphonse Daudet, painter and writer.

Daumier, Honoré, 1808–1879, painter and caricaturist.

Debureau, Gaspard, 1796–1846, and Charles, 1829–1873, father and son, both famous mimes.

Decamps, Gabriel-Alexandre, 1803–1860, painter of the romantic-Orientalist group.

Decau, Eugène, 1829–1894, landscape painter and sculptor.

Degas, Edgar, 1834–1917, Impressionist painter.

Déjazet, Pauline-Virginie, 1798–1875, actress at the Nouveautés.

Delaage, Marie-Henri, 1825–1882, poet, writer on magnetism and spiritualism.

Delaborde, Jules, Comte, 1806–1889, a Goncourt cousin, lawyer at the Cour de Cassation, historian.

Delacroix, Eugène, 1798–1863, painter of the romantic school, famous as a colorist.

Delpit, Albert, 1849–1893, novelist, journalist, playwright.

Delzant, Alidor, 1848–1905, author of studies on Saint-Victor and the Goncourts.

Dennery, Adolphe Philippe, known as Dennery, 1811–1899, dramatist.

Dentu, Edouard, 1830–1884, publisher and bookseller.

Déroulède, Paul, 1846–1914, poet and politician.

Desbordes-Valmore, Marceline, 1786–1859, poet.

Descaves, Lucien, 1861–1949, journalist, novelist, playwright, member of the Académie Goncourt.

Desprez, Louis, 1861–1885, novelist and author of *L'Evolution Naturaliste.*

Devéria, Achille, 1800–1857, and Eugène, 1805–1865, brothers, both painters.

Diaz de la Pena, Narcisse-Virgile, 1807–1876, painter.

Doche, Marie-Charlotte de Plunkett, known as Eugénie Doche, 1821–1900, actress, created the role of La Dame aux Camélias in 1852.

Doré, Gustave, 1833–1883, famous illustrator, especially of Rabelais and Dante.

Dorsy, Lucienne, actress at the Théâtre Libre, successively mistress of Antoine and Bauër.

Dostoevsky, Fyodor, 1821–1881, the celebrated Russian novelist.

Doucet, Camille, 1812–1895, playwright, secretary of the Académie Française, 1876.

Dreyfus, Alfred, 1859–1935, army officer, victim in the notorious Dreyfus case.

Drumont, Edouard, 1844–1917, journalist and politician, leading anti-Semite, author of *La France Juive.*

Du Camp, Maxime, 1822–1894, man of letters, traveling companion of Flaubert in the Middle East.

Dumas, Alexandre *père*, 1802–1870, author of historical novels.

Dumas, Alexandre *fils*, 1824–1895, popular playwright.

Dumas, Madame Alexandre *fils*, 1826–1895, formerly Princess Naryschkin.

Duményy, Camille, 1857–1920, actor, debut in *Henriette Maréchal*, 1885.

Duperré, Victor-Auguste, Baron, 1825–1900, admiral commanding Mediterranean Squadron.

Dupuy, Charles, 1851–1923, professor, Deputy, President of Chamber of Deputies.

Durand-Ruel, Paul, 1831–1922, patron of Impressionist painters.

Duret, Théodore, 1838–1927, traveled in the Orient with Cernuschi, art critic defending Japanese art and the Impressionists.

Duruy, Albert, 1844–1887, Bonapartist journalist and historian.

Duse, Eleanora, 1859–1924, famous Italian actress.

Eggis, Etienne, 1830–1867, Swiss poet, friend of Houssaye, Du Camp, Jules Janin, on staff of *L'Eclair*, author of *Contes Etranges*.

Emperor Alexander, Alexander II of Russia, 1818–1881, freed the serfs.

Emperor Louis-Napoléon, Napoleon III, 1808–1873, President of the Republic, 1848, seized power by the coup d'état of December 2, 1851, abdicated after the defeat at Sedan in 1870.

Empress Eugénie, wife of Napoleon III, née Eugenia de Montijo, 1826–1920.

Enault, Louis, 1824–1900, author of books on travel, on *Le Constitutionnel*.

Ephrussi, Charles, 1849–1905, art critic, editor of *La Gazette des Beaux Arts*.

Fantin-Latour, Théodore, 1836–1904, painter and lithographer.

Favart, Pierrette-Maria Pingaud, known as Madame Favart, 1833–1899, actress at the Comédie Française, organized companies for provincial tours.

Favre, Dr. Henri, 1827–1916, George Sand's physician, friend of Drumont.

Fenayrou (Gabrielle Gibon, Madame Marin), b. 1853, condemned to hard labor for murder of her lover in 1882.

Feuillet, Octave, 1821–1890, popular novelist.

Feydeau, Ernest, 1821–1873, man of letters, author of the novel *Fanny*.

Flaubert, Dr. Achille, b. 1813, brother of Gustave, succeeded his father as head of the Rouen hospital.

Flaubert, Gustave, 1821–1880, celebrated author of *Madame Bovary*, close friend of the Goncourt brothers, one of the intimates of Princess Mathilde's salon.

Fleury, Dr. Maurice de, 1860–1931, specialist in nervous diseases, writer on medical subjects.

Follin, Dr. François, 1823–1867, surgeon.

Forgues, Paul-Emile Daurand, known as Forgues, 1813–1883, journalist on *Le National*, friend of Gavarni.

Fouquier, Jacques-François-Henry, 1838–1901, publicist and politician, founder of *Le Petit Parisien.*

Fournier, Dr. Alfred, 1832–1914, pupil and successor of Dr. Ricord.

Français, François-Louis, 1814–1897, landscape painter, pupil of Corot.

France, Anatole, 1844–1924, novelist, author of *Le Lys Rouge.*

Fromentin, Eugène, 1820–1876, painter, Orientalist.

Gaiffe, Adolphe, journalist associated with Hugo's sons on *L'Evénement,* later on the staff of *Paris* and *La Presse.*

Galbois, Marie, Baronne de, 1828–1896, reader to Princess Mathilde.

Galland, Victor, 1822–1892, painter and decorator.

Gallé, Emile, 1846–1904, worker in glass and wood, inspired the school of Nancy.

Galliera, Madame de, 1811–1888, famous hostess of the Orleanist faction.

Gambetta, Léon, 1838–1882, political leader after the war of 1870.

Gatayes, Joseph-Léon, 1805–1877, harpist, composer, writer.

Gautier, Théophile, 1811–1872, romantic poet, novelist, and critic.

Gautier, Judith, 1850–1917, daughter of the above, married Catulle Mendès, 1866, divorced, 1896, author of Oriental novels, elected to the Académie Goncourt.

Gavarni, Sulpice-Guillaume Chevalier, known as Gavarni, 1804–1866, caricaturist and painter.

Gavarni, Pierre, b. 1846, son of the above, painter and sculptor.

Geffroy, Gustave, 1855–1926, journalist, art critic, novelist, administrator of the Manufacture des Gobelins.

Gérome, Léon, 1824–1904, painter and sculptor.

Gille, Philippe, 1831–1901, playwright, literary and art critic.

Girardin, Emile de, 1806–1881, journalist and politician.

Giraud, Eugène, 1806–1881, painter and engraver.

Goblet, René, 1828–1905, politician, in various ministries after 1879.

Got, François-Jules-Edmond, 1822–1901, comic actor at the Comédie Française.

Gounod, Charles, 1818–1893, composer of operas and religious music, including *La Reine de Saba.*

Gouvet, Louis-Maurice, childhood friend of Daudet, his second in duels.

Gouzien, Armand, b. 1839, dramatic and musical critic on *L'Evénement.*

Gozlan, Léon, 1803–1866, man of letters.

Grassot, Jacques-Antoine, 1800–1860, actor in comic roles.

Greffulhe, Comtesse Henri, née Elisabeth Riquet de Caraman-Chimay, 1859–1952, cousin of Robert de Montesquiou, principal model of Proust's Duchesse de Guermantes.

Grosclaude, Etienne, 1858–1932, journalist and author.

Grousset, Paschal, 1845–1909, republican journalist.

Guiches, Gustave, 1860–1935, novelist, disciple of Zola.

Guizot, François, 1787–1874, historian and statesman.

Guys, Constantin, 1802–1892, artist celebrated for his sketches of social life under the Second Empire.

Halévy, Fromental, 1799–1862, composer of operas, notably *La Juive.*

Halévy, Ludovic, 1834–1908, nephew of the above, author, with Meilhac, of operettas such as *La Belle Hélène.*

Halperin-Kaminsky, Ely, 1858–1936, Russian man of letters and translator.

Haraucourt, Edmond, 1856–1941, novelist, poet, playwright.

Haussmann, Georges-Eugène, Baron, 1809–1891, celebrated for rebuilding Paris.

Haussonville, Joseph-Othenin-Bernard de Cléron, Comte d', 1809–1884, politician and writer, married to Louise de Broglie, 1818–1882.

Hayashi, Tadamara, 1854–1906, Japanese art dealer, resident in Paris after the Exposition of 1878.

Hébert, Ernest, 1817–1908, twice director of the French Academy in Rome, a painter.

Heine, Heinrich, 1797–1856, German lyric poet, resident in Paris.

Helleu, Paul, 1859–1927, painter and engraver.

Hennequin, Emile, 1859–1888, writer on scientific subjects.

Henner, Jean-Jacques, 1829–1905, well-known painter.

Hennique, Léon, 1851–1935, writer of the naturalist school.

Heredia, José Maria de, 1842–1905, born in Cuba, poet of the Parnassian group.

Hervieu, Adolphe, 1818–1879, painter mostly of watercolors, appreciated chiefly by Gautier, Burty, etc.

Hervieu, Paul, 1857–1915, novelist and playwright.

Hervilly, Ernest d', 1839–1911, man of letters, comic writer.

Hirsch, Moritz, Baron von, 1831–1896, Bavarian financier.

Houssaye, Arsène, 1815–1896, man of letters, director of the Comédie Française, 1849–1856.

Houssaye, Henry, 1848–1911, son of the above, critic and historian.

Hugo, Charles-Victor, 1826–1871, son of the poet, man of letters, in exile with his father.

Hugo, Madame Charles, née Alice Lehaene, widowed in 1871, married Edouard Lockroy in 1877.

Hugo, Georges, 1868–1925, son of the above.

Hugo, Jeanne, 1869–1941, daughter of Charles Hugo, married Léon Daudet in 1891, was divorced and subsequently married Jean Charcot.

Hugo, Victor, 1802–1885, the celebrated poet and novelist, returned from exile in 1870.

Huret, Jules, 1864–1915, journalist on *L'Echo de Paris* and *Le Figaro,* author of *Enquête sur l'Evolution Littéraire* concerning the demise of naturalism, 1891.

Huysmans, Joris-Karl, 1848–1907, novelist who broke with naturalism.

Ibsen, Henrik, 1828–1906, the celebrated Norwegian playwright, his plays introduced in Paris by Antoine.

Ingres, Jean-Auguste-Dominique, 1780–1867, celebrated painter.

Isabey, Jean-Baptiste, 1767–1855, painter of miniatures, favorite painter of the *Incroyables* during the Empire.

Janin, Jules, 1804–1874, literary critic on *Le Journal des Débats.*

Janvier de la Motte, Eugène, 1823–1844, prefect prosecuted for questionable electoral and administrative acts, acquitted, 1872.

Johannot, Tony, 1803–1852, painter, caricaturist, and illustrator.

Jourdain, Frantz, 1847–1935, architect, novelist, and art critic.

Judic, Madame, Anna-Marie-Louise Damiens, 1850–1911, singer and actress, wife of the singer Israel, known as Judic.

Julie, Madame Charles Edmond, usually known as Julie.

Juliette, Madame, Juliette Drouet, 1806–1883, actress, Hugo's mistress for fifty years.

Karr, Alphonse, 1808–1890, man of letters known for his humor and satire.

Koning, Victor, 1842–1894, dramatic author, theatre director.

Lacroix, Paul, 1806–1884, erudite scholar known as "le bibliophile Jacob."

La Farge, John, 1855–1910, American painter.

Laffitte, Jules, editor of *Le Voltaire,* 1878–1886.

Lafontaine, Louis-Marie-Henri Thomas, known as Lafontaine, 1826–1898, actor.

Lafontaine, Madame, Victoria, 1840–1918, actress appearing in *Henriette Maréchal* in 1865 and in Daudet's *Froment Jeune et Risler Aîné.*

Lagier, Suzanne, 1833–1893, actress and singer of songs of her own composition.

La Guéronnière, Arthur Dubreuil-Hélion, Vicomte de, 1816–1875, journalist, Senator, diplomat.

Lamartine, Alphonse de, 1790–1869, poet of the romantic movement, involved in politics up to December 2, 1851.

La Roncière-le-Noury, Camille, Baron Clément de, 1813–1881, celebrated naval officer, distinguished himself during the siege of Paris.

La Rounat, Charles Rouvenat de, 1818–1884, dramatic author, director of Odéon.

Larroumet, Gustave, 1852–1903, historian of the theatre, associated with Lockroy in Ministry of Public Instruction, professor at the Sorbonne.

Latouche, Hyacinthe-Joseph-Alexandre Thabaud de, known as Henri de Latouche, 1785–1851, editor of *Le Mercure du XIXe Siècle* and later *Le Figaro.*

Latour-Dumoulin, Pierre-Célestin, 1823–1888, official of Ministry of Police, Deputy.

La Valette, Madame Samuel Welles de, née Marie Rouher, d. 1891.

Lavedan, Henri, 1859–1940, popular playwright.

Lavoix, Henri, 1820–1892, curator of medals at the Bibliothèque Nationale, reader at the Comédie Française.

Leblanc, Léonide, 1842–1894, actress celebrated for her liaisons with Prince Napoleon, Clemenceau, the Duc d'Aumale.

Lebrun, Pierre-Antoine, 1785–1873, dramatist, author of *Mary Stuart*, 1820.

Lecomte, Georges, 1867–1958, man of letters, secretary of the Académie Française, 1950.

Leconte de Lisle, Charles, 1818–1894, poet of the Parnassian group.

Lefebvre, Armand-Edouard, 1800–1864, art collector, diplomat, historian.

Legouvé, Ernest, 1807–1903, playwright, author of *Adrienne Lecouvreur.*

Lemaître, Jules, 1853–1914, literary critic.

Lemerre, Alphonse, 1838–1912, publisher of *Le Parnasse Contemporain.*

Lépine, or L'Epine, Ernest, 1826–1893, secretary of Morny, collaborated on Daudet's first plays.

Lerch, Louise, sister of Léon Lerch, a school friend of Edmond de Goncourt.

Lescure, François-Adolphe Mathurin de, 1833–1892, man of letters writing on historical subjects.

Lévy, Michel, 1821–1875, well-known publisher.

Limayrac, Paulin, 1817–1868, literary critic on *La Revue des Deux Mondes* and *La Presse*, political editor of *Le Constitutionnel.*

Lirieux, Auguste, 1810–1870, one of the founders of *La Patrie*, 1841, dramatic editor of *Le Constitutionnel.*

Littré, Emile, 1801–1881, philologist, involved in controversy over the dictionary.

Lockroy, Edouard Simon, known as Lockroy, 1840–1913, politician and man of letters, married Madame Charles Hugo.

Lorrain, Paul Duval, known as Jean Lorrain, 1855–1906, novelist and journalist.

Loti, Pierre, pseudonym of Julien Viaud, 1850–1923, naval officer and novelist.

Loynes, Madame de, see Tourbey, Jeanne de.

Lurine, Louis, 1810–1860, playwright, novelist, director of the Vaudeville.

Luynes, Honoré, Duc de, 1802–1867, archeologist, Deputy.

Magnard, Francis, 1837–1894, manager of *Le Figaro* after death of Villemessant.

Magne, Dr. Alexandre, b. 1818, ophthalmologist.

Magnier, Edmond, b. 1841, founder of *L'Evénement*, 1872, imprisoned for bankruptcy, 1895.

Magny, restaurateur, whose restaurant, founded in 1842, was the site of dinners of the Goncourts and their friends for many years.

Mallarmé, Stéphane, 1842–1898, Symbolist poet.

Malot, Hector, 1830–1907, novelist.

Manceau, Alexandre, 1816–1865, engraver, companion of George Sand until his death.

"Manchotte," Célina Debauve or Deboves, nicknamed "La Manchotte" because she had only one hand, protégée and possibly mistress of Sainte-Beuve.

Manet, Edouard, 1832–1883, important Impressionist painter.

Mangin, d. 1864, well-known itinerant peddler of pencils and notions.

Marchal, Charles, 1825–1877, painter, friend of Dumas *fils* and George Sand.

Margueritte, Paul, 1860–1918, man of letters.

Maria, a midwife, mistress of Jules and Edmond, supplied them with information about their servant Rose which they used in *Germinie Lacerteux.*

Mariéton, Paul, 1862–1911, poet of the *Félibrige* movement.

Markowski, proprietor of a dance hall of bad reputation in 1857.

Marmottan, Paul, 1856–1932, art critic, historian.

Marpon, Lucien, d. 1888, bookseller, associate of Flammarion.

Martin, John, 1789–1854, English engraver and painter, *Belshazzar's Feast.*

Massenet, Jules, 1842–1912, composer of operas, *Manon, Le Jongleur de Notre-Dame*, etc.

Maupas, Charlemagne-Emile de, 1818–1888, Minister of Police under the Empire.

Maupassant, Guy de, 1850–1893, novelist and short story writer, friend and pupil of Flaubert.

Mayer, Henry, b. 1857, actor at the Vaudeville and the Comédie Française.

Meilhac, Henri, 1831–1897, playwright in collaboration with Halévy.

Meissonier, Ernest, 1815–1891, genre painter.

Mendès, Catulle, 1841–1909, Parnassian poet, married Judith Gautier.

Méténier, Oscar, 1859–1913, novelist and playwright.

Meurice, Paul, 1820–1905, journalist on *L'Evénement* and *Le Rappel*, novelist and playwright, executor of Victor Hugo.

Mévisto, friend of Antoine, actor at the Théâtre Libre.

Meyer, Arthur, 1844–1924, editor of *Le Gaulois*, supporter of Boulanger, anti-Dreyfus.

Michel, Louise, 1839–1905, revolutionary, active during the Commune.

Michelet, Jules, 1798–1874, historian and man of letters.

Millet, Jean-François, 1815–1875, painter of landscapes and peasant life.

Mirbeau, Octave, 1848–1917, novelist and playwright.

Mistral, Frédéric, 1830–1914, Provençal poet, author of *Mireille.*

Monet, Claude, 1840–1926, landscape painter, leading Impressionist.

Monnier, Henri, 1805–1877, writer and caricaturist, creator of *Joseph Prudhomme.*

Montégut, E. H., cousin of Daudet, on staff of *L'Intransigeant*, manager of the Théâtre Libre, 1887–1890.

Montégut, Louis, b. 1855 or 1857, brother of the above, illustrator.

Montesquiou-Fezensac, Robert, Comte de, 1855–1921, poet and patron of letters.

Moore, George, 1852–1933, English novelist who took naturalism to England.

Morel, Eugène, 1869–1934, editor of *La Revue d'Art Dramatique*, librarian at the Bibliothèque Nationale.

Morny, Charles, Duc de, 1811–1865, bastard brother of Napoleon III, one of the chief figures in the coup d'état of December 2, 1851, and in the Second Empire, patron of the arts.

Murger, Henri, 1822–1861, writer famous for his *Scènes de la Vie de Bohème.*

Musset, Alfred de, 1810–1857, poet and playwright, his plays long better known in Russia than in France.

Nadar, Félix Tournachon, known as Nadar, 1820–1910, caricaturist and photographer.

Naquet, Alfred, 1834–1916, chemist and politician with populist tendencies.

Nathalie, Nathalie Martel, known as Nathalie, 1816–1885, actress at the Gymnase and the Comédie Française.

Nicolle, Dr. Charles, 1866–1936, friend of Léon Daudet, bacteriologist, Nobel laureate.

Nieuwerkerke, Alfred-Emilien, Comte de, 1811–1892, sculptor, superintendent of Beaux Arts under the Empire, lover of Princess Mathilde.

Nittis, Giuseppe de, 1846–1884, Italian painter and engraver established in France after the Salon of 1869.

Offenbach, Jacques, 1819–1880, composer of many popular operettas.

Ohnet, Georges, 1848–1918, novelist.

Osmoy, Charles Le Boeuf, Comte d', 1827–1894, politician, friend of Flaubert and Bouilhet.

Ozy, Julie Pilloy, called Alice, 1820–1893, actress, mistress of the Duc d'Aumale, Charles Hugo, etc.

Page, Adèle, d. 1882, noted beauty, stage debut in 1842, played in *La Vie de Bohème.*

Paillard de Villeneuve, Adolphe-Victor, 1802–1874, specialist in literary lawsuits, lawyer of Victor Hugo, Karr, etc.

Palizzi, Giuseppe, 1813–1887, Italian landscapist residing in France.

Pardo Bazán, Emilia, Condesa de, 1852–1921, Spanish novelist, defender of contemporary French realists.

Passy, Louis, 1830–1913, historian, politician, childhood friend of Jules de Goncourt.

Pasteur, Louis, 1822–1895, famous chemist and bacteriologist.

Patin, Henri, 1793–1876, literary critic, professor at the Sorbonne.

Paulus, Jean-Paul Habans, known as Paulus, 1845–1908, popular singer.

Pélagie (Denis), b. 1831, went into service with the Goncourts in 1868, and remained with Edmond until his death.

Peragallo, Léonce, d. 1882, general agent for the Society of Dramatic Authors.

Persigny, Jean-Gilbert-Victor Fialin, Duc de, 1808–1872, Minister of the Interior under Napoleon III.

Philips, Dr. Charles P., b. 1811 at Lüttich, urologist established in Paris after 1850, Sainte-Beuve's physician.

Pillaut, Mademoiselle Germaine, daughter of Léon Pillaut, musician and musicologist, a friend of the Daudets.

Pingard, Antonius-Louis, 1797–1885, secretary of the Académie Française, 1841.

Pipe-en-Bois, pseudonym of Georges Cavalier, 1841–1878, a Latin Quarter bohemian whom Goncourt considered responsible for the cabal against *Henriette Maréchal.*

Pissarro, Camille, 1830–1903, Impressionist painter.

Pixérécourt, René-Charles Guilbert de, 1773–1844, playwright known for his melodramas.

Planche, Gustave, 1808–1857, much-feared critic on *La Revue des Deux Mondes.*

Plessy, Jeanne-Sylvanie, 1819–1897, actress at the Comédie Française.

Poe, Edgar Allen, 1809–1849, known in France mainly by his prose, translated by Baudelaire.

Poincaré, Raymond, 1860–1934, statesman, President of France, 1913–1920.

Ponsard, François, 1814–1867, playwright.

Pontmartin, Armand de, 1811–1890, novelist and playwright.

Popelin, Claudius, 1825–1892, painter, enamelist, writer, lover of Princess Mathilde succeeding Nieuwerkerke.

Porel, Désiré-Paul Parfouru, known as Porel, 1843–1917, actor, director, husband of Réjane.

Potain, Dr. Pierre-Carl-Edouard, 1825–1901, a pathologist.

Pouchet, Georges, 1833–1894, friend of Flaubert, professor of comparative anatomy.

Pouthier, Alexandre, painter, childhood friend of Edmond de Goncourt, model for Anatole in *Manette Salomon.*

Pradier, Jacques, known as James, 1792–1852, sculptor.

Prévost, Marcel, 1862–1941, popular novelist and playwright.

Primoli, Joseph, d. 1927, nephew of Princess Mathilde.

Prince Napoleon, (Jérôme Bonaparte), 1822–1891, brother of Princess Mathilde.

Princess Mathilde, 1820–1904, daughter of King Jérôme Bonaparte, married to Anatol Demidov, from whom she was separated in 1846; her town house on the Rue de Courcelles and her villa at Saint Gratien were meeting places of literary and artistic society.

Proust, Antonin, 1832–1905, journalist, Minister of Beaux Arts, involved in the Panama affair.

Puvis de Chavannes, Pierre, 1824–1898, painter celebrated for his murals, e.g., at the Boston Public Library.

Quantin, Albert-Marie-Jérôme, 1850–1933, publisher for the Chamber of Deputies.

Quesnay de Beaurepaire, Jules, 1838–1923, prosecuting attorney in Court of Appeals, adversary of Dreyfus, novelist.

Rachel, Elisabeth-Rachel Félix, known as Mademoiselle Rachel, 1821–1858, tragic actress.

Raffaelli, Jean-François, 1850–1924, French painter of scenes on the outskirts of Paris.

Ramelli, Edmée, d. 1899, actress at the Gymnase, Odéon, and Comédie Française.

Regnault, Henri, 1843–1871, painter, Orientalist.

Régnier, Henri de, 1864–1936, poet and critic.

Réjane, Gabrielle-Charlotte Réju, known as Réjane, 1856–1920, celebrated actress, created the role of Germinie Lacerteux.

Renan, Ernest, 1823–1892, historian and philosopher, involved in controversy by *La Vie de Jésus*, 1863.

Renoir, Auguste, 1841–1919, Impressionist painter.

Ricord, Dr. Philippe, 1800–1889, surgeon, specialist in treatment of syphilis.

Rochefort, Henri, 1830–1913, political journalist.

Rodenbach, Georges, 1855–1898, Symbolist poet of Belgian origin.

Rodin, Auguste, 1840–1917, celebrated sculptor.

Rollinat, Maurice, 1846–1903, poet, follower of Baudelaire.

Rose (Rosalie Malingre), d. 1862, in service with the Goncourt family, 1837–1862, provided the basis for the portrait of Germinie Lacerteux.

Rosny, J.-H., joint pseudonym for Joseph-Henri, 1856–1940, and Séraphim-Justin, 1859–1948, born in Brussels, novelists, at first disciples of Zola but later in opposition to him.

Rothschild, Alphonse de, 1827–1905, head of the Paris house, art collector.

Rouher, Eugène, 1814–1884, lawyer and politician, strong supporter of Napoleon III.

Rouland, Gustave, 1806–1878, magistrate, Minister of Public Instruction and Senator under Napoleon III.

Rousseau, Théodore, 1812–1867, landscape painter.

Rouvroy, Louise, d. 1884, singer at the Gaîté Lyrique.

Royer, Paul-Henri-Ernest de, 1808–1877, prosecuting attorney, Minister of Justice, 1857–1859.

Royer-Collard, Pierre-Paul, 1763–1845, philosopher and political orator.

Sabatier, Apollonie-Aglaé Savatier, known as Madame Sabatier, 1822–1890, famous hostess, friend of Baudelaire, Flaubert, Gautier, etc.

Sacy, Samuel-Ustazade Silvestre de, 1801–1879, editor of *Le Journal des Débats*, librarian at the Mazarine Library, Senator.

Sagan, Charles-Guillaume-Boson de Talleyrand-Périgord, Duc de, known as Prince de Sagan, 1832–1910, famous man of fashion.

Sainte-Beuve, Charles de, 1804–1869, the most authoritative literary critic of his time; his "Lundis" ran in *Le Constitutionnel* or *Le Moniteur* from October 1, 1849 on; a Senator under the Empire.

Saint-Victor, Paul Bins, Comte de, 1825–1881, art and literary critic, Lamartine's secretary, 1848.

Salvandy, Narcisse-Achille, Comte de, 1795–1856, Minister of Public Instruction, 1845–1848, refused to follow Napoleon III.

Samary, Léontine-Pauline-Jane, 1857–1890, actress at the Odéon, later a *sociétaire* of the Comédie Française.

Samson, Joseph-Isidore, 1793–1871, actor at the Comédie Française.

Sand, George, pseudonym of Aurore Dupin, Baronne Dudevant, 1804–1876, renowned novelist of the sentimental romantic school.

Saqui, Madame, née Marguerite-Antoinette Lalanne, 1786–1866, famous rope walker under the First Empire, still appearing at the Hippodrome in 1861.

Sarcey, Francisque, 1827–1899, the dominant dramatic critic of his time.

Sardou, Victorien, 1831–1908, playwright, author of *Madame Sans-Gêne*.

Scherer, Edmond, 1815–1889, politician and literary critic, attached to *Le Temps* from its inception in 1861.

Schoelcher, Victor, 1804–1893, Senator, author of the decree for abolition of slavery, 1848.

Scholl, Aurélien, 1833–1902, journalist and famous wit.

Scribe, Eugène, 1791–1861, playwright, perfecter of the "well-made play."

Séverine, Caroline Rémy, known as Séverine, 1855–1929, wrote for *Le Gil Blas*, etc., predominant interest in relief of poverty.

Sichel, Auguste and Philippe, dealers in Oriental art.

Silvestre, Paul-Armand, 1837–1901, man of letters, later works Rabelaisian.

Simon, Jules, 1814–1896, philosopher and statesman.

Soulié, Eudore, 1817–1876, curator of the museum at Versailles.

Spuller, Jacques-Eugène, 1835–1896, statesman and writer on politics.

Stevens, Alfred, 1828–1906, Belgian painter.

Strindberg, Johan August, 1849–1912, Swedish dramatist whose plays were introduced in Paris by Antoine.

Sue, Eugène, 1804–1857, novelist, *Les Mystères de Paris, Le Juif Errant.*

Sully-Prudhomme, René-François-Armand Prudhomme, known as Sully-Prudhomme, 1839–1907, Parnassian poet, Nobel laureate, 1901.

Swinburne, Charles Algernon, 1837–1909, English poet with many French connections.

Tailhade, Laurent, 1854–1919, poet, defender of anarchists, wounded by an anarchist bomb.

Taine, Hippolyte, 1828–1893, philosopher, historian, and literary critic.

Tessandier, Aimée-Jeanne, 1851–1923, actress, triumphed in *L'Arlésienne.*

Texier, Edmond, 1816–1887, novelist and journalist on *L'Illustration.*

Thérésa, Emma Valadon, known as Thérésa, 1837–1913, singer of burlesques at the Alcazar.

Theuriet, André, 1833–1907, poet and novelist.

Thiboust, Lambert, 1826–1867, actor and playwright.

Thierry, Edouard, 1813–1894, dramatic critic, manager of the Comédie Française, librarian at the Arsenal.

Thiers, Adolphe, 1797–1877, active in politics from the beginning of the July Monarchy, put down the Commune, elected President of the Third Republic, 1871.

Thomas, Ambroise, 1811–1896, composer of *Mignon.*

Tolstoy, Leo, Count, 1828–1910, the celebrated Russian writer.

Toudouze, Gustave, 1847–1904, novelist.

Tourbey, Marie-Anne Detourbay, known as Jeanne de Tourbey, 1837–1908, married Count Victor-Edgar de Loynes, whose name she retained after their separation; a famous courtesan; had an early salon frequented by Renan, Flaubert, etc., a later one dominated by Lemaître.

Troubat, Jules-Auguste, 1836–1914, journalist on *L'Artiste*, secretary to Sainte-Beuve until his death.

Turgenev, Ivan, 1818–1883, Russian novelist, lived in Paris a great part of his life.

Vacquerie, Auguste, 1819–1895, husband of Léopoldine Hugo, journalist on *L'Evénement*, playwright.

Vallès, Jules, 1832–1885, writer and revolutionary figure.

Valtesse, Lucie Delabigne, known as Valtesse, 1850–1910, actress and courtesan, model for Nana.

Velpeau, Dr. Louis, 1795–1867, celebrated surgeon and physiologist.

Verdi, Giuseppe, 1813–1901, the great Italian composer of operas.

Verlaine, Paul, 1844–1896, a major lyric poet, notorious for his irregular life.

Vernet, Horace, 1789–1863, painter of battle scenes.

Veuillot, Louis, 1813–1883, Catholic publicist.

Viardot, Louis, 1800–1883, journalist, historian, theatre director, translator.

Viardot, Madame Louis, née Pauline Garcia, 1821–1910, singer, Turgenev's mistress.

Viaud, Julien, see Loti, Pierre.

Vidal, Jules, 1858–1895, painter, novelist, playwright, collaborated in adaptation of *Soeur Philomène* for the theatre.

Vignier, Charles, on *La Revue Moderniste*, adversary of Robert Caze in fatal duel.

Vigny, Alfred, Comte de, 1797–1863, poet and novelist of the romantic school.

Villedeuil, Pierre-Charles Laurens, Comte de, 1831 or 1835–1906, a cousin of the Goncourts, man of letters, founder of *L'Eclair*, 1852, and *Paris*, 1853.

Villemessant, Jean Cartier de, 1812–1879, journalist, founder of *Le Figaro.*

Villiers de l'Isle-Adam, Auguste, Comte de, 1838–1889, poet.

Viollet-le-Duc, Eugène-Emmanuel, 1814–1879, architect famous for his restoration of Notre Dame de Paris, Pierrefonds, and Carcassonne.

Vitu, Auguste, 1823–1891, journalist on *Le Constitutionnel.*

Vogüé, Eugène-Melchior, Vicomte de, 1848–1910, author of *Le Roman Russe.*

Walewski, Alexandre, Comte, 1810–1868, natural son of Napoleon I, Minister of Foreign Affairs under Napoleon III.

Whistler, James McNeill, 1834–1903, American painter and etcher.

Wilde, Oscar, 1856–1900, English poet and playwright.

Wolff, Albert, 1835–1891, on staff of *Le Figaro,* playwright.

Xau, Fernand, 1852–1899, journalist, editor of *Le Gil Blas.*

Yriarte, Charles, 1833–1898, art critic, historian, on staff of *Le Monde Illustré.*

Zola, Emile, 1840–1902, author of the Rougon-Macquart novels, close associate of Edmond de Goncourt and Daudet.

Zola, Madame Emile, née Alexandrine Meley, 1839–1925.

Index

Abbatucci, Marie, 198
About, Edmond, 206, 207, 229, 304
Académie Française, 5, 24, 52, 81, 105, 110, 113, 139-144, 161-163, 178, 184, 198, 203, 207, 263, 273, 275, 289, 294, 296-298, 304, 309-310
Achard, Amédée, 59
Ajalbert, Jean, 254, 280
Alexis, Paul, 174, 201, 262, 275, 280
Allan, Madame, 18-20
Allard, Jules and Léonide, 284, 289
Ambroy, Timoléon, 280
Antoine, André, 7, 245, 246, 251-252, 277, 287, 311, 319
Arago, Emmanuel, 161, 264 (mistakenly for Etienne)
Arago, François, 35
Aristophanes, 120
L'Artiste, 36, 37
Art Nouveau, 327, 335
Augier, Emile, 143, 193, 240
Autran, Joseph, 105

Bach, J. S., 76
Baffier, Jean, 299
Balzac, Honoré de, 1, 4, 40, 44, 60, 64, 90, 93, 151-152, 163, 194, 203, 297
Banville, Théodore de, 26, 35, 161, 163, 197, 238-239
Bapst, Germain, 177
Barbey d'Aurevilly, Jules, 155-156, 165, 225-226
Barbier, Auguste, 110
Bardoux, Agénor, 175-178
Barrès, Maurice, 321
Barrière, Théodore, 37
Barye, Louis-Antoine, 159-160, 233
Baudelaire, Charles, 4, 39, 42, 55, 122, 206, 247, 330
Bauër, Henry, 267, 301-302, 311
Beaulieu, Anatole-Henri, 198, 221
Beaumarchais, 46
Beauvoir, Roger de, 36, 156
Becque, Henry, 240
Béhague, Comte de, 132
Bellanger, Marguerite, 148
Bellay, Joachim du, 39
Benedetti, Vincent, 140, 173
Béranger, Pierre-Jean de, 52, 61, 90
Bernard, Dr. Claude, 111, 137-138, 223, 279
Bernardin de Saint-Pierre, 41, 55, 102, 194
Bernhardt, Sarah, 175, 196, 213-214
Bernis, Cardinal, 40
Berthelot, Marcelin, 91, 111, 176
Bertin, Jean-Victor, 299
Berton, 117
Bescherelle, Louis-Nicolas, 127
Bibliothèque Nationale, 9, 164, 307
Le Bien Public, 172, 173
Bing, S., 157, 175, 207, 213, 229, 265, 270, 287, 293, 300, 334-335
Bizet, Madame, 230
Blanc, Charles, 132
Blavet, Emile, 180, 215, 267
Boileau, 90
Boisdeffre, General, 312
Boissieu, 183
Boitelle, Edouard, 128

Bonheur, Rosa, 37
Bonnard, Pierre, 332, 333
Bonnat, Joseph-Léon, 295
Bonnetain, Paul, 241, 254
Bonnières, Robert de, 236-237, 240, 265, 303
Borel, Pétrus, 48, 81
Bossuet, 248
Boucher, 65, 328
Les Bouffes, 60
Bouilhet, Louis, 53, 95, 114, 117, 130
Bourget, Paul, 193, 207, 243, 273-274, 275
Bracquemond, Félix, 182-183, 232, 238, 263, 305, 328, 330, 333
Brainne, Madame, 201-202
Brandes, Georg, 8, 275, 317
Brandès, Marthe, 278
Brébant dinners, 8, 180
Bressant, Jean-Baptiste, 98
Brindeau, Louis, 20
Brisson, Eugène-Henri, 226
Broglie, Duc de, 105, 309
Broussais, Dr. François, 138
Bruneau, Alfred, 317
Brunetière, Ferdinand, 246, 309
Buffon, 48
Buloz, François, 246
Burty, Philippe, 10, 116, 125, 137, 173, 183, 190, 206
Busnach, William, 179-180, 226
Busquet, Alfred, 84
Byl, Arthur, 244
Byron, 39

Caesar, Julius, 36
Café Américain, 311
Café de Madrid, 204
Café de la Nouvelle Athènes, 253
Café Riche, 41-42
Cahu, 21-22
Calamatta, Madame, 82
Callot, Jacques, 85
Calmann-Lévy, 200, 204, 208
Camescasse, Jean-Louis, 228
Camondo, Isaac de, 157
Canrobert, Marshal, 141
Caraguel, Clément, 217
Carnot, President Sadi, 271
Carré, Albert, 320
Carrière, Eugène, 302, 313-314
Cassatt, Mary, 279, 333-334
Caze, Robert, 230-232, 242
Céard, Henry, 174, 201, 225, 237, 238, 243, 246, 275, 287, 308, 319
Cellini, 139
Cernuschi, Enrico, 156-157, 213-214, 334
Cervantes, 302
Cézanne, Paul, 327
Chabrillat, Henri, 179-180
Champagny, Frantz, 110
Champfleury, 2, 122
Champsaur, Félicien, 230-231
Charcot, Dr. Jean-Martin, 196-197, 202, 237, 270
Chardin, 102
Charles Edmond, 46-47, 60, 74, 112
Charpentier, Georges, 92, 172, 173, 185-188, 194-195, 200, 204, 206, 222, 226, 238, 241, 252, 306, 314
Chateaubriand, François-René, 48, 54, 61, 99, 102, 248
Chauchard, General, 140
Chennevières, Marquis de, 69
Chéret, Jules, 299
"Chien Vert," 185-186
Claretie, Jules, 220-221, 317
Claudin, Gustave, 209-210
Claye, Jules, 143
Clemenceau, Georges, 249, 280, 301, 319
Colet, Louise, 46
Colombey, 317
Colombier, Marie, 267
Comédie Française, 7, 18, 20, 209, 271
Commanville, Madame Ernest, 178, 188, 190-192, 309
Commerson, Jean, 60
Le Constitutionnel, 72
Coppée, François, 165, 239, 303
Corneille, 48, 142, 189, 195
Corot, Camille, 298-299
Le Corsaire, 25, 28
Cottin, Madame, 79, 91
Courbet, Gustave, 2, 103-104, 327
Cousin, Victor, 39, 162-163
Couture, Thomas, 295
Cratinus, 120
Crémieux, Hector, 60
Croizette, Sophie, 144
Crosnier, Irma, 266

Curel, François de, 317
Cuvier, 73
Cyrano de Bergerac, 35

Dailly, Joseph-François, 293
Dalloz, Paul, 160-161, 163
Dalou, Jules, 232, 237
Daly, César, 183
Dante, 234
Darzens, Rodolphe, 320
Daudet, Alphonse, 4, 5-6, 9, 11, 128-129, 133, 145, 150-151, 154-155, 166-169, 170, 176, 177-178, 181, 185-188, 190, 192, 194-195, 197-198, 201, 203, 204-206, 208, 210, 211, 214-215, 216, 218-219, 222, 224-225, 228, 231, 234, 235-236, 238, 241-242, 244, 245, 249-250, 251, 254-261, 262, 265-268, 269, 275, 278, 281-286, 286-287, 289, 296-297, 298, 301, 307-308, 312, 314-315, 316, 317-318
L'Arlésienne, 222
Froment Jeune et Risler Aîné, 150
L'Immortel, 296,
Lettres de Mon Moulin, 281
Le Nabab, 175
L'Oeillet Blanc, 224
Les Rois en Exil, 178
Sapho, 6
Daudet, Madame Alphonse, 6, 206, 214-215, 237, 249-250, 254-261, 265, 280, 283, 297, 298
Daudet, Edmée, 227, 259, 282-283
Daudet, Ernest, 201, 284, 285
Daudet, Léon, 6, 204, 205, 241, 244, 251, 255, 258, 259, 260, 261, 266, 277, 280-281, 281-286, 312-313, 321
Daumier, Honoré, 51-52, 94, 159, 222, 253
Le Décadent, 263
Decadents, 272, 290
Decau, Eugène, 298-299
Deffand, Madame du, 87
Degas, Edgar, 4, 133-135, 253-254, 279, 300, 331-332, 334
Déjazet, Pauline-Virginie, 267
Delaage, Marie-Henri, 26
Delaborde, Jules, 31
Delacroix,—Eugène, 4, 81-82, 89, 206, 222, 233-234, 295, 327
Delâtre, Auguste, 45, 183
Delpit, Albert, 204-205
Delzant, Alidor, 304-305
Dennery, 46, 64
Dentu, Edouard, 36
Déroulède, Paul, 143, 317
Désaugiers, Marc-Antoine, 73
Desbordes-Valmore, Marceline, 301
Descaves, Lucien, 198, 241, 244, 246, 275-277, 278, 279-280
Desprez, Louis, 216, 228, 232
Diaz, Narcisse-Virgile, 27-28, 295
Dickens, Charles, 75, 183
Diderot, 4, 42, 77, 90, 93, 302
Didot (booksellers), 246
Doche, Eugènie, 46, 165
Doré, Gustave, 304
Dorsy, Lucienne, 311
Dostoevsky, Fyodor, 262, 290
Doucet, Camille, 275, 296, 309-310
Dreyfus, Alfred, 3, 312, 313-314
Drumont, Edouard, 225, 229-230, 234-236, 243-244, 256, 274-275, 315-316
Du Camp, Maxime, 184, 191, 196-197
Dumas, Alexandre *père*, 1, 39, 83, 163, 271
Dumas, Alexandre *fils*, 29, 82-83, 126, 139, 141-145, 163, 176, 207, 212, 223, 240, 269, 303, 310
Dumény, Camille, 267
Duperré, Admiral, 292
Dupuy, Charles, 217
Durand-Ruel, Paul, 300
Duret, Théodore, 227, 321
Duruy, Albert, 234
Dusautoy, 66, 229
Duse, Eleanora, 312

Ebner, Jules, 204, 282
L'Echo de Paris, 263, 264, 289, 312
L'Eclair, 12, 21-22
Eggis, Etienne, 26
Eiffel Tower, 272, 280
Emperor Alexander, 120
Emperor Napoleon III, 2, 49, 51, 110, 113, 148-149
Empress Eugènie, 2, 99, 110, 113
Enault, Louis, 26

Ephrussi, Madame, 193
L'Evénement, 217, 242, 254-260, 264

Fantin-Latour, Théodore, 122, 330
Favart, Madame, 220
Favre, Dr. Henri, 212
Fenayrou, 198
Feuillet, Octave, 208
Feydeau, Ernest, 37, 38, 50, 62, 126-127
Le Figaro, 8, 46, 102, 173, 195, 208, 211, 215, 216, 220, 228, 241, 259, 264, 265, 270, 274, 282, 292, 294
Flaubert, Dr. Achille, 84, 181
Flaubert, Gustave, 2, 4, 5, 6, 36, 37-38, 46-49, 52, 53, 55, 58, 61, 64-65, 75, 78, 84-86, 88, 95, 100, 101, 103, 109, 117, 119, 121, 122, 127, 129-132, 133, 138, 139, 144, 145, 148-149, 150, 153-154, 155, 165-169, 171, 174, 176, 178, 181-182, 185-187, 188-192, 201, 248, 262, 290, 297, 300
  Bouvard et Pécuchet, 188
  Le Candidat, 6, 135-137
  Un Coeur Simple, 170
  L'Education Sentimentale, 114
  Madame Bovary, 2, 6, 38, 46, 48, 49, 54-55, 57, 59, 61, 65, 84, 86, 115, 131, 209, 281
  Salammbô, 53, 57-58, 68, 70, 72-73, 84, 281
  La Tentation de Saint Antoine, 117-118
Fleury, Dr. Maurice de, 255
Follin, Dr. François, 52
Fontanes, Louis de, 177
Fouquier, Jacques-François, 267
Fournier, Dr. Alfred, 251
Foyot restaurant, 201
Français, François-Louis, 299
France, Anatole, 159, 271, 281
La France, 289
Fromentin, Eugène, 211

Gaiffe, Adolphe, 36
Gakutei, 254
Galbois, Madame de, 140
Galland, Victor, 135
Gallé, Emile, 317
Galliera, Madame de, 110
Gambetta, Léon, 197, 223
Gatayes, Joseph-Léon, 26
Gaubast, Brinn, 259, 263
Le Gaulois, 217-218, 228, 234-235
Gautier, Judith, 5, 125
Gautier, Théophile, 4-5, 18, 36, 37-39, 47, 62-65, 66, 78-80, 81, 82-83, 87-88, 90, 94-95, 100, 101, 105, 106, 113, 119-120, 125-126, 173, 211, 247, 304, 323-324
Gavarni, 2, 4, 20, 22-23, 42, 49-50, 52-53, 62, 68-69, 73, 80, 104, 126, 151, 221, 328
Gavarni, Pierre, 253, 298
Gayda, Joseph, 215, 216
Geffroy, Gustave, 198, 242, 243, 244, 258, 268, 280, 300, 309
Gerdès Press, 17-18
Gérome, Léon, 193
Le Gil Blas, 196, 209, 248
Gille, Philippe, 211, 259, 260, 317
Girardin, Emile de, 26, 110, 176-177
Giraud, Eugène, 70, 99
Le Globe, 79
Goblet, René, 226
Goethe, 73, 125, 151, 302
Gogol, Nikolai, 262
Goncourt, Edmond and Jules de, Académie Goncourt, 5, 9, 198; collaboration, 321-323; *Grenier*, 8, 214, 215, 216, 231, 232, 240, 274, 276, 280, 307, 312, 322; testimonial dinner, 314-321; trial, 27-32
  L'Art Français, 62, 328
  Charles Demailly, 275
  Chérie, 200, 209
  En 18 . . , 17-18, 106-107, 323
  La Faustin, 192-193, 196-197, 290, 312
  La Femme au Dix-huitième Siècle, 71-72
  La Fille Elisa, 7, 170, 172-173, 174, 185, 319
  Les Frères Zemganno, 274, 290
  Gavarni, 4, 104, 132
  Germinie Lacerteux, 4, 7, 89, 92, 93, 94, 209, 252, 263-272, 290, 319

Goncourt, Edmond and Jules de (*cont.*)
Henriette Maréchal, 6, 8, 97-99, 133, 202, 216-220, 222
L'Histoire de Marie-Antoinette, 52
L'Historie de la Société pendant la Révolution, 33, 252-253
Journal, 2-11, 184, 206, 311-312, 313, 320, 322
La Lorette, 33
Madame Gervaisais, 106, 111, 112, 292, 319
Madame de Pompadour, 246
La Maison d'un Artiste, 292
Manette Salomon, 7, 159, 199, 253, 320, 332
La Nuit de la Saint Sylvestre, 18-21
Outamaro, 288
Les Portraits Intimes, 36, 37
Renée Mauperin, 195, 209, 237-238
La Révolution dans les Moeurs, 328
Soeur Philomène, 7, 52, 59, 244-245
Venise la Nuit, 65, 247
Got, François, 98
Goujon, Jean, 65
Gounod, Charles, 63-64, 230
Gouvet, Louis-Maurice, 205, 256, 259
Gouzien, Armand, 227, 264
Goya, 253
Gozlan, Léon, 20
Gramont, Madame de, 87
Grassot, Jacques-Antoine, 70
Greffulhe, Comtesse, 268, 301
Greuze, 67-68
Grosclaude, Etienne, 294
Grousset, Paschal, 231
Guiches, Gustave, 241, 249
Guillaume (publisher), 250
Guizot, François, 110
Gung'l, 320
Guys, Constantin, 42-44

Hachette, 75
Halévy, Fromental, 60
Halévy, Ludovic, 201, 222, 229, 235, 269
Halperin-Kaminsky, Ely, 290
Haraucourt, Edmond, 268
Haussmann, Georges, 70
Haussonville, Comte d', 110, 143-144
Haussonville, Madame d', 141
Havard, 201
Hayashi, Tadamara, 229, 248, 288, 299, 310
Hébert, Ernest, 176
Heffernan, Jo, 330
Heine, Heinrich, 34, 41, 56, 74-75, 126
Helleu, Paul, 317
Hennequin, Emile, 232
Henner, Jean-Jacques, 295
Hennique, Léon, 174, 198, 280, 312
Heredia, José, 191-192, 198, 211, 225, 303, 309-310, 319
Hervier, Louis, 63
Hervieu, Adolphe, 240
Hervilly, Ernest d', 122
Hiroshige, 299, 332
Hirsch, Baron, 235-236
Hobbema, 206
Hokkei, 299
Hokusai, 229, 254, 292, 299, 322, 329, 333
Homer, 42, 68
Houdon, 22
Houssaye, Arsène, 19-20, 35
Houssaye, Henry, 259, 310
Hugo, Charles, 116
Hugo, Madame Charles, 161, 163, 227, 244, 277-278, 313
Hugo, Georges, 116, 161, 268, 277-278, 285, 313, 321
Hugo, Jeanne, 161, 227, 261, 277-278, 280, 281, 281-286, 312-313
Hugo, Victor, 1, 4, 5, 10, 24, 35, 58, 64, 66-67, 79-80, 81, 84, 89, 91, 97, 100, 103, 104, 114, 116, 124-125, 160-165, 179, 184, 192, 222-224, 234, 239, 244, 247-248, 278, 281, 313
Hugo, Madame Victor, 79-80, 81
Huret, Jules, 289-290
Huysmans, J.-K., 174, 198, 201, 211, 231, 240

Ibsen, Henrik, 287, 288, 302
Impressionists, 253, 291, 300, 327, 331
L'Indépendance Belge, 92
Ingres, Jean-Auguste, 4, 65, 107, 182, 206, 221, 331
L'Intransigeant, 285

Janin, Jules, 18, 24, 28, 32, 323-324
Janvier, Eugène, 124, 180
Japanese art, 62, 83, 91, 102, 106-107, 137, 149-150, 156-158, 171, 175, 199, 207, 227, 229, 238, 253, 288, 292, 299, 300, 322, 327-335
Johannot, Tony, 216
Jourdain, Frantz, 256-257, 317
Le Journal des Débats, 37, 177
Judic, 184
Julie, 46
Juliette, Madame, 161

Karr, Alphonse, 26, 27, 29, 31, 32
Koning, Victor, 228, 235, 267, 289
Korin, Ogata, 254, 333

La Bruyère, 48, 248
Laclos, 104, 302
Lacroix, Paul, 151
Lacroix (publisher), 201
La Farge, John, 8, 322, 329
Laffitte, Jules, 189
Lafontaine, 179, 316
Lagier, Suzanne, 129, 174, 320
La Guérronière, Vicomte de, 99
Lamartine, Alphonse de, 1, 38, 64, 224
Lambert-Thiboust, 142
Lancret, 328
La Roncière-le-Noury, Baron, 70
La Rounat, Charles, 46
Larroumet, Gustave, 317
Latouche, Henri de, 151-152
La Tour, Maurice Quentin de, 102
Latour-Dumoulin, Pierre, 29-30, 33
Launay, Mlle de, 87
La Valette, Madame de, 141
Lavedan, Henri, 235, 317
Lavoix, Henri, 144, 223
Leblanc, Léonide, 209-210, 220
Lebrun, Pierre-Antoine, 110
Lecomte, Georges, 311
Leconte de Lisle, Charles, 159, 176-177, 303, 311
Lefebvre, Armand-Edouard, 30
Lefilleul (bookseller), 197
Legouvé, Ernest, 222
Lemaître, Jules, 216, 227-228, 229, 281
Lemerre, Alphonse, 159
Le Nain, 74
Lépine, Ernest, 129
Lerch, Louise, 308
Lescure, François, 51
Lévy, Michel, 56, 59, 71, 155
La Liberté, 110
Liberty, Arthur L., 334
La Librairie Nouvelle, 59, 201
La Libre Parole, 315
Limayrac, Paulin, 49
Lirieux, Auguste, 19-20
Littré, Emile, 127
Lockroy, Edouard, 227, 268, 271, 277, 281, 282-285, 313
Lorrain, Jean, 312
Loti, Pierre, 198, 207-208, 211, 249-251, 274, 288, 289, 296-298

Magnard, Francis, 264, 265, 292, 294
Magne, Dr. Alexandre, 180
Magnier, Edmond, 255, 257, 259
Magny dinners, 8, 73, 74, 76, 78, 81, 82, 83, 92, 95, 96, 100, 111, 229
Maintenon, Madame de, 87
Maison d'Or restaurant, 25, 225
Mallarmé, Stéphane, 8, 240, 303, 322
Malot, Hector, 311
Manceau, Alexandre, 212
Manet, Edouard, 4, 133, 180, 193, 327, 329, 331
Mangin, 171, 210
Manifeste des Cinq, 5, 241-243
Manzi, 292
Marchal, Charles, 82, 126
Marchangy, Louis-Antoine, 81
Margueritte, Paul, 198, 241, 317
Marie-Antoinette, 37, 152, 224, 319
Mariéton, Paul, 268, 310
Marmottan, Paul, 284
Marpon, Lucien, 172, 197, 204, 235, 271
Massenet, Jules, 177, 230
Le Matin, 252
Maupassant, Guy de, 145-148, 174, 186, 191-192, 197, 201-202, 213, 236-237, 248-249, 291-292, 308-309, 311
Meilhac, Henri, 222
Meissonnier, Ernest, 193

Mendès, Catulle, 125, 209, 240, 278, 303
Méténier, Oscar, 275, 278, 280
Meurice, Paul, 116, 124
Mévisto, 317
Meyer, Arthur, 217, 234-236
Michel, Louise, 244
Michelangelo, 233, 234
Michelet, Jules, 67, 84, 86-88, 94, 113-114, 142
Millet, Jean-François, 70-71, 295-296
Mirbeau, Octave, 174, 198, 274, 302
Mistral, Frédéric, 210
Molière, 23, 78, 97, 99, 120
Mommsen, Theodore, 75
Monet, Claude, 4, 274, 292-293, 300, 327, 329, 331
Le Moniteur, 63, 160
Monnier, Henri, 53, 201, 248
Montégut brothers, 280, 282, 285
Montesquieu, 48-49
Montesquiou-Fezensac, Robert, 8, 211-212, 216, 300-301, 305-306
Moore, George, 253
Morel, Eugène, 307
Morny, Duc de, 2, 60, 128-129, 150-151
Moronobu, 227
Murger, Henri, 2, 23-24, 25-26, 34, 56-57
Musset, Alfred de, 18, 39, 56, 70

Nadar, 185
Napoleon, 113, 193
Naquet, Alfred, 261
Nathalie, 27-28, 37
Naturalism, 3, 171-172, 174, 185, 240, 289-290, 294, 301-302
Nicolle, Dr. Charles, 282, 285, 286
Nieuwerkerke, Alfred, 29, 70, 74, 99, 139
Nettis, Giuseppe de, 192, 193, 197, 254

Odéon, 7, 53, 117, 218-220, 237, 239, 264-272, 280
Offenbach, Jacques, 60, 238
Ohnet, Georges, 235
Ollendorff, 201, 235
Osmoy, Comte d', 191, 198
Ozy, Alice, 304-305

Page, Adèle, 267
Paillard de Villeneuve, Adolphe, 31-32
Palizzi, Giuseppe, 24
Paradol, 229
Pardo, Bazán, Emilia, 8, 274
Paris, 7, 24-27
Parmigiano, 65
Passy, Louis, 32, 37, 38
Pasteur, Dr. Louis, 138
Pater, Jean-Baptiste, 328
Patin, Henri, 162
La Patrie en Danger, 291
Paulus, 239
Pélagie, 173, 188, 219, 268
Peragallo, Léonce, 225
Persigny, Duc de, 128
Le Petit Journal, 270
Philips, Dr. Charles, 129
Pillaut, Germaine, 261
Pingard, Antonius-Louis, 140, 162, 303
Pipe-en-Bois, 217
Pissarro, Camille, 302, 331
Pixérécourt, René, 64
Planche, Gustave, 246
Plessy, Jeanne, 98
Poe, Edgar Allen, 35, 249, 262
Poincaré, Raymond, 309, 314-315, 316-319
Ponsard, François, 271
Pontmartin, Armand de, 246
Popelin, Claudius, 139, 188, 291-292
Porel, 7, 220, 245, 263, 264, 265, 266, 269-270, 271-272
Potain, Dr. Pierre, 197, 261, 284-285
Potonié, Madame, 309
Pouchet, Georges, 182, 189, 191
Pouthier, Alexandre, 21, 25
Pradier, James, 85
Prévost, Marcel, 317
Primoli, Joseph, 312
Princess Mathilde, 8, 10, 69-70, 78, 88, 98, 99, 105, 106, 109-110, 113, 138, 139, 139-140, 144, 220, 231, 292, 310, 321
Prince Napoleon, 29, 73

Proust, Antonin, 301
Pushkin, Alexandre, 123
Puvis de Chavannes, Pierre, 4, 240-241, 317

Quantin (publisher), 252-253
Quesnay de Beaurepaire, Jules, 276

Rachel, 28, 29
Racine, 80, 90, 136, 195
Radziwill, Prince, 66
Raffaelli, Jean-François, 245, 322
Ramelli, Edmée, 117
Raphael, 206
Le Rappel, 124
Realism, 2, 36, 62, 74, 104, 125, 219, 220, 327
Regnault, Henri, 122, 171
Régnier, Henri de, 307, 319, 321
Réjane, 7, 252, 263, 264, 266, 267, 269, 270
Rembrandt, 62
Reminy, 95
Renan, Ernest, 51, 76-77, 79, 90-91, 92, 178, 184, 216, 224, 281, 294, 300
Renoir, Auguste, 300, 302, 331
Le Réveil-Matin, 242
La Revue Blanche, 332
La Revue Bleue, 216
La Revue d'Architecture, 183
La Revue des Deux Mondes, 18, 102, 196-197, 246
La Revue Indépendante, 253
La Revue Nouvelle, 298
Richelieu, 142
Ricord, Dr. Philippe, 113, 251
Ritsono, 254
Rochefort, Henri, 294
Rodenbach, Georges, 289, 311, 314
Rodin, Auguste, 4, 232-234, 238, 247-248, 249, 274, 292, 309, 320
Rolland, Romain, 272
Rollinat, Maurice, 240, 268
Romanticism, 2, 21, 33, 36, 94, 101, 102, 180, 197, 289
Rose, 10, 69
Rosny brothers, 198, 240, 241, 242, 249, 258
Rossetti, Dante Gabriel, 333
Rossini, 64
Rothschild, Alphonse de, 157, 214, 274
Rouher, Eugène, 110
Rouland, Gustave, 32, 33
Rousseau, Jean Jacques, 77, 79, 102, 320
Rousseau, Théodore, 206, 258, 295
Rouvroy, Louise, 22
Royer, Paul, 30, 32
Royer-Collard, Pierre-Paul, 162-163
Rubens, 82, 206

Sabatier, Madame, 47
Sacy, Samuel, 143
Sade, Marquis de, 58-59, 147, 212
Saint-Aubin, Augustin de, 45
Sainte-Beuve, Charles de, 30, 38, 39-40, 41, 60-62, 72-73, 73-74, 76-77, 79-80, 81, 83, 87-88, 90, 92, 95, 100, 103, 105, 109-111, 112-113, 129, 228
Saint Margaret Mary Alacoque, 92
Saint-Simon, 41, 248
Saint-Victor, Comte de, 46, 60, 71, 79-80, 82, 90, 160-161, 305
Salvandy, Comte de, 177
Samary, Léontine, 237-238
Sand, George, 1, 40-41, 62, 79, 82, 89, 91, 100, 107-108, 117, 129, 212, 247, 309
Saqui, Madame, 25
Sarcey, Francisque, 108, 206, 229, 239, 302
Sardou, Victorien, 127-128, 212, 223, 269, 284
Sarrut, 276
Saye, Madame, 330, 333
Scherer, Edmond, 79-80
Schoelcher, Victor, 125, 285
Scholl, Aurélien, 26, 46, 259, 265, 316
Scribe, Eugène, 124
Scudéry, Madame de, 41
Séverine, 215-216
Shakespeare, 39
Sichel brothers, 157, 207, 213
Le Siècle, 157, 264
Silvestre, Paul, 198
Simon, Jules, 284-285
Soulié, Eudore, 79, 103

Spuller, Jacques-Eugène, 223
Staël, Madame de, 41, 62, 105
Stendhal, 1, 4, 243
Stevens, Alfred, 149, 273, 294-296, 317
Strindberg, Johan, 302
Sue, Eugène, 1, 67
Sully-Prudhomme, 317
Swinburne, Charles Algernon, 145-147, 203
Symbolists, 290

Tacitus, 162, 324
Tahureau, 28, 30
Tailhade, Laurent, 317
Taine, Hippolyte, 9, 10, 75, 77, 78-80, 95, 96, 112, 178, 184, 222-223, 239, 275, 294, 303, 304
Talleyrand, 36
Le Temps, 51, 110, 112, 159, 270, 272
Tessandier, Aimée-Jeanne, 222
Texier, Edmond, 107
Tézénas, 280
Théâtre des Délassements, 34
Théâtre du Gymnase, 320
Théâtre Libre, 7, 244-245, 246, 277, 311
Théâtre Lyrique, 22
Théâtre des Menus-Plaisirs, 269
Théâtre des Variétés, 142, 280
Thérésa, 209-210
Theuriet, André, 317
Thiers, Adolphe, 39, 81, 90, 124, 128, 203
Thomas, Ambroise, 176
Thuillier, Mlle, 24
Tiffany, Louis C., 334
Le Tintamarre, 173
Titian, 206
Tolstoy, Leo, 2, 262, 301-302
Toudouze, Gustave, 304, 311
Toulouse-Lautrec, 332
La Tourbey, 294
Toyokuni, 287, 332
La Tribune, 108
Troubat, Jules-Auguste, 103
Turgenev, Ivan, 2, 74, 75, 119-122, 122-124, 129-130, 151, 154, 165-169, 201, 202, 203, 207, 245-246, 262

Utamaro, 254, 288, 300

Vacquerie, Auguste, 116, 244
Vallès, Jules, 195, 198, 215
Valtesse, 174
Van Eyck, 50
Van Gogh, Vincent, 332
Le Vaudeville, 128, 320
Véfour restaurant, 129, 300
Verdi, Giuseppe, 64, 310
Vergil, 61, 68, 258
Verlaine, Paul, 116, 122, 306, 308
Vernet, Horace, 118
Veuillot, Louis, 201
Viardot, Pauline, 309
Vidal, Jules, 244
Vignier, Charles, 254
Vigny, Alfred de, 83
Villedeuil, Charles, 21-22, 25-26, 27, 29
Villemessant, Jean, 13, 16, 25, 34, 60, 149
Villiers de l'Isle-Adam, Auguste, 303, 322
Viollet-le-Duc, Eugène, 70
Vitu, Auguste, 267, 269
Vogüé, Eugène-Melchior, 229, 262, 294
Voltaire, 35, 42, 48, 76-77, 78, 90, 104
Le Voltaire, 189, 195, 196
Vuillard, Edouard, 332

Wagner, Richard, 291
Walewski, Alexandre, 56
Watteau, 68, 86, 91, 102, 132, 254, 328
Whistler, James, 193, 306, 330-331, 333
Wilde, Oscar, 203, 306, 321
Wolff, Albert, 81, 173, 268, 292

Xau, Fernand, 214

Yriarte, Charles, 301

Zola, Emile, 3, 4, 5, 6, 7, 8, 10, 108-109, 115, 137, 148, 153-154, 167-169, 170, 171-172, 174, 181, 184-185, 185-186, 190, 191, 192-193, 194-195, 197, 198, 199-200, 201-

Zola, Emile (*cont.*)
202, 203, 211, 222-223, 228, 241-243, 245, 246, 248, 262, 263, 268-269, 275, 278-279, 286, 287, 290, 293-294, 304, 307-308, 310, 314-315, 319, 324
L'Argent, 279
L'Assommoir, 170, 179-180, 290, 293
La Bête Humaine, 278
La Curée (Renée), 240
La Débâcle, 279, 293
Le Docteur Pascal, 279, 293
La Faute de l'Abbé Mouret, 153
Germinal, 209, 226-227, 252
La Joie de Vivre, 195, 208-209
Lourdes, 293-294
Madeleine Férat, 109
Nana, 182, 184
Pot-Bouille, 241
Le Rêve, 290
Rome, 319
Thérèse Raquin, 132
Zola, Madame Emile, 185, 241, 307-308

Paris and the Arts, 1851–1896: from the Goncourt Journal

Designed by R. E. Rosenbaum
Composed by Vail-Ballou Press, Inc.
in 11 point linotype Janson, 3 points leaded,
with display lines in Palatino.
Printed letterpress from type by Vail-Ballou Press
on Warren's 1854 text, 60 pound basis
with the Cornell University Press watermark.
Bound by Vail-Ballou Press
in Joanna Arrestox B book cloth
and stamped in All Purpose foil.